Heaven Can Wait

HEAVEN CAN WAIT

Purgatory in Catholic Devotional and Popular Culture

DIANA WALSH PASULKA

OXFORD
UNIVERSITY PRESS

OXFORD
UNIVERSITY PRESS

Oxford University Press is a department of the
University of Oxford. It furthers the University's objective
of excellence in research, scholarship, and education
by publishing worldwide.

Oxford   New York
Auckland   Cape Town   Dar es Salaam   Hong Kong   Karachi
Kuala Lumpur   Madrid   Melbourne   Mexico City   Nairobi
New Delhi   Shanghai   Taipei   Toronto

With offices in
Argentina   Austria   Brazil   Chile   Czech Republic   France   Greece
Guatemala   Hungary   Italy   Japan   Poland   Portugal   Singapore
South Korea   Switzerland   Thailand   Turkey   Ukraine   Vietnam

Oxford is a registered trade mark of Oxford University Press
in the UK and certain other countries.

Published in the United States of America by
Oxford University Press
198 Madison Avenue, New York, NY 10016

Library of Congress Cataloging-in-Publication Data
Pasulka, Diana Walsh.
Heaven can wait : Purgatory in Catholic devotional and popular culture /
Diana Walsh Pasulka.
pages   cm
Includes bibliographical references and index.
ISBN 978-0-19-538202-0 (hardcover : alk. paper) —
ISBN 978-0-19-970042-4 (ebook)
1. Purgatory—History of doctrines.   2. Sacred space.
3. Catholic Church—Doctrines.   4. Purgatory.
5. Popular culture—Religious aspects—Catholic Church.   I. Title.
BT843.P37   2014
236'.509—dc23   2014011175

1 3 5 7 9 8 6 4 2
Printed in the United States of America
on acid-free paper

To my husband, Daniel; my mother, Heather Walsh; and my brothers, Daniel and Dennis. Thank you for the conversations and inspiration.

Contents

Acknowledgments

DURING THE TIME period that I wrote this book, I experienced several life events, including having children and earning tenure at my university. I would like to acknowledge the support provided by my family, colleagues, and students, and the people whom I met while doing research. I would first like to thank Cynthia Read, who has been a very positive, patient, and helpful editor and guide during the process of writing the book. I am very grateful to the anonymous reviewers of the early manuscript for their insightful comments. I traveled far out of my historical area of research in the first two chapters of the book, and I owe a debt of gratitude to Isabel Moreira, whose own work on purgatory proved my invaluable guide through the complex theological worlds of late antiquity and the early medieval eras. I would also like to thank Dr. Moreira for her generosity and for providing helpful comments on these sections of the manuscript that resulted in several crucial adjustments. As I finished writing my manuscript I read Jeffrey J. Kripal's book *Authors of the Impossible: The Paranormal and the Sacred* (Chicago: University of Chicago Press, 2010). It influenced the way I thought about my research on the Catholic supernatural and motivated me to edit parts of my manuscript to reflect my deepened understanding. My students have made my journey fun and interesting. Jamie Brummitt, Everett Fulmer, Kerry Sullivan, Eugene O'Dea, Garrison Libby, and Bryan Hendershot helped me collect archival material. My former student Hope Bordeaux read parts of the manuscript and provided valuable feedback, and Christopher Moreland offered helpful comments and suggestions on the introduction to the book.

My colleagues at the University of North Carolina Wilmington were instrumental in providing me with the time and resources I needed to finish the manuscript. I am grateful to David Webster and George Zervos, and the University of North Carolina Wilmington for assisting me in securing a sabbatical leave in the fall 2013, which allowed me time to finish. My colleagues Patty Turrisi, Walter Conser, and Teddy Burgh provided intellectual support. My colleague Herbert Berg helped me navigate through several theoretical problems. George Zervos has been a very supportive chair, and I thank him for that. I am grateful to the Honors College at the University of North Carolina and Kate Bruce for providing the support that my students needed to engage in research with me. I would also like to thank William A. Christian Jr., whose writings on visionaries helped frame my approach to my subject, and who provided moral support at the very end of the project, typically when I needed it most.

I have met wonderful people who have shared their experiences and perspectives with me. Susan Tassone is a remarkable person and researcher. Several ministers of the purgatory apostolates, including Mike Humphrey and Brian Bagley, were generous with their knowledge. I am also grateful to the members of the Ark of the Covenant, who provided encouragement and support. The archivists at the Philadelphia Archdiocese Historical Research Center were incredibly helpful in locating periodicals and pamphlets. Poet and teacher Sarah Messer helped me discover the beauty of my subject by directing my attention to the elements of medieval purgatory: fire, water, stone. During the last months of this project I met screenwriters Chad Hayes and Carey Hayes. Their fascination with purgatory inspired me and helped me understand purgatory's timeless appeal for artists and authors of all kinds.

Finally, I would like to thank my family. This book could not have been written without the help of my husband, Daniel, who took care of the home hearth while I disappeared into the cave of a computer screen. My mother, Heather Walsh, helped me conduct archival research in Charleston, South Carolina, while I was seven months pregnant with twins. She deserves special thanks for that trip. My brothers Daniel and Dennis have always inspired me and I look forward to many future conversations with them about philosophy and religion. I am indebted to Marcia Czopek, Bill and Melanie Pasulka, and Joe and Linda Pasulka for sharing their memories of pre-Conciliar Catholicism. Thank you, Joe Pasulka, for reading parts of my early manuscript and for offering editorial comments. I would like to thank my sister-in-law, Brigid Pasulka, who was the best of sports while accompanying me on several research adventures. My children are too young to read this book, and will be for several years to come. However, when they do read it, and if they do, I hope that they know that I dedicate all of my work to them, with love.

Heaven Can Wait

Introduction

THE PROBLEM WITH PURGATORY

IN 2007, JOSEPH Ratzinger, the residing Pope Benedict XVI, surprised a group of Catholics who were gathered for a church service in Rome by declaring that if believers remained unrepentant then they risked "eternal damnation—the Inferno." He raised eyebrows further by saying that hell "really exists and is eternal, even if nobody talks about it much anymore."[1] Vatican officials scrambled to soften his statements. Church historian Agostino Bagliani said that the pope was merely speaking as a "parish priest" and as such was using "straightforward" language.[2] Not long after this, Pope Benedict shocked many people again by reconsidering the Church's position on "limbo," the afterlife location traditionally reserved for deceased unbaptized babies and virtuous pagans.[3] Popular media reflected shock and confusion. A headline from London's *Telegraph* read, "Pope Ends State of Limbo after 800 Years." Another headline declared, "The Pope Abandons Limbo! Will Purgatory Follow?"[4] These developments left Catholics and non-Catholics wondering, *what about purgatory? Does that still exist?*

Purgatory is a doctrine of the Catholic Church, which means that Catholics are obligated to believe in it. However, most American Catholics are unsure about its doctrinal status, and many even wonder what it is. I recently gave an informal presentation to a group of young Catholics at my university's Catholic Student Center that illustrates American Catholic perceptions about purgatory. The subject was the Catholic observance of Lent. Sister Mary, of the Ursuline Order of Sisters, officiated at the lecture. She told me I could talk about my research as long as it concerned the subject of Lent. In the Catholic religion Lent is an annual penitential observance that encompasses the forty days prior to Easter Sunday. Catholics are encouraged to make a sacrifice or give up a bad habit in recognition of the sacrifice of Jesus. I intended to speak about sacrifice and its meaning. Ten minutes into my discussion, I noticed that Sister Mary was unhappy. She was shaking her head and frowning. I was confused, but continued. She tapped me on the arm and said, "We don't talk about sacrifice during Lent. Instead, we focus on doing good works and helping people. Sacrifice is an old, and very cruel concept."

"Oh," I replied. That was not a problem for me, as I am always prepared with more material than I can possibly cover. I segued into my discussion about purgatory, which is the subject of my research. Again, I felt a gentle tap on my arm. This time Sister Mary was a little more forceful.

"Purgatory is not a doctrine of the church anymore," she said, "is it?" The question was posed as a statement.

This was a dilemma. On the one hand, I knew that indeed purgatory was still a doctrine of the church, and on the other hand, I didn't want to risk exposing Sister Mary's ignorance before the students whose spiritual consciences she was charged with forming. So I said nothing.

She continued, "I believe that purgatory can be interpreted as being here on earth." "In fact," she said, "purgatory is definitely earthly."

Having said that, she smiled.

This was helpful. My research focuses on the ways in which people have imagined purgatory as a material, concrete, and often physical place. The earthly purgatory has a long history, and I knew it well. I then launched into a discussion about the medieval belief that purgatory existed in a cave, on an island in Ireland. Sister Mary was happy. I was happy too, and the students enjoyed the discussion.[5]

This exchange highlights the issues raised in the following chapters, which attend to the *materiality* of purgatory, as characterized in some of its most popular narrative representations. Purgatory's *materiality* refers to the persistent set of characteristics associated with purgatory that have been a continuous problem from its inception as a doctrine in the thirteenth century to the present. It has been variously described as a location on earth, as a place where souls are at once physical and spiritual, and as a condition that demands bodily mortifications and severe penances. In this sense, materiality is a category that encompasses three important sites where purgatory has presented theological, scientific, and logical difficulties for church theologians, scholastic philosophers, and others who have been responsible for working out the philosophical support for the doctrine: place, body, and performance. From the twelfth century to the present, representations in various sources, including medieval *chronicles*, *exempla*, early modern periodicals, and, later, in pamphlets, books, and magazines, and today on websites and in books, have depicted purgatory variously as a location on earth, a place simultaneously spiritual and physical, and, most recently, as a more abstract condition of souls experiencing the pain of loss. The version of purgatory as a physical location persisted into the nineteenth century. Pre-doctrinal representations of purgatory shifted so much with respect to historical context that it is impossible to identify a linear progression from that of a physical place to a condition of soul. However, this progression becomes pronounced in the modern era and by the mid-nineteenth century conceptions of purgatory as a place were subject to anti-Catholic polemicists and were actively discouraged by Church authorities. I have not encountered anyone, currently, who believes purgatory is a place on earth. Taking a "long view," of purgatory suggests that material representations of purgatory have been discouraged in favor of representations clothed with abstract words such as *process, state of soul,* or *condition*. The progression from a "place" to a "condition" has been fraught with dramatic twists and intrigues, and even today the issue of purgatory's material status is not definitively settled. Contemporary Catholic devotional literature about purgatory focuses on the material locations of place, body, and performance that were the focuses of purgatory devotions in eras past.

Sister Mary's statements about purgatory participate in a long tradition of interpretations of the doctrine that seem to have little in common with official definitions. Papal statements about purgatory, from its official codification as a Roman Catholic doctrine until today, emphasize its status as an afterlife "state" or condition, and deemphasize its material, concrete characteristics. Writing during the Council of Trent (1545–1563), Pope Pius IV insisted that attention to purgatory's material aspects, such as where it is located and what types of punishments occur there, should be discouraged. "The more difficult and subtle questions, and which tend not to edification, and from which for the most part there is no increase of piety, [should] be excluded from popular discourses before the uneducated multitude."[6] Currently, papal discussions of purgatory, while briefer, are substantively no different. In his General Audience address of 1999, Karol Wojtyla, Pope John Paul II, stated that the term "purgatory," "does not indicate a place, but a condition of existence." And, on January 12, 2011, Pope Benedict XVI noted that the fifteenth-century mystic St. Catherine of Genoa did not focus on "purgatory as a place of transit in the depths of the earth," or "as an exterior fire." Rather, purgatory was an inner state.[7] Shortly after, the Catholic News Service published an article that eliminated any possibility that the pope would be misunderstood as to purgatory's physical reality. It was titled "Purgatory Is a Process, Not a Place."[8]

Despite papal statements about it, authors of popular narratives about purgatory have characterized it very differently. In their reports and anecdotes, purgatory is a physical place of suffering. Souls in purgatory are depicted engulfed in real, not symbolic, fire, the evidence of which include burned charcoal–colored handprints on tables for the living to consider, such as can be found in the Purgatory Museum in Rome. It is tempting to suggest that these narratives are in tension with official, cleric-authored proclamations about purgatory. While in some instances this is the case, in other contexts it was clerics and theologians who wrote about purgatory as a place, and scholastics also wrote about the physical evidence left by souls in purgatory. What persists throughout these various narratives and their historical contexts, however, is the problem presented by purgatory's materiality. Purgatory's place, which has been described variously as being in Ireland, or in Italy, in the middle of the earth, or as a place next to hell, has been a problem for those who attempt to locate it, and also for those who have participated in a tradition that downplays its concrete features. The following chapters examine several cases where the physicality of purgatory is its best advocate *and* its most problematic feature. In other words, this book is a history of the problem of purgatory—it's characterization as a physical place of real, not symbolic, suffering.

In my exchange with Sister Mary, she expressed her belief that purgatory is "earthly." While it may have been more common to associate purgatory with an actual earthly location in medieval Europe, as stated previously this belief persisted into the nineteenth century. For hundreds of years, and contrary to the proclamations of most popes on the subject, purgatory was believed to be either on earth or in the middle of the earth. I was not surprised to hear of Sister Mary's belief that purgatory was on earth, and I am certain that her belief is not like the belief that prompted medieval knights to undertake journeys to Ireland in search of the real purgatory. But nonetheless what is important is that Sister Mary associates purgatory with an earthly place, not a condition. This inclination to attribute spatial and physical characteristics to purgatory, and the problems this creates, is intrinsic to its history. Scholastic theologians of the thirteenth century, who were most responsible for providing the theological support for the new doctrine, questioned where it was on earth, and they rarely questioned *if* it was on earth. William of Auvergne (1180–1249) posited the existence of two purgatories, one on earth, and the other somewhere else, perhaps near heaven. As recently as 1863, the French periodical "Le Liberateur des Ames du Purgatoire," edited by the French priest Celestin Cloquet, described how the souls in purgatory resided inside the earth. Purgatory's place on medieval and early modern world maps, or *mappa mundi*, persisted even as the Garden of Eden and heaven, the two most mapped religious destinations, gradually disappeared.

Processes of "disenchantment" had a profound effect on representations of purgatory as an earthly location. In the late nineteenth century, sociologist Max Weber argued that societies of early modern Europe became disenchanted, as a former, religious or "enchanted" worldview was replaced with one that emphasized natural mechanisms as the prime cause of empirical phenomena. In other words, empirical processes replaced divine intervention as the primary explanatory framework for natural events. In the twentieth century, the "disenchantment of the world" became a catchphrase for scholars of religion to describe secularization, and although Weber's thesis has been shown to be too general and fraught with teleological assumptions, it is an apt description of the progress of modern representations of purgatory, which gradually focused less on thaumaturgical and material elements. Among the various and often contradictory ways in which purgatory has been represented, a pattern emerges in the modern era that gradually takes root, particularly after the French Enlightenment, that points to a decline in its association with hell and "real," not figurative, tortures inflicted by demons and angels. In European Catholic devotional culture of the early modern era to the present, there is a move away from imagining purgatory as a material, punitive place to a more gentle, abstract process of purgation. This trajectory is absent in vision narratives and other sources from late antiquity through the medieval eras, where purgatory is consistently varied in its spaces and places.[9] In later representations, purgatory became a site where souls no longer endured visceral tortures, but instead experienced a more abstract pain of loss. In this sense, representations of purgatory reflect larger cultural developments regarding belief in the afterlife, particularly hell.[10]

There are exceptions to this trend, however. Contemporary advocates of purgatory have revived medieval and early modern popular narratives about purgatory and republished them for popular consumption. *The Way of the Cross for the Holy Souls in Purgatory*, which was first published in 1928, is being edited and reprinted by the popular author of Catholic devotional literature, Susan Tassone, and has been one of Our Sunday Visitor Press's best-selling books for fifteen years. There are some new narratives about purgatory, as well. On a website managed by the Missionary Sons of Mary, dedicated to Saint Jude Thaddeus, viewers can read an account of a mother and daughter, who, while praying for their deceased husband and father, are surprised when the floor opens up into a crevice of flames. The article, "A True Story about Purgatory Involving One of Our Priests," describes how the father cries out in agony and asks them to have a traditional Requiem Mass performed for his soul.[11] In contemporary devotional books about purgatory, which is the subject of chapter 5, authors insist that purgatory is a physical place: "Various manifestations of souls from Purgatory to saints and mystics, however, prove beyond reasonable doubt that the physical nature of the suffering in Purgatory is real and it is much more intense than anything one can imagine in this world."[12] The issue of purgatory's materiality vexed theologians in the thirteenth century and continues to be an important issue for Catholics concerned with reviving a declining and, within most American parishes, often nonexistent devotion and belief.

Susan Tassone and others like her, who emphasize the materiality and reality of purgatory, are resisting a gradual development that is hundreds of years old, and their resistance is illustrative of issues within the contemporary American Catholic culture. My exchange with Sister Mary, again, is revealing in this instance. Sister Mary received her religious training during the tumultuous years of the Second Vatican Council (1962–1965). She is not sure if purgatory is still a doctrine of the Church and she encouraged me to focus my discussion on issues of engagement in the world, rather than on sacrifice and penance, which in her estimation belonged to an older era of Catholicism. In many ways, Sister Mary and authors of contemporary purgatory literature—who insist that purgatory is real and requires penance—represent two very different interpretations of the Catholic tradition. This issue speaks to what has been termed a "hermeneutic of discontinuity," which involves the interpretation of the massive changes that swept the Church after Vatican II.[13] In this sense, the history of the problem of purgatory, which I will argue is a history of its materiality, illustrates a broader issue within American Catholicism that has to do with these changes. Contemporary efforts to revive a tradition of purgatory that focus on its spatial and material qualities and link these to the sacred reflects an implicit, and often explicit, critique of the Church reforms of Vatican II. In interviews with Catholics who are engaged in reviving old purgatory literature, it was apparent that they believed that the Church has lost its focus on the afterlife, the salvation of souls, and the reality of the supernatural. The reforms of Vatican II, according to many whom I interviewed, placed too much emphasis on pastoral efforts that replaced a view of the Church as the mediator between worldly matters and the supernatural. The efforts by contemporary Catholics to recover the material culture and texts associated with a "foregone era" illustrates how purgatory's materiality—its spatial, concrete aspects, and its location—is directly linked to practitioners' understanding of their connection to the deceased, their view of the afterlife, and, most significantly, their interpretation of Catholic history. While this book traces the purgatory problematic—its status as a place and/or condition through history—I end with contemporary culture and reveal that the problem of purgatory's materiality continues to be an issue, and one that is at times controversial. As a historian, I have no stake in this debate, other than to reveal, to the best of my ability, the frameworks that have contributed to this development.

The Second Vatican Council: From Tabernacle and Purgatory *to* Spirit and Life

The Second Vatican Council, convened by Pope John XXIII in 1962 and closed by Pope Paul VI in 1965, represents a significant turning point in Catholic history.[14] It has been variously interpreted as a watershed moment where the Magisterium of the Catholic Church chose to adapt to modern times, or critiqued as an inorganic "rupture" instigated as a top-down movement by a handful of clergy.[15] By all accounts, however, it represents one of the most decisive moments in Catholic history. A church distinguished by services conducted in Latin that mandated penances such as forbidding practitioners meat on Friday metamorphosed into a church that initiated inclusive liturgical services conducted in the languages of the laity, all within approximately eight years. Foremost among the changes was a restructuring of the liturgy and the eradication of much of the material support for devotional practices involving intercessory prayers to saints and devotions for the dead.[16]

The change of title of the second-oldest continuously published American Catholic periodical *Tabernacle and Purgatory* is illustrative of the effects that the Vatican Council had on beliefs and practices associated with purgatory. The Benedictine periodical, published since 1905 as a forum for Catholics, featured narratives about the "holy souls" in purgatory.[17] In 1965 the editors changed the title of the periodical to *Spirit and Life*. Elaborating on the change, the editors noted that the old title reflected "a former era's devotion to the souls in Purgatory." Explaining why this reference was no longer relevant, they wrote that the new title reflected a different emphasis, one now "caught up in the surge of renewal which the Spirit of God is breathing upon our era, our magazine too reaches out toward new horizons and new perspectives."[18] The change of title was a seamless adaptation to the new standards set by the Council, as the reference to the concrete structure of the tabernacle was replaced with the more abstract term "spirit," and the this-world emphasis on "life" supplanted the otherworld connotation of purgatory.

In changing the name of *Tabernacle and Purgatory*, the editors were aligning the mission of their periodical not just with the new "spirit" of Vatican II, but also with a development that gained traction after the French Enlightenment. The dichotomous framing of spirit over matter received vigorous support through the works of eighteenth-century philosophers like Immanuel Kant, whose essay *Religion within the Limits of Reason Alone* was highly influential and argued that religion should be based solely on reason and belief rather than on ritual and revelation. Kant's ideas influenced many Enlightenment thinkers and had a profound effect on representations of religion. Brigit Meyer argues that during the 1840s and afterward, the empirical sciences dictated the terms of how religion would be viewed, particularly with respect to a spirit and matter dualism. She notes, "The opposition has continued to shape public opinion up to our time."[19] As the change in title of the periodical suggests, the shift in emphasis toward social engagement with issues like poverty and injustice in the world instead of otherworld concerns, inaugurated by the theologians of the Vatican Council, had profound effects on beliefs and practices associated with purgatory.

On cue with the new emphasis on spirit during the 1960s, the Church hierarchy shifted its relationship to Catholic material culture. Statues of saints were removed and relegated "to the periphery of Catholic attention."[20] Some of the most significant changes occurred with respect to the liturgy or religious service for the dead called the Requiem Mass (Mass for the Dead), performed at funerals and during The Commemoration of All Faithful Departed or All Souls' Day. The traditional, pre-Conciliar Requiem Mass was a solemn affair that made use of material supports such as the catafalque, beeswax candles, and the color black. The catafalque is a structure that typically supports a coffin and functions as a visible sign of the invisible presence of the deceased.[21] In the post-Conciliar Requiem Mass it was removed because it was perceived to be an impediment to reflections upon resurrection. Similarly, the priests' robes, or vestments, which were traditionally black, were changed to white or violet. Priests were encouraged to wear the new colors because they were thought to reflect ideas of resurrection as well as to incorporate the traditions of non-Western cultures where black was not associated with death. In the former Requiem Mass, congregants chanted the *Dies Irae* (Day of Wrath), which was a medieval Latin hymn about the Day of Judgment. The chanting of this hymn was also discouraged, as it was said to convey an "unduly fearsome concept of death."[22] The new liturgy removed material components that supported a specific image of the afterlife—instead of emphasizing a view that the deceased would suffer for their sins and were in need of prayers and supplications, it advocated for a hopeful view of the afterlife as a state of resurrection.

The changes consequential to the Council were shocking on many levels to American Catholics, and even those who favored the changes acknowledged that the shift, while surprising, "may be a good antidote for us."[23] One parishioner stated that although she abhorred "the downgrading of the Renaissance art to ninety yards of fabric crowded with pasted-on banners and butterflies," she was for the most part resigned and happy to "allow the younger generation their expression of faith."[24] Studies conducted during the changes revealed, for the most part, support for the changes among the laity.[25] For some Catholics the change from Latin to English and the vernacular "could not come too quickly."[26] The new Mass allowed for more opportunities for celebrants to participate and parishes reported having record numbers of volunteers. However, the removal of material support for the devotions that had structured the lives of many American Catholics was not a "matter of small consequence."[27] The pre-Conciliar presence of the saints in the churches, as well as regular, public devotions, even while already in decline prior to the Council, nonetheless provided the appearance of the stable and consistent support of supernatural helpers.[28] It also reinforced the doctrine of the Mystical Body of Christ. The realms of the Mystical Body of Christ, purgatory, and earth and heaven are all interactive, and devotions play an important role as a means of contact between the members of each realm. This doctrine, fully elaborated by Pope Pius XII in 1943, emphasized the role of the laity in maintaining the church, the Mystical Body, through their devotions and actions.[29] The removal of the signs, images, and practices that articulated doctrines that supported the invisible structures of the visible church had an effect on belief in the doctrine of purgatory.

Belief in purgatory had enjoyed the support of a rich heritage of material structures like chantry chapels that allowed priests or religious to perform

FIGURE I-I Privileged St Cross altar, 18th century Kosmonosy (Czech Republic, Central Bohemia) Church of the Piarist order. Reprinted with the permission of the Department of Art History, Faculty of Arts, Masaryk University Brno, photo Tomasz Zwyrtek.

Masses or prayers for deceased souls, privileged altars, and a myriad of iconographic forms such as murals, paintings, and engravings. It had also been supported by written discourse, the most famous of which is Dante Alighieri's *Purgatorio*, and later as purgatory periodicals and pamphlets. As a central component of the doctrine of the Mystical Body of Christ, the realm of purgatory contained the souls of the Church Suffering. The removal of the saints and material support for this doctrine had a profound impact on belief in the doctrine of purgatory. It was this very aspect of the Church, the emphasis on otherworldly suffering, that underwent a significant change. This was most evident in the changes that impacted the liturgy of the Mass—the primary sacrament and weekly devotion of Catholics.

The liturgical changes instituted by the council members of Vatican II directly and indirectly affected rituals and practices associated with purgatory. Among those who had instigated the liturgical reforms was Archbishop Annibale Bugnini, who was a member of the committee responsible for drafting *Sacrosanctum Concilium* or the Council's *Constitution on the Sacred Liturgy*, the document that outlined the liturgical changes. Commenting years after the Council, he noted that Council members "got rid of texts that smacked of a negative spirituality inherited from the Middle Ages. Thus they removed such familiar and even beloved texts as the *Libera me* (Deliver Me), *Domine* (Our Lord), the *Dies Irae* (Day of Wrath), and others that overemphasized judgment, fear, and despair. They replaced these with texts urging Christian hope and arguably giving more effective expression of faith in the resurrection."[30] Purgatory, which by definition is a place where souls experience expiation and is between death and heaven, didn't fare well amid these changes. On the one hand, the removal of the material supports for the Mystical Body of Christ, which supported the Church Suffering, or the souls in purgatory, dealt one blow to the material structures that supported the belief. And on the other hand, the removal of the psalms and scriptures that emphasized expiation and suffering post-death dealt another blow to belief in the doctrine.

The Catholic Response to the Liturgical Reforms and a Hermeneutic of (Dis)Continuity

The reform of the liturgy illustrated in stark relief the importance of material culture to sustaining certain Catholic beliefs. Nowhere was this more evident than in Catholic reactions to the reforms. In one instance, reaction to the reforms resulted in schism. Archbishop Marcel Lefebvre, who had been a member of the Second Vatican Council, was so troubled by the changes in the liturgy that he founded a society of priests in 1970, the fraternal Society of St. Pius X, who refused to celebrate the new form of the Mass, called the *Novus Ordo*. Lefebvre felt that the new Mass was not valid and did not transmit the true and living spirit of the tradition. He felt he had no choice but to foster the transmission of the true tradition sacramentally passed down through the liturgy of the Tridentine, or old Roman Rite Mass, officiated in the Latin.

In 1988 Lefebvre consecrated four priests as bishops, enabling another generation to transmit the tradition within the line of Peter. Pope John Paul II was presiding at the time. He called Lefebvre's actions an affront to the Roman lineage of Peter and to the Roman pontiff. He declared the consecrations illicit and schismatic. The same year that Lefebvre ordained the bishops, John Paul II excommunicated him from the Roman Catholic Church. Although the excommunications were a bold and public gesture communicating a policy of intolerance toward disobedience, John Paul II did recognize that the Tridentine liturgy, or the Roman Rite in its extraordinary form (Latin), was important for many who had grown up with it and for many within the Catholic hierarchy, such as the followers of Lefebvre. In an attempt to reach these Catholics, John Paul II took decisive action to heal the wound caused by the liturgical reforms and by the excommunications and to prevent the formation of a parallel church.[31] He wrote an apostolic letter in the form of *motu proprio* (on his own impulse), *Ecclesia Dei Adflicta*, which in this case was a letter to the whole Church, acknowledging that there were many who wished to preserve the old liturgical tradition and also wished to remain faithful to the true "Successor of Peter," John Paul II. For their benefit he instituted a Pontifical Commission *Ecclesia Dei* that would oversee these groups, allow them to celebrate the Tridentine Mass, and address their specific needs and concerns.

Twenty years later, in 2009 and amid a growing movement of Catholics who in varying degrees shared Lefebvre's interpretation of tradition and desired access to the sacramental repository of the church as manifested in the Roman Rite and the Tridentine Mass, Pope Benedict XVI nullified the excommunications of Saint Pius X Society's bishops. Earlier, in 2007, Pope Benedict XVI issued the encyclical *Summorum Pontificum* (of the Supreme Pontiffs) that addressed the use of the Roman Rite. In this letter, Benedict directly dealt with the divisive issues of "discontinuity" of tradition by declaring that although there may be the appearance of discontinuous traditions surrounding the two liturgies, there is really just one Rite, not two. He explained that the one Rite has two forms, the ordinary form (officiated in the vernacular) and the extraordinary form (officiated in the Latin). Even before 2007, Benedict was attempting to ameliorate the "hermeneutics of discontinuity." In his 2005 Christmas address to the bishops, he reflected upon the past forty years since the Second Vatican Council:

> Why has the implementation of the Council, in large parts of the Church, thus far been so difficult?
>
> Well, it all depends on the correct interpretation of the Council or—as we would say today—on its proper hermeneutics, the correct key to its interpretation and application. The problems in its implementation arose from the fact that two contrary hermeneutics came face to face and quarreled with each other. One caused confusion, the other, silently but more and more visibly, bore and is bearing fruit.
>
> On the one hand, there is an interpretation that I would call "a hermeneutic of discontinuity and rupture"; it has frequently availed itself of the sympathies of the mass media, and also one trend of modern theology. On the other, there is the "hermeneutic of reform," of renewal in the continuity of the one subject—Church which the Lord has given to us.[32]

During his tenure as pope, Benedict consistently attempted to ameliorate the perception that Vatican II initiated a "new tradition," thus earning him the title of the "reformer of the reform."[33] He received both criticism and accolades for his efforts. Catholics in favor of the older traditions were happy that he allowed the Roman Rite to be made available, where it had previously been subject to special permission. He acknowledged that new and young Catholics were intrigued and attracted to the beauty of the Roman Rite, admiring its aesthetic value that was manifest in its material forms, and for that reason he believed that it should be made freely available and supported by bishops. Critics wondered if he was going back on the *Spirit* of the Council. His message, however, attempted to keep the church unified. In all of his efforts he expressed hope that "in the history of the liturgy there is growth and progress, but no rupture. What earlier generations held as sacred, remains sacred and great for us too, and it cannot be all of a sudden entirely forbidden or even considered harmful."[34]

Although Lefebvre's Society represents an extreme response to Vatican II, the critique expressed by its members, that Vatican II inaugurated a "pastoral" form of Catholicism—not one dedicated to the salvation of souls, and that this is reflected in liturgical and material culture—is shared to varying degrees by those involved in contemporary efforts to revive the material aspects of purgatory.

Materiality Matters: The New Traditionalists and the Purgatory Apostolates

The case of the Society of Saint Pius X reveals that many Catholics have interpreted the *appearance* of historical discontinuity as reality. In other words, where some see continuity, others see rupture. In sociological studies of American Catholics, those who came of age before and during the Second Vatican Council's generation have proven to be the most committed parishioners.[35] They are distinctive from other cohorts in that they were raised within a family where parents discussed religion with their children and lived within an extended Catholic community. They report that they often had teachers and coaches as religious role models. Demographic studies reveal that in the United States cohort differences are more significant than racial, ethnic, or gender differences.[36] Although the pre-Conciliar cohort accepts the changes that were made after the Council, they report regret over the disappearance of the culture that supported public devotions such as praying the rosary and devotions for the holy souls in purgatory. In general, this generation reports more experiences of God's presence than other cohorts and they link this experience to devotions and going to private confession.[37] Although they are mostly in favor of the changes wrought by the Second Vatican Council, they share a common cause with a loosely affiliated group of Catholics whose members span all generations: traditionalist Catholics. Uniting the two groups is the assumption that the material aspects of the Catholic faith—the statues and relics of saints; the images, smells, and music of the Roman Rite; as well as the various devotions involving images and pilgrimages to shrines—are not mere additions to the faith, but are constitutive of the presence of the sacred. In the words of Marshall McLuhan, who was a Catholic and scholar of the mass media, for these practitioners "the medium *is* the message."

Traditionalist Catholicism began with the first liturgical reforms of the Second Vatican Council and proliferated among Marcel Lefebvre's society as well as among the followers of other well-known priests like Italian Francesco Forgione, *Padre Pio,* who asked for special permission to continue the Roman Rite. The movement is universal in scope, spanning the ranks of clergy and the laity, international and intergenerational. Many of my students consider themselves traditionalist Catholics. When I ask them what that means, they respond by relating how they were exposed to the aesthetic dimensions of Catholicism through videogames, movies, songs, and other venues. In other words, the material representations of pre-Conciliar Catholicism are important to them. One student explained that his introduction to traditionalist Catholicism came through hearing Gregorian chant in Japanese anime. Mainstream newspapers comment on the trend toward traditionalism, noting that the traditional Mass is "not a fogey's hangout. The congregation is young and international. Like evangelical Christianity, traditional Catholicism is attracting people who were not even born when the Second Vatican Council tried to rejuvenate the church."[38] It hasn't been the first time that Catholic aesthetic culture inspired conversions. English Catholic convert and architect Augustus Welby Pugin ignited the early nineteenth-century Gothic Revival that resulted in the spread of neo-Gothic Protestant and Catholic church structures throughout England and the United States because he felt that the material structures of medieval churches literally manifested the presence of the sacred. The American intellectual Orestes Brownson converted to Catholicism amid widespread shock and dismay, citing as part of his motivation Catholicism's aesthetic charms.[39]

Several of my students were introduced to the doctrine of purgatory through a popular videogame called *Dante's Inferno*. In the game, players have to move through the nine circles of hell in a boat called *Charon* and they eventually come upon the island of purgatory. The protagonist, Dante, is reimagined as a knight of the Crusades who battles demons, helps absolve sinners of their sins, and punishes the worst of them. Other students remembered Cole Sear, the youthful protagonist of M. Night Shyamalan's movie *The Sixth Sense* (1999), who made the line "I see dead people" a modern idiom. Cole's proclivity for seeing dead people disturbs him, and he seeks refuge in a makeshift tent in his bedroom that he arms with small statues of Catholic saints and a statue of Jesus he has stolen from a church. In one scene, Cole seeks sanctuary in the church, which is distinctively medieval, as noted in the screenplay: "Its old stone and huge towers make it stand out from the modern buildings all around it."[40] In the church Cole recites, in Latin, the Hebrew Psalm 130, *De Profundis*, which, besides being a psalm, is a Catholic prayer for the holy souls in purgatory. Cole utilizes the church and his tent as a refuge from the dead people he sees. This is clarified by the exchange he has with Malcolm, the psychologist who is attempting to help Cole with his issues (and who, it is revealed later, is dead). "In olden times, in Europe, people used to hide in churches. Claim sanctuary," Malcolm says. Cole asks him, "Nothing bad can ever happen in a church, right?"[41] Were the dead people that Cole

saw in purgatory? Regardless of the answer, many modern representations of afterlife scenes, like those in *The Sixth Sense*, appropriate medieval Catholic imagery and attract new followers to a movement whose
members resonate with imagery that evokes an older, and, what many
perceive to be, a more authentic tradition.

The appropriation of medieval Catholic imagery and narratives is not
only a phenomenon within youth culture. Contemporary devotional literature
about purgatory features medieval, early modern, and nineteenth-century
images of souls in purgatory. The most popular author of contemporary
purgatory devotional literature is Susan Tassone. In my interviews with her,
I found that she and I shared knowledge of many of the primary sources
about purgatory that were only to be found in one or two archives in the
world. She has edited and republished many of them for an enthusiastic
audience. When her bestselling book, *Praying with the Saints for the Holy
Souls in Purgatory*, was about to be published, she related how she and her
editors chose the artwork for the cover. The artist, Jed Gibbons, agreed to
paint a piece inspired by the Communion of Saints where holy souls are
languish underneath the Virgin Mary, the Queen of Purgatory, and other
members of the Church Triumphant. Susan wanted to capture what she
considered an authentic tradition and appearance, and to recapture a pre-
Conciliar aesthetic. Susan's book revives many of the pre-Conciliar devotions. In my conversations with her, I never had the impression that she
considered herself to be a traditionalist Catholic, but she did envision her
vocation as publishing books on purgatory that utilize old sources and
clarify misunderstandings about purgatory, for an enthusiastic audience.
Her texts recover several aspects of past purgatory devotions relating to
place, body, and performance. In her recapitulations of the narratives of
purgatory, she attends to its location and issues like its physical torments.
She also prescribes old devotions related to penance and rituals, in the form
of intercessory prayers, in an effort to ameliorate the suffering of the souls
in purgatory. These texts help practitioners form connections to the deceased and they provide them with a view of the nature of the otherworld.

Susan is one of many "apostolate" leaders who edit and republish old books
about purgatory. An apostolate is a ministry, often lead by laity, which furthers
the aims of the Church in various ways. There are different types of apostolates, such as those intended to end hunger or to help the poor. The purgatory
apostolate leaders educate Catholics about the doctrine and promote devotions for the holy souls in purgatory. They are selective about the books they
republish, choosing texts that emphasize purgatory's concrete aspects as

opposed to texts that promote purgatory as a process or condition of the soul.⁴² The purgatory apostolate movement is significant in that it reflects, on a practical level, issues about competing interpretations of Catholic history. To apostolate leaders, Vatican II inaugurated a rupture in tradition with respect to the doctrine of purgatory. Before Vatican II, Catholics knew what the doctrine was, how to avoid purgatory, and why praying for souls in purgatory was necessary. After Vatican II, purgatory disappeared for most Catholics. The concrete and spatial aspects of purgatory are important to the apostolate leaders and their communities and are utilized as means of educating about the reality of purgatory. Many of the revived stories feature souls in purgatory that are portrayed in real, not figurative, fire, where holy souls visit the living and ask for prayers and intercessions and leave physical evidence of their visits, like burned handprints on tables, or windows left open. Put simply, the material features of purgatory and its associated rituals and devotions are being revived or reinterpreted, and interpretations of purgatory as an abstract condition are often rejected. Most apostolate leaders feel they must reach into the treasure trove of the past and bring old images and rituals into the present, where they are then reinterpreted as linking current Catholics to what they imagine as a continuous and unruptured past. Others, like Susan Tassone, view their vocation as correcting old interpretations of purgatory as a place and replacing them with the new interpretation of purgatory as a process.

Within the context of debates about the hermeneutic of continuity, the activities of the members of purgatory apostolates reveal that purgatory and its representation is one example of how contemporary American Catholics are articulating a hermeneutic of rupture without explicitly disagreeing with official statements from Joseph Ratzinger and others who insist that there is one continuous, unbroken Catholic tradition. Without exception, each of the ministers I interviewed insisted that he is loyal to the Catholic Magisterium. Yet they reject the current representation of purgatory—some would say "non-representation"—in favor of an older version perceived to be more authentic. The more authentic version, they believe, has physical features complete with visceral punishments. The apostolate minister's focus on the materiality and recuperation of old versions of purgatory participates in the general reassessment of Vatican II promoted by traditionalist Catholics, who, among other things, shed light on the issue of how the sacred intersects with, and is embodied in, Catholic materiality.

The contemporary status of purgatory's representation is just the latest in a long tradition of problems associated with its materiality. Although purgatory was officially defined by the Roman Catholic Church in documents leading up to and during the Second Council of Lyon between 1245 and 1274, it had existed as a concept for several hundred years. In her study of purgatory in the texts of late antiquity, Isabel Moreira notes that "before these conciliar pronouncements, purgatory's existence was hardly doubted. For centuries purgatory's features and purpose were fleshed out by religious groups, political players, writers, poets, visionaries, and by clerics and ordinary people telling ghost stories. For centuries, purgatory did not need an official stamp, because it had gradually seeped into common Christian understanding of where dead Christians went."[43] It was later, during the "long twelfth century," that the place and location of purgatory became an issue debated by scholastic philosophers.

Theorizing the Problem: Purgatory as "Betwixt and Between"

As a transitional state between death and heaven, purgatory is liminal, a threshold between two ostensibly stable conditions. Liminality, from the Latin, *limen*, meaning threshold, is a space, place, or state of ambiguity, "betwixt and between" two stable categories of meaning.[44] It has been suggested that "liminal" categories construct the appearance of stability.[45] There are liminal stages, such as coming-of-age ceremonies and rites of passage, where participants are neither children, nor adults; liminal processes, such as pilgrimage; and liminal beings, like cyborgs or monsters, and monks or nuns. Mary Douglas's work on liminal beings reveals that they can be dangerous, yet possess potential benefits.[46] The shaman is a liminal figure who bridges the worlds of the sacred and profane. He or she can elicit healings or inflict curses. The liminal, in this sense, confers power. Liminal places are powerful places as well, and potentially dangerous. Sacred caves, mountains, and pilgrimage sites confer a spiritual benefit to those who can withstand their tests.

Purgatory's status as a liminal condition and place is made more complicated because throughout its history it has been liminal in different ways. Purgatory is generally conceived of as an afterlife condition of transition, between death and heaven. However, for hundreds of years purgatory was believed to be a place on earth, accessed through a cave, itself a literal threshold. As such it was both this-worldly and otherworldly. As theologians solidified its status as otherworldly and Catholics were encouraged to interpret it as a condition, not a place, they nevertheless read narratives featuring souls scorched by fire, suspended in blocks of ice, and engaged in epic battles with demons. In other words, purgatory's specific type of liminality is not just that it is a transitional state for souls, but possesses qualities that appear to make it simultaneously material and immaterial. Some of the more popular visions about purgatory possess this quality. The seventh-century Irish monk Fursey had a vision of an aerial purgatory and retained a physical scar from his visit. The medieval "bestseller" *The Treatise of Saint Patrick's Purgatory*, written by the Cistercian monk H. of Saltrey, recounts the tale of a knight/visionary who literally walks through a cave into purgatory, which is represented as a physical place. He is fully awake, not dreaming or having a vision, and the tale inspired many pilgrims to journey to Ireland in search of the real entrance to purgatory. Most medieval visionary literature features a visionary who, in her mind's eye, or in a dream, travels to an otherworld. Not so with the *Treatise*, which also emphasizes the scars remaining on the knight's body when he returns.

Within the field of religious studies, the subject of religion and its material features has received recent interest from scholars. In 2000 David Chidester announced a *material turn* within the study of religion.[47] With respect to Catholic history, Colleen McDannell elaborated the terms of the study of materiality of religion in her book *Material Christianity: Religion and Popular Culture in America* (1995). She identified a bias within the study of religion that downplayed the material aspects of religion and religious practice. In his work, historian Robert Orsi focuses on the ways in which Italian American Catholics embody their faith and connect with the sacred through objects such as images of saints. The *material turn* inaugurated several exciting ways to consider the liminal within religious traditions that specifically addressed its status as simultaneously material and immaterial. Many theorists place the body at the center of analyses in attempting to overcome a mind/body, spirit/matter dualism.[48] David Morgan's work elaborates a theory of religious images and the cultural work they perform in the construction of meaning, taking into account cultural biases that privilege the text over the image. Jeremy Biles coined the term "paramediation," to explain how a physical object, a body or a telephone, for example, functions as a form of mediation between the visible and the invisible.[49] In his analysis of the body and senses in apparitions and visions, he concludes that "far from confirming some Cartesian dualism, mystical raptures dramatically exhibit the ultimate inseparability of mind, spirit and body, for such experiences are shot through with imagery and grounded in bodies practiced in 'techniques of ecstasy.'"[50] The techniques of ecstasy Biles refers to are ascetic practices intended to initiate mystical states. Jeffery Kripal, while not generally included within the materialist turn in religious studies, advocates a theory of religion in his book *Authors of the Impossible: The Paranormal and the Sacred*, which grapples with the material elements of the paranormal. Coining the term "The Impossible," he interprets supernatural/paranormal phenomena as "not dualistic or intentional experiences at all, that is, they are not about a stable 'subject' experiencing a definite 'object.'" Instead, he argues that these events are narrative experiences that are most often encountered in texts. He recommends viewing the paranormal or supernatural as semiotic, hermeneutical phenomena often embedded in certain texts.

Within different historical contexts, purgatory's materiality has functioned in various ways. Within scholastic texts, purgatory was a necessary construct to foster the separation of the philosophical categories of spirit and matter. It is significant that during the medieval era, at which time purgatory was affirmed as a Roman Catholic doctrine, scholastic theologians were rediscovering the works of Aristotle and his work regarding two substances in the universe: matter and spirit. From its inception as a doctrine, purgatory's materiality has functioned simultaneously as a benefit and a problem. For hundreds of years the "place" of purgatory, which was potentially on earth, helped sustain a belief in the doctrine. Tales of adventurous knights and nobleman who traveled through purgatory acted as an advertisement for the destination for clergy and practitioners. These tales fueled the fires of medieval imaginings about purgatory, lending support to the newly established doctrine. Its location, which, for many, was arguably in Ireland, was a problem too, especially throughout the thirteenth century as the scholastics ramped up their efforts to place it within the framework of an emerging philosophical category of Dualism as they understood it. As Jacques Le Goff notes, "One senses a desire to rationalize Purgatory, to tidy it up, to control it—in a word, to purge it of its offensive popular trappings." These trappings included references to "the senses."[51] Was purgatory on earth, or was it an afterlife state? Was it somehow both? These questions vexed medieval scholars like Thomas Aquinas and William of Auvergne.

The materiality of representations of purgatory has puzzled scholars as well. In Carol Zaleski's substantive analysis of medieval vision narratives, she notes that the *Treatise* (*Tractatus de Purgatorio Sancti Patricii*) differs from other vision narratives in that its protagonist, a knight of the crusades, Owen, journeys into a real purgatory. In this sense the *Tractatus* "stands apart."[52] Courtney Kunshuh also notes this difference. In most medieval visionary narratives, the visionary travels through otherworld destinations through his or her mind's eye, while the person's body, in bed or sitting, remains perfectly still.[53] Contrary to this, Owen's experience of traveling through a cave of purgatory takes place "physically rather than in a dream," which "is unlike most other visionaries."[54] Le Goff also notes the various ways in which purgatory was thought to be a physical place. Gregory the Great (540–604) claimed that purgatory had its foundations in various sites in Italy, including Sicily and the Lipari Islands.[55]

The materiality of purgatory is its most persistent, and, I will argue in this book, problematic feature. From its inception as a doctrine, I trace the gradual shift away from its status as a physical place of tactile punishment to its status as being perceived, as Benedict XVI declared in 2011, as a "process," devoid of spatiality. How did this shift come about? Which texts were instrumental in instigating this change? What political and social developments supported this move away from interpreting purgatory as a material place with physical features to viewing it as a condition? Through answering these questions, I hope to contribute to an understanding of purgatory as a permanent site of liminality, as Victor Turner argues in *Betwixt and Between*, as a state perceived to be at once "pure"—spiritual in the Cartesian sense of "pure spirit"—while at the same time polluted by materiality, or place. Purgatory is generally represented simultaneously as a spiritual state associated with non-corporeal souls, and a place where these souls have the capacity to feel real fire and to leave physical evidence of their experiences. In other words, souls in purgatory are represented as simultaneously non-corporeal *and* corporeal. Today, there are relatively few new representations of purgatory. The emergence of the purgatory apostolates and the loosely affiliated group of communities associated with them—traditionalist Catholics, homeschool communities, young people interested in the aesthetic elements of the Catholic tradition, and others—contribute to a growing interest in the tradition of purgatory as a physical place. With few exceptions, they do not invent new ways of imaging purgatory, but harken back to older traditions.

Dynamics of power are evident as one explores the problems associated with purgatory's materiality. Authors and communities that support the view of purgatory as a condition and not a physical place are generally associated with the Church hierarchy, as starkly illustrated in the nineteenth century, when influential Catholic converts, former Anglicans John Henry Newman and William Henry Faber, promoted a view of purgatory

that was distinctly nonmaterial and contrary to the views espoused by
mid-level Catholic nuns and clerics, like the abbot Celestin Cloquet, who
argued that purgatory was in the middle of the earth. The latter's publications were shut down by the Church and ridiculed by non-Catholic polemicists. Newman's and Faber's works on purgatory, on the other hand, were
incorporated into Catholic periodicals like *Tabernacle and Purgatory*, and
continue to be published today.

Much of the scholarship about purgatory spans the periods of late antiquity through the medieval era and focuses on precedents and potential
foundational texts that informed the official, thirteenth-century doctrine.
Le Goff's *The Birth of Purgatory* remains an important history of purgatory. Le Goff argued that thirteenth-century theologians first used the
term "purgatory" to refer to a place of purgation that was neither heaven
nor hell.[56] Delving further into the past, Peter Brown, working with
sources from late antiquity, argued that it was during the seventh century
that a significant shift in Christian ideas of the afterlife came about. This
shift involved a change from imagining the otherworld, including demons
and angels, as imminent and close at hand, if invisible, to a belief in the
otherworld as being something one encounters when one is dead, and is
therefore inaccessible to the living. Brown argued that this new view is
seen in the works of Gregory the Great, where one observes "a perceptible
tilt away from a world rustling with invisible, contiguous powers toward
a world beyond the grave."[57] Did any one cultural tradition or set of texts
ultimately leave an indelible mark on the doctrine? This is a matter for
interpretation. Le Goff speculates that the doctrine drew from a Celtic
penitential worldview: "A theme common among Celts was that of the
voyage to the islands of the blessed, the earliest example of which seems
to be the voyage of Bran." He suggests that perhaps this and other similar
tales may have played an important role in purgatory's formation.[58] Isabel
Moreira's work reveals that this position is problematic, as visions of the
afterlife that focused on "intense sinfulness" were already in circulation in
the fifth and sixth centuries.[59] She argues that cultural diffusion makes
searching for one cultural tradition of purgatory, like an Irish tradition,
problematic, as many Irish monks were proficient in Latin, and many
Continental clerics and theologians were indebted to Irish influences.

The sources most often used to compile the early history of purgatory
are "ghost stories" and medieval vision narratives, most of which are Latin
texts authored by clerics. Important studies of vision literature of purgatory
and otherworld journeys include the works of Carol Zaleski and Jean-Claude

Schmitt. Zaleski's *Otherworld Journeys: Accounts of Near Death Experience in Medieval and Modern Times* examines patterns within vision narratives about purgatory and Schmitt's *Ghosts in the Middle Ages* is an examination of several stories about purgatory and the souls who populate it. Schmitt calls his analysis a "social history of the imaginary," and speculates that medieval Catholics "bestowed in certain of their dead a semblance of existence, a bodily appearance and a face." Although he concedes that they perhaps did so to better understand their relationship to the deceased, he also suggests that they were motivated to "control the society of the living, the transference of inheritances, and the imposition of moral and social norms." In other words, he uncovers issues of power at work in the social contexts that birthed these narratives.

Expanding on the types of sources that contain information about medieval belief in purgatory, Carl Watkins explores medieval *chronicles*, which are illustrated histories, and *exempla*, lists of morality-themed anecdotes used by priests in their homilies.[60] Rejecting the "two-culture model" that assumes that elite cultures possess distinct religious beliefs and practices that differ from provincial or folkloric cultures, his work reveals a community of believers "bound together by shared belief, ritual and practice," where complexity and diversity of belief characterized both clerical and lay communities.[61] The development of shared ideas and practices "generated tension as churchmen tried to tighten religious observance in the localities," but also generated collusion as well. For Watkins, while diversity of belief and practice dominates the era, cultural trends do emerge, and he cautions that "the mistake here might be to imagine that the theologians drove change when in reality they followed developments which they were obliged to accommodate."[62] What this means for the doctrine of purgatory is that its development can't just be pinned to certain narratives or visionary tales that informed theologians, who then formulated the doctrine, but instead also involved the Church's responses to local customs, practices, stories, and anecdotes.[63]

In the last ten years, several studies of purgatory have emerged that stress material culture, rather than texts, as sources for understanding beliefs and practices associated with purgatory. These studies focus on objects like privileged altars, which emerged after the reforms of the Council of Trent, and still dot the religious landscape of Europe today. Privileged altars functioned as a public connection between the living and the dead in that prayers or masses said at the altar were indulged—that is, the rituals performed at the altar were believed to help souls achieve a quicker entrance into heaven from purgatory. The Council of Trent was convened to address the criticisms and ruptures brought about by the Protestant Reformation, and as a consequence the Church sought to unify belief through rituals like those performed at the privileged altar. Art historians Tomáš Malý and Pavel Suchánek, working with Moravian art and texts spanning the sixteenth through the seventeenth centuries, explore the ways in which material structures like the privileged altar, engravings, and other objects manifested the Council of Trent's injunction to bring cohesion to the memory of the dead and practices relating to purgatory. Their work has produced an informative database of images that illustrate this development.[64] Kristen Poole's work also identifies ways in which material culture—spaces and locations—formed perceptions of the afterlife in early modern England. In *Supernatural Environments in Shakespeare's England*, she focuses on early modern beliefs about the location of purgatory and reveals that as clergy attempted to bring local beliefs and practices about purgatory more in line with official definitions, older ideas about it, such as the belief that it existed on an island in Ireland, persisted.[65]

Guillaume Cuchet described the nineteenth century in France as the century "par excellence of the cult of souls in Purgatory," and has argued that there was an increase in the practice of intercessory prayers to souls in purgatory due to a social climate that placed Catholicism in competition with the metaphysical doctrines of Spiritualism.[66] Spiritualism emphasized communication between the living and the dead and presented an alternative framework to traditional Catholic means of connecting with the deceased. After this revival, however, devotions to purgatory declined, as Cuchet reveals in *The Twilight of Purgatory*, and is illustrated in discussions of the literalism of the fire of purgatory, which he terms the gradual *spiritualization* of purgatory. The spiritualization of purgatory involved a change from externalized devotions as manifested in rituals that occurred at the privileged altar, to interpretations of purgatory as an inward devotional disposition. Taking a longer view, I argue that the spiritualization of purgatory, or what I will term its gradual de-materialization, occurs as soon as the doctrine is codified, in the thirteenth century, and gains momentum after the European Enlightenment. It is important to note that what has been described here are histories of purgatory. There is no one, linear history of purgatory. A study of purgatory as it developed in other geographic locations would necessarily look different from this study, which identifies a specific problematic that has played out historically within Western European and, later, North American Catholicism.

Purgatory: An "Impossible" Place

The history of purgatory is the history of tales of the supernatural and the impossible. The material features of purgatory, such as holy souls who leave physical evidence of their visits or visionaries who arrive back from purgatory burned and scarred, qualify as supernatural events, in the strictest sense, as they occur outside of what has been considered, since the medieval era, as ordinary or possible. Watkins notes that even though the "supernatural" as a formal category had not yet been established in medieval Europe, "the embryo of the idea had already come into being."[67] Following the work of Alexander Murray, Watkins reveals that in this time period "distinctions were steadily being drawn between the observed patterns of nature and the anomalies within them."[68] Extraordinary, supernatural events were designated by language of "awe and wonder." The doctrine of purgatory was codified during this time period, and while its mention in documents from the councils where it was formulated downplay its features inspiring awe and wonder, purgatory literature, which included visionary tales, references, and anecdotes in *chronicles* and *exempla*, as well as its articulation in the more formal treatises of the scholastic theologians, was dominated by language of awe and wonder. Reports of souls from purgatory occurred within circumstances that were deemed extraordinary.

During the "long twelfth century," religion in its parochial setting was a "blend of local and universal practice."[69] Even as clergy were accommodating reports of the supernatural, they were also utilizing these accounts in didactic literature. In doing so, they utilized the material, concrete elements of the supernatural as evidence for an unseen, invisible world. Beyond its function as a means to secure belief among those who needed to "see to believe," the materiality of purgatory empowered practitioners to change or ameliorate their afterlife destinations. In this respect there is no better case than the purgatory caves in Ireland, located on Saints Island and Station Island in Lough Derg (Red Lake) to illustrate the problems *and* benefits of purgatory's materiality. The caves at Lough Derg, which became known as St. Patrick's Purgatory by the twelfth century, were sites of penitential activity. Practitioners engaged in ascetic exercises and utilized sacred space to expiate their sins so as to avoid hell after they died. In effect, the caves functioned as concrete purgatories. Chapter 1 is an examination of the practices that occurred at the caves and the fame that the site achieved throughout Europe. At first, the location of purgatory in Ireland did not present a problem since purgatory as a concrete place of penance was easily reconciled with early medieval theological frameworks. However, as chapter 2 reveals, while at first the purgatory caves were a boon to belief regarding the doctrine, they soon became a problem and an embarrassment for Church authorities and were suppressed several times. Despite suppression, practitioners utilized the site as a means to control their afterlife fates as late as the eighteenth century. Chapters 1 and 2 further address how the shift in late medieval penitential theology brought about a change in how purgatory was interpreted among theologians. As this shift gained momentum in the late thirteenth century, the materiality of purgatory became a problem, and places like Lough Derg were viewed with suspicion by Church authorities.

Chapter 3 examines how Lough Derg was represented in the popular press, and specifically in the works of Bishop John England, a priest who was born in Ireland at the end of the eighteenth century and became a bishop in the United States. England was deeply influenced by two events: English colonization of Ireland, and the French and American revolutions. Enlightenment thought profoundly influenced his ideas of religion and purgatory, and his writings reflect a greater process at work within Catholicism and specifically with respect to representations of purgatory. England distanced himself from what he considered to be the superstitious views of purgatory as a place, and indeed from having any knowledge whatsoever of souls in purgatory. On the one hand, he condemned the pilgrimage site of his homeland, the caves at Lough Derg, for fostering superstition, while on the other hand he lauded the pilgrimage for being a devotional practice that inspired faith among Irish Catholics during the trying years of English colonization. Significantly, John England's purgatory, devoid of space and time, reveals a model of purgatory that would become standard for future authoritative representations. England's work is also representative of the beginning of the end of purgatory, or, as Cuchet termed the development, purgatory's spiritualization, where representations of purgatory become abstract and rituals associated with the doctrine focus less on public demonstrations and more on practitioner's subjectivity. In chapter 4 I further trace the impact of Enlightenment thought on representations of purgatory within the Catholic press. Periodicals in France and North America reveal that the version of purgatory that relied on its material elements gradually gave way to more abstract versions of purgatory as a condition where souls experience the pain of loss. Anecdotes of souls in purgatory, which were common in periodicals devoted to the doctrine, are interspersed with references to "reason" guided by faith and other idioms representative of Enlightenment thought.

The gradual process of the displacement of purgatory from earth to its status as an afterlife condition took hundreds of years, yet it is in the present that the problem of purgatory's materiality is most clearly evident. This is illustrated in chapter 5 by the efforts of contemporary Catholics who are reviving a physical version of purgatory and rejecting an abstract version that they associate with modernism. Amid the little commentary about purgatory by church authorities, lay apostolates and ministers publish websites, tracts, and books that are beholden to old texts about purgatory that focus on its physical attributes and literal, not allegorical, punishments. This revival, led by the apostolate leaders mentioned earlier, belongs to a larger critical response to the liturgical reforms and the changes consequential to the Second Vatican Council. Even as the development of empiricism dealt a severe blow to the version of purgatory as a place, as people used increasingly more sophisticated instruments to ascertain earthly locations and places, it is ultimately the senses that guide what is known about the sacred, and thus the afterlife, and advocates for a literal purgatory insist on representing purgatory's physical features as a means to gain knowledge about it and to establish it as a real, not imaginative, place. At issue for these contemporary practitioners is the loss of knowledge of the supernatural, and the material aspects of purgatory provide the means to this knowledge.

I

When Purgatory Was a Place on Earth

THE PURGATORY CAVE ON THE RED LAKE IN IRELAND

THE MOST FAMOUS depiction of purgatory is found in Dante Alighieri's fourteenth-century epic poem *The Divine Comedy*.[1] Dante's purgatory is a rocky, cone-like island that juts out of the sea and is located in the Southern Hemisphere. (See fig. 1-1.) At the bottom of the island is an ante-purgatory where souls languish who repented too late in life or who died without the benefit of last rites. (See fig. 1-2.) Purgatory consists of seven terraces, each corresponding to the seven sins of wrath, greed, sloth, pride, lust, envy, and gluttony. On the lower terrace, souls wallow in tortures matching the sins of envy, pride, and sloth. Those who were envious in life and misused their eyes by coveting the possessions of others now stumble blindly around their terrace with their eyelids sewn shut with hot wire. The formerly prideful are hunched over, barely able to walk due to the weight of heavy stones strapped to their backs. The formerly gluttonous now weep, gaunt and starving, in constant view of a fertile tree loaded down with ripe and colorful fruit they cannot eat. At the top of the mountain is a paradise, heaven, for which each of these souls is ultimately destined. Dante's *Divine Comedy* is one of the most influential books in the Western world and has provided artists, poets, and visionaries a fount of graphic images of the afterlife.

Dante placed his purgatory on an island, yet his vision was just that—a vision. Dante never claimed that the island of purgatory *actually* existed somewhere in the Southern Hemisphere. Yet prior to Dante's visionary poem, many medieval Europeans would not hesitate to say that, indeed, the entrance to purgatory *is* located in a cave on a rocky island floating on a blood-red lake in Ireland called "Lough Derg" (Red Lake).[2] Dante was well aware of the purgatory in Ireland. Throughout medieval Europe it

FIGURE I-I Dante, Virgil, and Stazio among the souls devoured by the flames. Dante Alighieri, *Divine Comedy*, Purgatory, Canto XXIII/XXIV. Venice, 13th century. Biblioteca Marciana, Venice, Italy. SEF/Art Resource, NY.

was the most famous Irish destination.[3] If one were to ask a Catholic today about the location of purgatory, she would likely find the question absurd. Like heaven and hell, purgatory is assumed to be an otherworld state, *not* a physical, let alone earthly, location.[4]

Despite contemporary beliefs about purgatory, medieval and modern Europeans flocked to the island on Lough Derg hoping to journey through a cave that was believed to be a real purgatory. Monks and papal emissaries, or nuncios, traveled to the island to determine if the cave really was an earthly portal to purgatory. The Irish purgatory has had a long, fascinating history in the pages of religious devotional literature and Catholic periodicals. European belief in a terrestrial location of purgatory persisted throughout the medieval era and well into the nineteenth century. Its popularity is attested to by the copious extant manuscripts in England and Continental Europe, references in homily manuals used by priests, in *chronicles* written by clerics, and in

FIGURE 1-2 Cagnola, Francesco, and Sperindio, 16th century. "The Last Judgment, Purgatory," 15th-century fresco, "the poor man's Bible," Church of the Trinity, Piedmont. Gianni Dagli Orti/The Art Archive at Art Resource, NY.

collections of medieval *exempla*, which are stories and anecdotes intended to inspire moral action and that are used by pastors in their sermons.[5] As thirteenth-century chronicler Caesarius of Heisterbach remarked to the incredulous, "Let anyone who doubts the existence of Purgatory go to Ireland and enter the Purgatory of Patrick and he will have no further doubts about the punishments of Purgatory."[6] For many Europeans, from the medieval era through the nineteenth century, purgatory was a place on earth.

The problem of purgatory's materiality is best exemplified by the case of Lough Derg. As a portal to purgatory, and perhaps to heaven and hell, it is represented as a location that participates simultaneously in a spiritual and physical reality. According to the earliest references about Lough Derg written in the late twelfth century, the issue of its spiritual and earthly status does not appear to be a problem for pilgrims who visit the location seeking absolution of their sins through extreme penance. However, the issue of its location does become a problem in the thirteenth and fourteenth centuries, as theologians, fueled by the philosophy of Aristotle, attempt to categorize the purgatory cave at Lough Derg as either physical or spiritual. The problem for them is that it cannot be both, and ultimately the dogmatic formulation of purgatory is completely severed from its association to any terrestrial location. Lough Derg and its fame as a real purgatory challenged the official definition of purgatory as a spiritual place or state, not an earthly place, and the cave was ostensibly shut down several times.[7] Yet pilgrimage to Lough Derg continued, as pilgrims made use of the location as an earthly purgatory where they believed they could absolve their sins through penance. Pilgrims continued to visit the location throughout the eighteenth century, and clerics continued debating the terrestrial location of purgatory until 1860. What practices sustained the belief in this portal to the afterlife? What rituals occurred there? What connections or impact did belief in the purgatory at Lough Derg have on the formulation of the definition of purgatory, which occurred at the Second Council of Lyon in 1274 and was more fully developed in the Councils of Florence (Basel, Ferrara, and Florence 1431–1449) and Trent (1545–1563)? The case of Lough Derg illustrates the connections between the emerging doctrine of purgatory and earthly penance.

The visionary literature that emerged from the penitential experience of Lough Derg focuses on the realism of the purgatory cave and is therefore distinct from other visionary literature. In most medieval visionary tales a person typically travels to otherworld destinations "in their mind's eye" while remaining stationary in their rooms or beds. The literature of Lough Derg, in contrast, emphasizes *real* journeys through a concrete purgatory. In the cave at Lough Derg penitents waged a spiritual battle against their own bodies and psyches. Through extreme ascetic practices and throughout an experience of enclosure lasting twenty-four hours in the cave, penitents endured hunger and extreme pain believing that they were acquiring spiritual virtues to be used as weapons against Satan and evil. After their enclosure in the cave they believed that they were sin-free and saved from punishment in the afterlife. They utilized the purgatory cave to become agents of their own salvation. This important aspect of the purgatory cave motivated a rich literature that bears the marks of this physical experience.

The interpretation of the Irish purgatory as a place where one could avoid the pains of hell by enduring and surviving extreme penitential rites was not without its detractors, however. Catholic penitential theology shifted dramatically in the late medieval era and new ideas of penance challenged

the theological frameworks that sustained this terrestrial portal and the practices associated with it. This resulted in a schism between local practices of
penance and official theological doctrine, and as chapter 2 will reveal, the
purgatory cave became a site of controversy. Yet change was slow, and sources
indicate that even after the Council of Trent and its injunctions to priests
and clergy to bring about uniformity in rituals and practices, the pilgrimage
site at Lough Derg was still being utilized as a "purgatory," where practitioners believed they could avoid hell by practicing penance, in this life.

Medieval World Maps, Religious Landmarks, and Earthly Purgatories

European belief in entrances to purgatory was part of a larger medieval
religious worldview reflected in several sources, including *mappa mundi*,
or world maps, as well as texts. World maps reflected known spatial locations and additionally incorporated religious ideas that reflect theological
notions of space and time. From the seventh century until the early modern era T.O. maps provided Europeans with a geography of the known
world, which consisted of three continents: Europe, Asia, and Africa.
These continents formed the "T" of the map bordered by the "O" or ocean
surrounding the known world. This map, the *orbis terrarium*, or circle
around the land, served as a model for other world maps.

Supernatural elements were a common feature on world maps and
historians of cartography have argued that the distinguishing feature of
medieval world maps was the presence of religious landmarks, including
heaven, hell, purgatory, and the Garden of Eden.[8] The Hereford map, created in approximately 1300 at the Hereford Cathedral in England, places
the Garden of Eden as a real location at the top of the map. The map is
constructed to appear like the body of Christ with his head at the top and
his feet at the bottom of the map, in the west. Medieval world maps reflected not only what was known to exist but also what was speculated to
exist. Locations like the Garden of Eden occupied a place on the map, but
not as an exact location, because although theologians like Augustine
Aurelius (354–430) believed the Garden of Eden to be a real earthly location, nobody had yet discovered it. In this way the Garden occupied an
important *possible* place on medieval world maps.

Similarly, medieval cartographers depicted purgatory on their maps as
a borderland and also as a real place on the island on Lough Derg. Many
world maps portrayed figures from heaven and purgatory near or within

actual geographical locations. A fragment of a world map found in 1986 among the records of the Duchy of Cornwall and dated to approximately 1150 illustrates how world maps integrated geography and depictions of purgatory. The fragment shows the edge of Africa bordered by people in various life stages—"a woman at vespers, an old man bent with age, a figure in purgatory holding a bowl of fire, and an angel."[9] In this way, cartographers, through their depictions of persons within a religious universe of space and time, integrated these images with concrete locations, revealing a world populated not just by physical locations but also by monsters, angels, and portals to the afterlife. As the historian of cartography Evelyn Edson notes, the maps were not practical for actual travelers but provided an "excellent overview of one's place in the world and in relation to world events."[10]

By the early modern era, cartographers began to represent concrete locations and de-emphasize supernatural elements. Historians have shown that by the early 1500s the "supernatural" elements of world maps began to disappear and the location of the Garden of Eden was removed almost entirely. Sea maps, created by mariners on their journeys, relied on information gathered through new tools like the compass, which by 1400 was a standard guide to mariners. Whereas the world map functioned to educate Europeans about the universe and their place within it, the mariner's map functioned to help guide sailors in their explorations of the actual world. At approximately the same time that early modern mariners utilized new maps and technologies, theologians questioned whether or not Biblical places like the Garden of Eden were also earthly locations. Martin Luther concluded that the Garden of Eden was no longer in existence due to the "deluge" and thought that efforts to locate it were foolish.[11] In many ways the history of cartography reflects theological debates about the location of the Garden of Eden on earth, and, as Edson notes, "When the earthly paradise no longer appears on the world map, we have a new mapping tradition, one devoted to the physical measure of time and space [rather] than to its transcendent theological meaning."[12]

Surprisingly, and despite developments that contributed to the removal of the location of the Garden of Eden from world maps, the purgatory cave on the island of Lough Derg continued to be represented as an earthly location on world maps and mariner maps. There are several extant maps from the early modern era showing the location of St. Patrick's Purgatory on the island of Lough Derg in the North of Ireland. A 1513 Ptolemy map of England, Ireland, and Scotland prepared by cartographer Martin

Waldseemüller represents the purgatory at the northern end of Ireland. Abraham Ortelius's map of 1585 includes St. Patrick's Purgatory along with fifteen other Irish towns. Significantly, St. Patrick's Purgatory is the only Irish location on cartographer Martin Behaim's 1492 world map. Among Behaim's important innovations to cartography was his creation of a globe of the earth inclusive of the Southern and Northern Hemispheres, and his maps reflect the rapidly expanding knowledge of global geography. Behaim did not include the Garden of Eden on his map, so his inclusion of the Irish purgatory is significant in that it suggests that the cave was a real, not speculative, destination for Europeans.[13] In 1790 Edward Ledwich published a map of the island that included reference to the purgatory cave as well as the religious landmarks that were associated with the penitential prayers.[14] (See fig. 1-3.)

In addition to maps, popular European texts about the Irish mariner and monk St. Brendan also supported speculations about portals to the afterlife. The ninth-century *Navigatio Sancti Brendani*, or *The Voyage of St. Brendan*, was a popular medieval tale about St. Brendan's search for an earthly paradise and includes several scenes in which Brendan is linked to portals to the otherworld. The *Navigatio* belongs to the genre of Irish immrama—or literature about navigation pilgrimages that were journeys taken by monks overseas in search of island paradises.[15] St. Brendan was said to have set off on a voyage in the sixth century in search of one such paradise. Although Brendan was a historical figure, it is impossible to determine truth from fiction in the tale, or even to what extent its audience maintained a belief in its more fantastic elements.[16] One early modern historian, sojourning through Ireland, recorded a popular rhyme about St. Brendan's purgatory that indicates that he was associated with a location that functioned like the purgatory cave at Lough Derg, *"For purging souls and sending them to heaven, there is a place by fame to Brendan given."*[17] Another source indicates that there may have been several purgatory caves in Ireland associated with Brendan: "There is one of St. Patrick in the Northern part of the Kingdom, and the other of St. Brendan's to be found in the Southern part of the Kingdom...together with what I have occasioned to add a third"[18]

In the *Navigatio* Brendan attempts to reach an earthly paradise and even comes upon an entrance to what the *Navigatio*'s author records as a cave to hell. One scene describes Brendan and his sailors coming upon a fiery island in a sea of boiling water. An inhabitant of the island lobs a fiery rock toward Brendan's boat and one of his sailors is then taken away by a demon

FIGURE 1-3 Map of Ireland, ca. 1560. As the Garden of Eden disappeared from world maps, St. Patrick's Purgatory remained a destination. Hibernia/British Library, London, UK/© British Library Board. All Rights Reserved/The Bridgeman Art Library.

and set afire. This description has led some historians to suggest that the author of the *Navigatio* most likely either heard about or landed in Iceland, where the volcano Hecla, spewing fire and lava, impressed him so much that he thought he was witnessing an entrance to hell.[19] Within the time frame that the *Navigatio* was written, there were at least fifteen explosive volcanic eruptions in Iceland.[20] Active volcanoes spewing fire and rocks may have reinforced medieval speculation that afterlife destinations were also geographical destinations, or at least the idea that entrances to these could be found on earth.[21] Other sources indicate that entrances to purgatory were also believed to exist on Mount Etna in Italy, and likely in many other places.[22]

The purgatory at Lough Derg was distinct from other purgatories represented on world maps. Most of the world maps that included the purgatory, including Behaim's map, provided mariners with a specific route to the cave. It was not represented as a possible location on the borders of the known world, as in the case of the Garden of Eden, but as a concrete place in this world. As we shall see, medieval European conceptions of the afterlife were by no means uniform or cohesive, in that some people believed that purgatory was accessed on the earth or existed in the earth, and others believed in an afterlife place of purgation, and still others believed in both. Within this context of diversity of belief, a pattern does emerge: the purgatory at Lough Derg was utilized as a real purgatory—a place where pilgrims could avoid hell by practicing an extreme, even brutal, form of penance.

The Medieval and Early Modern Theological Context: Schools of Satisfaction, Retreats of Penance

In 1370, a young Italian monk, Don Giovanni, described as "a hermit who [had] sinned violently in youth," hoped to end the emotional suffering caused by his sins by journeying to Lough Derg to perform the prescribed penitential exercises.[23] The abbot of his monastery, however, denied his request. In a desperate attempt to circumvent his abbot's authority, he wrote a plea to Catherine of Siena, a tertiary of the Dominican Order and scholastic philosopher who has since, in 1970, been declared a doctor of the Catholic Church. Don Giovanni hoped she might intervene on his behalf.[24] He expressed the urgency to end his pain by traveling to Lough Derg so he could perform the then-famous penance and become sin-free. Instead of supporting his desire, however, Catherine urged him to be obedient to his superior. She wrote that obedience and remaining in the monastery would be a far more efficacious penance then traveling to the famous site.

This exchange underscores the powerful attraction that Lough Derg exerted on pilgrims, and, significantly, two divergent views of penance. Catherine represents a position that had become orthodox in her era— salvation was not linked to actual places on earth. Don Giovanni's view, however, reflects another position entirely. It reveals a view that practitioners believed that earthly penance would exonerate them of sin and that certain places, such as the cave at Lough Derg, were particularly effective in facilitating this process. Don Giovanni's assumptions were not unique, but arose from some forms of early medieval penitential theology and belief in "fully satisfactory penance." A fully satisfactory penance could only be performed while a person was alive, and was severe enough to account for the offending sin. However, as Don Giovanni's exchange with Catherine reveals, the two competing ideas of penance, one suggesting that through earthly penance one could expiate one's sins, and the other linked to an afterlife purgation where sinners could be exonerated from their sins and even get help from the living through prayers and works of mercy, existed simultaneously for hundreds of years. Purgatory as an afterlife place of expiation was slow to be accepted throughout many local parishes and Lough Derg functioned as a purgatory on earth until the eighteenth century.

The view that penance or absolution on earth could ameliorate one's afterlife punishment was manifest in anecdotes recorded in several sources. Earthly penance was deemed so efficacious that even the dead were believed to be able to reanimate their bodies so they could perform penance or receive absolution from their sins in order to avoid afterlife torments. Medieval *exempla* record many such instances of penitential revenants. Cistercian abbot of Heisterbach, Caesarius, whom Jacques Le Goff calls "that great popularizer of purgatory," wrote in the early 1200s about a student who made a deal with Satan in order to pass his exams. When the student passed with flying colors, he promptly died and was transported to a valley where demons with sharp fingernails lacerated and tormented him. God took pity on him and returned him to his body and he promptly went through a conversion and became a Cistercian monk.[25] Another anecdote, found in William of Newburgh's chronicle *Historia rerum*, describes how a revenant is put to rest by obtaining a letter of absolution from a local bishop. In 1196, in the town of Buckingham, England, a dead man's corpse terrorizes the townspeople and the man's widow. Seeking to put the revenant to rest, the local residents attempt to burn its corpse, but the bishop suggests that they place a letter in the dead man's coffin, which effectively absolved him of the sins he committed in life.[26]

Stories of revenants returning from the dead to either perform or request earthly penance and then returning again to the realm of the dead, sin-free, underscores the early medieval connection between earthly penance and afterlife fate.

The question of when the concept of afterlife purgation, or the ability of the soul to undergo afterlife penance and avoid hell, made its way into the main theological schools, and which texts and traditions influenced its development, is ongoing.[27] What is clear, however, is that the belief that penance performed while one was alive could exonerate a person from a sin dominated the first twelve hundred years of Christian theology.[28] Satisfactory penance could absolve one of sin, and "Satisfactory" in this sense meant "full restitution" in that the pilgrims' suffering would "pay" for the sin committed. Parish priests made use of manuals called "penitentials" that prescribed penances for various sins, and lent support to this idea of penance. Within the penitentials, fully satisfactory penances ranged from fasting for up to ten years for homicide to fasting for three years while the penitent left behind "his homeland and his possessions and journey[ed] to Rome to the Pope and afterwards do as he advise[d] him." Harsher penances were prescribed for a person who had murdered a monk or kinsman.[29] Penitentials reflected the belief that there was only earthly penance and that these practices had to be performed while one was alive. As Isabel Moreira notes, "The entire thrust of... the penitentials and visions of the afterlife was to urge the need for present penance precisely because it was impossible to repent and make satisfaction after death."[30]

Penitents could satisfy God's wrath by enduring long pilgrimages. Weary pilgrims, traveling barefoot and wearing heavy chains and gray robes blazoned with black crosses, were easily identified as penitents. They made their way to sacred destinations in an act of penance called peregrination, or penitential pilgrimage. The goal of this penance was to expiate one's sins by traveling to locations known to be sacred and also dangerous—therefore exaggerating the penitential element. Pilgrims carried letters from their bishop identifying them as penitents and the letters also ensured that they would be the recipients of charitable meals and shelter from bad weather.[31] One Irishman, Aonghus Mac Niocaill, appealed to the dean of Armagh in northern Ireland for absolution for strangling his son. The dean demanded that he travel to several sacred penitential sites throughout Ireland, including the Skellig Michael, a monastery located on a seven hundred-foot treacherous rock off the coast; Glendalough, a monastery said to have been established by St. Kevin in the seventh century;

and Lough Derg. Mac Niocaill had to produce documentation assuring the dean that he had actually been to these places.[32] Penitents journeyed to locations where they believed they could expiate their sins in this life so as to avoid punishment after death.

Throughout the twelfth century, however, the idea that penance was connected not to earthly practices but to postmortem purgation, gradually took root, or more accurately, gained in ascendancy. Ideas that confession and intercessory prayers could affect postmortem punishment are evident in the writings of Bede in the eighth century, and later in the works of Anselm of Canterbury (1109) and Peter Lombard (1150), who formulated what would later become accepted penitential orthodoxy.[33] This was a gradual but permanent development, and the new idea that sins could be expiated postmortem developed into orthodoxy. It was approximately a hundred years after Anselm and Lombard proposed these ideas of penance that theologians solidified the doctrine of purgatory and the system of penance whereby the living could intercede on behalf of the dead. This development, which placed penance within an afterlife context, also separated it from any earthly provenance, technically. This development was not a linear, chronological process whereby practices followed from the utterances or writings of theologians. The case of Lough Derg reveals that, at least in this instance, local customs continued that reflected ideas of penance that linked it to penitential exercises, despite theological pronouncements.

Visionary tales emerged that supported the new penitential concepts. In 1209, an English chronicler named Ralph of Coggeshall translated into Latin an English laborer's vision of the otherworld. *The Vision of Thurkill* reflected the new penitential concepts, where "satisfaction for one's sins is not achieved through rigorous penitential activity on earth but in purgatorial places."[34] Carl Watkins describes how the visionary, Thurkill, passed through fire and through an icy lake to view tortured souls in purgatory. In this place, Thurkill reported that the suffering of the souls was relieved by prayers and the works of the living. Thurkill was also able to provide his church's parishioners information about the status of their deceased loved ones and whether they required Masses or intercessory prayers to ease their afterlife suffering and duration. In this way, the testimony of otherworld revelation worked to support the burgeoning rituals surrounding the liturgy of the dead to support an idea that penance occurred in an afterlife realm.

Yet despite texts like Thurkill's vision, which helped disseminate new ideas about penance, the new regime was not effectively communicated to

people throughout the local communities in Ireland. People still continued using the older methods of expiating sin and made little use of the
new system or rituals intended to absolve afterlife sin, including masses
for the dead and yearly confession.[35] Ireland did not have a centralized
Church and parishes functioned within a system that integrated pre-
Christian beliefs and motifs.[36] As part of this system Lough Derg was a
"retreat of penance" and a "school of satisfaction," where people engaged
in practices that were brutal enough to be "fully satisfactory" and that
were intended to exonerate them of sin and afterlife punishment.[37] Several
sources reveal that this is the prevailing meaning given to the site by pilgrims. The earliest texts about the site describe it as a place of penance,
and an examination of medieval Irish penance and later bardic poetry
reveals that the Irish site was a place where pilgrims did perform an austere penance that they believed would clear them of sins and thus afterlife
punishments. Thus, Lough Derg was a "school of satisfaction," in line
with early penitential theology, from at least 1180 until well into the 1700s.
In order to make sense of its liminal status as "betwixt and between" spirit
and matter, particularly as articulated in the copious literature about it, as
well as its curious place within the history of the doctrine of purgatory and
in more formal theological treatises, it is important to attend to what was
actually happening at Lough Derg. It is true that it was the location of
penitential activity, but what did that mean for pilgrims? As will be revealed, Lough Derg was a site where pilgrims' bodies merged with place
to effect their salvation, and this was interpreted to be purgatory on earth.

Medieval Anchorites and the Penance
on Saints Island

Recent scholarship about anchoritic traditions in Ireland, as well as indigenous poetry from the Irish bardic tradition and other texts about Lough
Derg, sheds light on the practices and rituals that were performed on the
island and their meanings for practitioners.[38] Anchorites were recluses,
monks and nuns who took vows of reclusion, which meant that they chose
to live their lives in a closed-up cell, or *reclusorium*, that was either attached
to a church, in a cave, or on an island. The lifestyle of an anchorite was
ascetic—he or she would spend time in meditative prayer and fasting. For
medieval communities, anchorites functioned as intercessors between
the sacred and the profane, that is, they lived in the world but were not "of
it." People journeyed to visit anchorites to obtain spiritual knowledge from

them. They were the conduits to the invisible world and were thought to have spiritual knowledge.

Anchoritic spiritual knowledge was directly linked to ascetic practices. Penitential practices accorded anchorites virtues that were then used in spiritual warfare. Through penance one was able to fight demons and ward off evil, as this Irish exemplum indicates: "how great is the power of penance and confession by which a sinner can thus be snatched from the devil."[39] Within Irish communities anchorites were sometimes perceived as having direct knowledge of sacred affairs. In the following account, written in approximately 1275, an anchorite overhears a demon boasting about a woman who has not confessed a sin and whom he will take to hell when she dies. "Truly, the anchorite heard everything. In the morning the anchorite sent for the priest and made known to him everything he had heard. On the advice of the anchorite the priest went to the woman, and she confessed."[40] In this episode the anchorite functions as the medium between the spiritual and the profane worlds, which is clearly a benefit to the members of the community who get access to hidden knowledge that can help them attain salvation.

The spiritual knowledge that anchorites obtained was directly linked to their penitential practices. Through their lifestyle, in which they performed fasts, bodily mortifications, and other penances, they obtained spiritual weapons—virtues that they then used to battle demons and other malefi-cent forces. The Lough Derg pilgrimage was a site of anchoritic activity, but it was also a place that provided non-anchorites with a truncated ver-sion of the anchoritic experience. At Lough Derg non-anchorites could endure a severe penance that enabled them to absolve their sins, but also accrue virtues. The penance was simultaneously spiritual and physical. Penitents experienced the limits of their physical endurance and as such obtained virtues.

The earliest texts about the cave were written in approximately 1180 and confirm that penitents traveled to the cave to perform extreme exer-cises that were intended to absolve them of sin and exonerate them from afterlife punishments. Each of the texts is written in Latin by a cleric. Giraldus Cambrensis, or Gerald of Wales, was a cleric who was appointed to be the royal clerk to King Henry II of England. He accompanied Henry's son, Prince John, to Ireland, and chronicled his travels in *The Topography of Ireland*.[41] The chronicle is peppered with interesting observations and anecdotes. To Gerald, who had been educated in Paris, Ireland was remote from civilization. He described a fantastic world where the Irish "wear black hooded robes," because the sheep in Ireland were black, not white, and they wore their hair long, which was not a custom of Europeans, yet they "by nature's gift are handsome."[42] They would have looked very different from the Cistercians and other monks who typically wore white or gray robes. Gerald was attentive to the stories that the Irish told, and he recorded information about Lough Derg, an island that "is stony and ugly and is abandoned to the use of evil spirits only. It is nearly always the scene of gatherings and processions of evil spirits, plain to be seen by all. If anyone ventures to spend the night in any one of them [the caves], he is seized immediately by malignant spirits, and is crucified all night with such severe torments...that, when morning comes, there is found in his poor body scarcely even the smallest trace of life surviving." However, if he or she survived, his sins would be remitted and he "would not have to endure the pains of hell."[43]

Although Gerald, due to his Parisian education, would have been aware of the new penitential regime, his interpretation of the Lough Derg penance confirms earlier ideas about earthly satisfactory penances: that it was a place where penitents suffered on earth to avoid afterlife punishments. The other text from the same era (~1180) is a vision narrative, the *Tractatus de Purgatorio Sancti Patricii*, written by the Cistercian monk H. of Saltrey.[44] In the *Tractatus*, a knight, Owen, journeys through the purgatory cave and encounters demons whom he must fight in order to absolve himself of the sins he accrued as a knight of the Crusades. The demons of Saltrey's account try to prevent Owen from finishing his journey of penance by using "terror and flattery," because they know that when he finishes it he will no longer be "theirs."[45] Instead, he is free from sin and begins a new life as a reformed sinner. The authors of these texts interpret the Lough Derg penance as occurring within an older penitential framework—that is, after performing the penance, the pilgrims are free from their sins and will avoid punishment after death. Additionally, the penitents are not only absolved from their sins, but they endure penances that are similar to the experiences of anchorites, that is, they are enclosed in a cell, the cave. As such they are literally closed up into another world, a world populated with evil spirits and demons.

Lough Derg was the site of an anchorite-like penance, but it was also the site where at least one anchorite lived. The *Tractatus* refers to an anchorite who lives on the island on Lough Derg, who is called "the prior with only one tooth," and is described as a "man of holy life." This man "had a cell arranged beside the canon's dormitory." The other men living in the community would often hear "angels in the old man's cell singing around him." According to the text, the angels confirmed that the anchorite was holy through his practices of abstinence: "'Blessed are you and blessed is the tooth which is in your mouth, which has never been touched by delectable food.' For his food was dry bread and salt and his drink was cold water."[46] Medieval Irish anchorites typically lived on remote islands and stony structures or caves.[47] Besides the reference in the *Tractatus*, there are other references to a hermit living on Station Island, which is one of two islands on Lough Derg associated with the purgatory cave.[48] The original cave was on Saints Island.[49]

Ascetic practices and penance would have equipped the anchorite with spiritual virtues, which were then used to fight evil. This benefit of penance is underscored in the *Tractatus*, as Owen journeys through the purgatory cave acquiring strength to fight off the demons that haunt him. When he enters the cave, the narrator states that Owen has "been instructed in a new type of chivalry, the knight, who in the past bravely fought men, is now ready to give battle bravely to demons." His weapons are not his hands or an ax, but instead "the breastplate of justice; as a head bears a helmet, his spirit is crowned with the hope of victory and eternal salvation and he is protected by the shield of faith. He holds the sword of the spirit which is the word of God."[50] After his ordeal Owen is "purified of sin" and his new virtues establish him as a holy penitent.

H. of Saltrey's description of the preparation one must take prior to enduring the penance further links Lough Derg to anchoritic practices. The preparation is so difficult it has been described, even in contemporary times, as "the hardest Christian pilgrimage in the world."[51] The "ritual of admission to the purgatory" is similar to medieval rites of the enclosure of a hermit or anchorite, which involved rituals performed before a man or woman was enclosed in a cell, room, or cave, for the duration of their lives. The *Tractatus*'s description of this ritual provides another clue that the location of the cave was a specific destination for extreme forms of penance in the medieval era.

The "ritual of admission to the purgatory" was a penance in itself and followed a specific formula. Nobody could enter the purgatory without first obtaining permission from his bishop, and then from the prior, or head priest, of the island. These authorities were then supposed to dissuade the potential penitent, for many did not survive the night in the cave. If the pilgrim persisted, and if his sin was grave enough, he would then be given a letter of admittance, in conformity to the common practice of distinguishing penitents from other travelers. The penitent would then show his letter to the prior, who tried one last time to dissuade him. If the penitent persisted, he would then spend fifteen days fasting and praying. The prayers, called stations because they involved walking and kneeling, were rigorous. Practitioners recited the "Our Father" and several sources indicate they did so while walking on stone and rock shards.[52] After fifteen days, if he was still able, the pilgrim attended a special mass where he was sprinkled with holy water and prayed for by "neighboring clergy." He would then be "led to the door of the Purgatory accompanied by a procession and litany." Some sources say that he would be given his last rites.

> As the prior opens the door in front of everyone he warns him once again about the attacks of the demons and about the many persons lost in this pit. If, however, the penitent is firm in his intention, after receiving benedictions from all the priests, he commends himself to the prayers of all, impresses the sign of the cross on his forehead with the correct hand, and enters. The prior immediately bolts the door.[53]

If the pilgrim survived this ordeal, he would endure another fifteen days of fasting and vigil. One medieval monk noted, "If, on the next day at the same hour, he does not appear to have returned, the prior bolts the door...certain of his loss."[54]

Christian rites of enclosure were recorded as early as the sixth century. The following description portrays a ritual similar to the preparation at Lough Derg. In this scene a nun is granted permission to enter a cell in which she would remain until her death. Her fellow nuns and priest lead a procession, singing as "they all bade her farewell and she gave to each the kiss of peace. Then she was enclosed in her cell and the door through which she had entered was bricked up."[55] Although Owen and pilgrims of Lough Derg do not actually stay in the cave for life, the ritual suggests a shorter version of the anchoritic retreat. The overnight stay in the cave was actually dangerous and potentially lethal, and in this sense, conformed to the rites of enclosures of anchorites who were shut away from the world, symbolically "dead." Irish religious nuns and monks did practice short rites of enclosure. In an eighth century manual of penance, nuns and monks were advised to spend "the night in cold churches or remote cells while keeping vigils and praying without respite, while not sitting or lying down to sleep, as though one were at the gates of hell."[56] In 1200, Peter of

Cornwall notes that on an island in Ireland "old men dwell permanently living an anchoretic life, who drink nothing but water mixed with milk."[57] The rite of enclosure described in the *Tractatus* aligns the penance at Lough Derg with Irish anchoritic traditions.

The purgatory cave at Lough Derg was associated with anchoritic practices, and although these practices did not conform completely to what is currently known about English and European anchoritic rules and rituals of enclosure, it appears that the enclosure in the cave was a shortened version of this practice. The penances allowed the pilgrim to develop the virtues of prayer and fasting as weapons for spiritual warfare with demons. Comparing the penance at Lough Derg to anchorite enclosure, the author of the *Tractatus* states, "Not even cloistered monks (who think they lead a harsh life on account of their confinement) know what sort of pains and torments are in the places we have described."[58] The life of an anchorite was physically austere, and the mini-version of the enclosure to the cave replicated, for a short duration, the anchoritic experience. The stress of an extreme fast, coupled with the rigorous prayers that included walking on sharp rocks and immersing oneself in the cold lake waters, and then, after fifteen days, being enclosed within a cave or cell that was most likely vaporous, would have pushed pilgrims to the very limits of their physical endurance. Within the medieval context, austerities like these were interpreted through a spiritual lens. Through austere penances, practitioners accrued spiritual strength. Importantly, the penance at Lough Derg was interpreted as an "earthly" purgatory in the sense that pilgrims could absolve themselves of their sins in this life to avoid hell in the next life. This interpretation of the site persisted, even as the new penitential orthodoxy took hold in the schools of Paris and England.

Irish Indigenous Poetry: Satisfactory Penance

In 1586 Englishman William Camden published a history of England and Ireland. It was his intention to "to restore antiquity to Britaine, and Britaine to its antiquity." In other words, he wanted to reveal how ancient traditions of England and Ireland continued and lived on in its present culture. With this in mind, and like chronicler Caesarius of Heisterbach before him, he recorded the oral traditions of the Irish, including rhymes about the cave at Lough Derg. In a section on the County Donegal he writes about a "vault" on a haunted island. There is "a Lake, where there appears above the water an Island, and in it a little Monastery, and a very narrow vault within the ground, which is much spoken about there being walking spirits and dreadful apparitions, or rather some religious horror." According to Camden the inhabitants associate the vault, or cave, with the Greek hero Ulysses. "Which cave, as some dream ridiculously, was digged by Ulysses when he went down to parlee with those in hell." Several things are notable about his record. First, practitioners associated the location with a tradition of mythical poetry, in this case Homer's *Odyssey*. Second, they specifically reference the hero Ulysses's journey into the underworld, where he encounters the "shades" of the dead, including his own mother, and returns with an important secret that allows him to journey safely home to Ithaca. Finally, Camden indicates contradictory stories about the origin of the vault. "Some affirm that Patrick, the Irishman's apostle," founded the place, whereas others say that "some Abbot of the same name" obtained the place from God.[59] In either case, the vault is a place where the Irish, like Ulysses, descend into an underworld.

Camden's recording of apparently incidental reports of an association between the Greek bardic tradition and the cave is significant. There are at least eleven extant poems about Lough Derg, written in the native Irish language, categorized within the Irish bardic tradition (1250–1650).[60] Irish bards and their predecessors, the filid, represented a respected caste within Irish society that was charged with maintaining cultural memory. They used mnemonic devices like metrical verse, rhyme, and alliteration to record and remember history associated with clans, kingdoms, geographical locations, and the stories about them.[61] The earliest recorded Irish poem is an elegy to St. Collumne Cille, written by his friend Dallan Forgaill in 597, and set to verse in order to be remembered. Bardic poets like Tuileagna O Maeolchonaire "attribute an ancient origin" to the site: "Loch Dearg aon Roimh na hEireann, mar fuair sinn sa seinleigheann," "Lough Derg the one shrine of Ireland as we have found in the old learning."[62] As records of cultural memory and oral literacy, bardic poetry represents another source of evidence, along with scholarship about Irish anchoretic practices, for unraveling the mystery of how the site of the cave was used by practitioners.[63]

Irish bardic poetry provides the most frank descriptions of the penance in the cave and what it meant for practitioners. Writing to the pilgrims in the early 1600s, Franciscan poet Aodh Mac Aingil insisted that the Irish should remember the special status of their purgatory. Although he is writing after the penitential reforms of the twelfth century, his understanding of the purgatory cave at Lough Derg conforms to previous penitential ideas of earthly "satisfactory" penance. He reminds the Irish that if a sinner endures horrible torments in the cave, he or she would be cleansed of his or her sins and could avoid purgatory in the next life.[64]

> There is many a sign of Patrick's constant prayer, and his harsh penance, and indication of his making satisfaction for his sins on Lough Derg....I myself saw the wells where he used to pray, the stones on which he used to sleep, the penitential bed where he used to beseech the one true God to have mercy and give grace to his people....It is certain that what motivated Patrick to this was his desire to save himself and his people from the everlasting pains of hell and the fierce fire of purgatory.[65]

Seventeenth-century poet Tomas Mac Gabrhrain, in *An Sgathan Spioradalta* (The Spiritual Mirror), reveals the same interpretation of the cave as functioning like purgatory on earth. According to Mac Gabrhrain, God appeared to St. Patrick and pointed out a cave, saying, "Whoever enters this cave for 24 hours with true sorrow for his sins shall be absolved from all the pain his sin deserves." Mac Gabrhrain continues, "The souls of those who enter the cave are cleansed from their sins and the pain in store for them. From the above it can be understood that God ordained many Purgatories in this life for the purgation of souls."[66] What these poems reveal is as late as the 17th Century the cave was understood as a location of earthly penance, in the same tradition as early medieval era penitential theology.

Bardic poetry also provides illustrations of the stark penances performed at Lough Derg, involving reclusion in the dark cave for twenty-four hours, and immersion in the icy lake waters, as well as constant prayer and stations. Writing in the late 1500s, Tullengne mc Torne O Mulconeree reveals that the immersion of his body in water is akin to the cleansing of his soul through penance. "O deceitful body of mine, Only Lough Derg can cleanse your sinfulness, Since a thing must be cleansed in water, I pity you as you lie....Wise doctors tell us, When a cancer is malignant, So now I must bathe my soul, In the lake which will heal my wounds."[67] In Mulconeree's text, his soul is bathed along with his body, or, more literally, he doesn't make a distinction between the soul and his body. The most famous native Irish poem about Lough Derg, "My Pilgrimage to Lough Derg Was in Vain," written in the seventeenth century, describes the experience of being in the cave. "O King of the cells and churches, Alas, after all my sins and pride, And I buried alive in a grave, A narrow, hard stone prison, Naked and fasting."[68]

Early modern anti-Catholic polemicists describe the very same practices, although unlike the bardic poets, the polemicist's descriptions mock the penitents. Along with Camden, who found the references to the cave and Ulysses "ridiculous," Henry Jones, a Protestant bishop of Clogher, whose diocese housed the island, found the behaviors of the practitioners "super-stitious" and their stories "fables, not worthy to be considered in serious discourse," yet he recorded rhymes and verses about the location in his anti-Catholic polemic "St. Patrick's Purgatory: Containing the Description, Originall, Progresse, and Demolition of that Superstitious Place." These rhymes emphasize penitential autonomy: "A purgatory for punishment here, and no other purgatory to be after." Another rhyme underscores this aspect of the penance, "by the prayers and merits of those who daily report to this purgatory to find some relief of their pains in the other purga-tory."[69] And like Camden, he noted that practitioners didn't always associ-ate the island with only St. Patrick, but with St. Davog, "where that Saint is said to be buried," or other saints, like St. Finatu, "as others would have it." The confusion about St. Patrick's patronage of the purgatory cave lends credence to a theory, suggested by Pontfarcy and many others, that Augus-tinian canons, who took over the location in the twelfth century, perhaps working together with Anglo-Norman knights like John D'Courcy, tied the preexisting penitential location with St. Patrick to curry favor with the in-digenous population.[70]

According to Jones, the cave into which the penitents descend is "two feet wide in most places, and three feet high, so that they are enforced to stoop that go into it." In Jones's account there was at first one cave for both men and women, although they went into it at different times: "Into this cave, not promiscuously, but men by themselves, and women by them-selves." In time, however, the canons created a second cave, "one for men, and other for women."[71] Most likely the original cave was a natural cave, yet through time and use it was altered and changed, and sources from Ceasarius of Heisterbach to Jones reveal that there were multiple fabri-cated caves, also called cells and prisons, all over Station Island.

Jones describes the penance leading up to the reclusion in the cave as being particularly brutal. "The entrance to the island is narrow, rockie and rugged." Penitents walk barefoot over shards of rock said to be the "guts of that great Serpent metamorphosed into stones." The "Serpent," dealt with at length in chapter 2, figures in the legends and origin myths of Lough Derg, and is a feature on world maps that represent the purgatory cave. After the penitents walk on rocks and perform their walking prayers, or stations, they then immerse themselves in the icy waters of the lake, which "heals the wounds occasioned by their going barefoote on sharpe rocks and stones." Jones also references the stones throughout the island that penitents incorporate in their stations. "There is a small trifling of ground, and a heap of stones, called an altar. Toward the narrow part of this island . . . there were six Circles from their figure, or Saints beds, or beds for penance. These cells or beds serve for a great part of their devotion in which there are often pacings and kneelings: to which end they are compassed with sharp stones and difficult passages for as go barefoot, as all must."[72]

It is clear from these sources, which span from the twelfth to the eighteenth centuries, that the cave on the island was an important site of penitential activity that was interpreted within the early medieval framework of providing for "satisfactory penances" where practitioners could absolve themselves of sin to avoid afterlife punishment. Chapter 2 will clarify that this interpretation encompassed native Irish as well as many Europeans until the fourteenth century, but that the continuance of this interpretation was much more localized by the fifteenth through the eighteenth centuries, and perhaps was confined just to some native Irish, as indicated by bardic poetry. The work of Kristen Poole, however, suggests that English references to St. Patrick's Purgatory, and other terrestrial purgatories, were common enough in the sixteenth century.[73]

The cave on the island of Lough Derg functioned as an important site of expiation and was, in effect, a purgatory on earth. Roman Catholic theologians would place the space of purgatory in the afterlife, but this move had little effect on the practitioners who traveled to Lough Derg. That this purgatory was on earth was not a problem, necessarily, for most medieval pilgrims or visiting clerics, as they were ensconced within a worldview dictated by early medieval penitential theology. What becomes significant, and problematic as we shall see for later theologians and even contemporary scholars, are the visions that accompany the austere practices. As will be revealed, the visions articulate a specific type of metaphysics. As in Tullengne mc Torne O Mulconeree's conflation of body and soul, the visions inspired by the penance at Lough Derg do not cohere to a neat separation between matter and spirit, but instead suggest a fusion of matter or spirit, or an ignorance of this dualism altogether. Although this doesn't represent a problem for penitents like Mulconeree, it will be a problem for scholastic theologians and others.

It is tempting to establish a causal relationship between the penitential exercises and the consequential visions that practitioners report, and many

have, suggesting that the harsh penances directly influenced the practitioners' minds and caused visions. However, there is another way to interpret
the interplay between the visions that are reported by pilgrims at Lough
Derg and the physical penances in which they engaged. This possibility
arises from attention to reports of how pilgrims' bodies interact with the
place of Lough Derg. Reports of this interaction, found in most of the primary sources, offer clues about the interaction between spirit and matter at
Lough Derg. The connections between the physical performance of these
rites and their spiritual benefits are more clearly illustrated in the narratives about the journey through the purgatory, where practitioners report
that they venture with their physical bodies and journey through a real,
concrete, spiritual realm. If this seems incongruous, it didn't appear to be
to the first clerics who penned the earliest narratives describing the journey, Gerald of Wales and H. of Saltrey. It will, however, become a problem
for later authors of Lough Derg, and remains perplexing to contemporary
scholars who try to make sense of this aspect of the Lough Derg pilgrimage
and who have suggested two traditions of Lough Derg history—one focused
on spiritual visions and adventures, and the other focused on penance, the
body, and Ireland. In the latter case, it seems as though historians have unwittingly assumed a matter/spirit opposition, and have associated spirit
with the Latin tradition, and matter with an indigenous, Irish tradition.

Physical Bodies in Spiritual Places:
The Treatise of Saint Patrick's Purgatory

As an outpost of purgatory, Lough Derg inspired literature that ranged
from the fantastic to the polemical. The distinguishing characteristic of
much of this literature is its emphasis on the physical experience of the
purgatory cave. By far the most fantastic and influential of this literature
and the best example of the emphasis on the concrete uses of the cave is
the *Tractatus de Purgatorio Sancti Patricii*, or the *Treatise of the Purgatory of
Saint Patrick*, and as noted earlier, written in approximately 1180 by the
Anglo-Norman Cistercian monk H. of Saltrey. H. of Saltrey retells a story
he has heard from another Cistercian monk, Gilbert, who had traveled
through Ireland with a knight named Owen who acted as his translator.
Gilbert was impressed with Owen's reserved and serious demeanor, and
found him to be "a man stamped by a profound religious experience."[74]
During their journey Owen gradually revealed the cause of his spiritual
strength. He told Gilbert that he had been through the most difficult of

Christian pilgrimages, and survived. Gilbert listened to Owen's story, committed it to memory, and would later tell fellow clergy in England.

The distinguishing characteristic of the Latin *Tractatus* is its emphasis on the physical experience of a spiritual realm, to which its author draws the reader's attention. In the prologue, which frames the treatise, H. of Saltrey writes that souls "have been pulled by the hands, dragged by the feet, hanged by the neck, scourged, thrown down and subjected to many more ordeals of this kind."[75] He notes that it is not a contradiction to think that souls can experience physical attacks or blessings. He further states that his account "confirms what is believed by some, namely that hell is under the earth or rather at the bottom of a cavity in the earth. It also shows that there is a paradise on earth towards the east where the souls of the faithful, freed from the purgatorial punishments, are said to stay for some time in bliss."[76] These statements establish a framework for interpreting Owen's journey. The framework is not dictated by ontological dualism, but by an acceptance that souls can pass between worlds—this world and the otherworld. The price of admission, so to speak, appears to be penance. The extreme penitential rituals would no doubt have helped leave an impression on the bodies and minds of practitioners, and the literature inspired by these experiences bear the marks as manifested in the emphases on the physical journey. Owen related to the knight his harrowing experience of traveling into and through the cave, which he called an entrance to purgatory, which also included a gate to hell as well as an earthly paradise. Gilbert then retold his tale to a fellow monk, H. of Saltrey, who wrote it down. H.'s tale is dramatic: "Many men entered the Purgatory; some of them came back but others died there."[77] The *Tractatus* became one of the most popular stories of the medieval era, circulating through hundreds of editions that were translated into more than six vernacular languages.[78] It is credited with putting Ireland on the medieval Christian world map and Owen's journey became known as one of the "daring deeds" (*l'audac imprese*) of medieval chivalry.[79] Due to the tale's fame, word spread about the pilgrimage and the cave, and it attracted knights and nobleman from all sectors of European society.

The key to the otherworld is Owen's penance. H. of Saltrey writes that Owen had been a knight in the Crusades, and a sinner who had plundered church property. Being remorseful and seeking penance from his bishop, Owen was ordered to suffer the trial of Lough Derg. During his enclosure, Owen believed that he traveled through purgatory, was brutally attacked by demons and scalded by the fires of hell, and finally came upon the earthly paradise while barely making it out of the cave alive and free of sin. He was then assured of heaven.

According to the text, Owen went through the customary preparations for the penance. He received his last rites and withstood the fifteen days of fasting and prayer. The prior of the island church enclosed Owen in the cave by shutting a makeshift door that was attached to the cave. Enclosed in darkness, Owen found himself in an interior region that expanded out before him. Fifteen monks in white clothes then appeared before him. They said, "Since you have come to the Purgatory to be purified of your sins you are perforce compelled to act manfully or else you will die body and soul because of your inaction."[80] They also provided him with a verbal talisman, saying that if he called out the name of Jesus when he felt he would perish, he would avoid catastrophe. As he descended into the interior regions of the earth, he encountered fetid odors and saw demon tormentors who clamored to bite and harass him. He also saw dark shapes with gleaming eyes and teeth that pulled and pushed him in the direction of a fiery pit. Shouting Jesus' name, he was able to beat back howling demons, who cringed and dispersed as he made his way through realms of tortured souls suffering for the sins they committed during their lives. He journeyed on and, encountering the gaping mouth of hell, peered into the roiling fires that continuously scorched the middle of the earth and the souls consigned there.

In all, Owen would endure ten torments inflicted upon him by demons that tried to compel him to quit his journey and leave the cave a broken and defeated man. The demons announced, "You came here to endure torments for your sins; so, you will obtain from us what you were looking for, namely pains and afflictions. Yet, because up to now you have served us, if you agree to our advice and turn back willingly, as a favor we will bring you unharmed to the door through which you entered so that you may continue to enjoy being alive in the world and not lose completely everything that is pleasant to your body."[81] Undaunted, and having "in his breast a manly heart," he continued his journey through the torments. He is dragged over a long stretch of land while being simultaneously blown by a burning wind that pierces his body "with its harshness." While being dragged he sees countless souls pinned to the ground and stomped upon by large toads with fiery fangs. Demons drag Owen through level after level of torturous sites. One plain is filled with souls hanging upside down from chains, screaming as their heads get dunked into sulfurous flames. H. of Saltrey comments, "No human language is adequate to express the moans and cries of the wretches and the wailing he heard," and then continues to describe other souls whose punishments include having demons stick nails in their eyes, nostrils, and genitals.[82] The text's messages conform to the penitential framework that suggests that one can absolve oneself by enduring extreme penance. It also provides vivid imagery of the otherworld and the penitent's relationship to that world. Demons and angels populate this world, portrayed in the text as real, not imagined, entities. Unlike the *Journey of St. Brendan*, there are copious extant texts and sources available to suggest that many Europeans believed that not only could one be absolved of sin in the purgatory cave, one could encounter the otherworld there.

The *Tractatus* figures in almost all scholarly analyses and historical treatments of the doctrine of purgatory.[83] Jacques Le Goff credits the *Tractatus* for its work in popularizing a place distinct from heaven and hell. "At last, there was a description of Purgatory, a place with a name of its own and an other world consisting of three regions."[84] Carl Watkins's work on penance and purgatory corrects the notion that the *Tractatus* supports a vision of the tri-level afterlife of heaven, hell, and Purgatory in between. Instead, he notes, "the *Tractatus* clearly included two middle places, the Purgatory of St. Patrick and the Earthly Paradise."[85]

The one element that differentiates the *Tractatus* from most other visionary literature and that has been a source of confusion for scholars is its emphasis on the concrete reality of purgatory. In a nuanced analysis of the *Tractatus*, Carol Zaleski writes that Owen's actual journey into a real purgatory differentiates the *Tractatus* from other medieval visionary literature. In this aspect, the *Treatise* "stands apart."[86] Owen's experience of traveling through a cave of purgatory takes place "physically rather than in a dream," which "is unlike most other visionaries."[87] In this sense the *Tractatus* incorporates beliefs about terrestrial otherworld destinations as actualities. It is a visionary tale, but exceeds this genre as it is a visionary tale about a physical journey through a spiritual realm.

The popularity of the *Tractatus* has overshadowed the location of Lough Derg and its history, leading some scholars to mistakenly associate the text's emphasis on adventure to an otherworld as being original to the Lough Derg purgatory and pilgrimage instead of its penitential aspects. Historian Ludwig Bieler suggests this: "What once was an adventure, at times suspected as of doubtful theological and spiritual value, has become a sober practice of penance."[88] Scholars have subsumed the *Tractatus* into a European visionary literary tradition, with much justification, yet at the same time unwittingly severed it from its indigenous context, leading some to believe that it is only peripherally associated with Lough Derg and Ireland and viewing Lough Derg's nationalist, Irish elements as a later accretion.[89] Victor and Edith Turner point to this issue in their examination of Lough Derg, *Image and Pilgrimage in Christian Culture*, noting "the failure to distinguish the Irish conception of Lough Derg from an alien, even exotic, view." They further suggested that "the 'real charm' of Louch Derg may well escape those not schooled in Irish tradition."[90] For their part, Irish historians of Lough Derg generally concur with this assessment. In Alice Curtayne's *History of Lough Derg*, she writes, "The foreign idea of the sanctuary was exciting and fantastic, the native one was wholly spiritual."[91] The historiography of Lough Derg follows the contours of the dualistic framework that posits matter over spirit and that has influenced most of religious studies scholarship in the last one hundred years. The consequence of this has been the articulation of two traditions of Lough Derg, one tradition focusing on visions that are assumed to be based on Latin manuscripts about the site—a Continental tradition, and the other that is an indigenous interpretation of the site that emphasizes the body and ascetic exercises.

However, even Curtayne acknowledges that many medieval Irish penitents were attracted to the island by the hope of having visions of the otherworld.[92] What is lost in this interpretation of the two traditions of Lough Derg theory is the simple fact that the visions of the otherworld, which most often included meetings with the deceased, occurred at Lough Derg within a context of extreme penance. The visions and the penitential exercises are best understood as occurring together and mutually influencing the literature that emerged from the penitent's experiences. As a contemporary priest commented about the experience of pilgrims, "The prayer of the Lough Derg pilgrims is not a prayer of the lips or the mind; it is a prayer of the whole body. It is the physical nature of the prayer on Lough Derg that so clearly defines the spirit of the place."[93]

What we find at what Le Goff calls "the birthplace of Purgatory" in Ireland, is that purgatory's earthly portal, at Lough Derg, was not a problem when viewed within the context of the older penitential theology. Lough Derg was understood by indigenous Irish to be a location where they could purge their sins in order to avoid hell in the afterlife. Attention to the historical context of medieval Irish religious life and its traditions of ascetic practices reveals that caves and reclusariums, or small cells attached to churches, were used for this purpose. Additionally, indigenous Irish poetry and rhymes, mostly written in the sixteenth and seventeenth centuries, and anti-Catholic polemic from the same era, indicate that Irish understood the cave in this way. Although the poems were written well after 1180, they overwhelmingly emphasize that the site was a space for physical purgation of sins.

The late medieval era was seminal for the doctrine of purgatory. It was the subject of papal discussions and in 1254 Pope Innocent IV, in a letter to his legate to the Greeks, defined purgatory as a state of afterlife purification. Later, in an effort to further establish doctrinal accord with the Greek Church, Pope Gregory X organized the Second Council of Lyon between 1272–1274. At the Council theologians defined purgatory as an afterlife destination where sinners could hope to suffer penances and then attain heaven and obtain aid through the prayers and suffrages of the living. Neither document mentioned purgatory's location or its physical aspects, or the nature of the purification, if it involved real fire, or other details. There was, however, no lasting accord with the Greek Church, and later at the Council of Basel, Ferrara and Florence (1431–49) the subject of purgatory was more contentious between the churches, as the Greek council members were reticent to define the fire of purgatory as a real fire.

Conclusion

As church officials made their declarations about purgatory, many Catholics believed that purgatory could be accessed in Ireland. In the cave on the island, practitioners engaged in severe penances they believed would save them from hell. This idea endured well into modern times. After fasting for fifteen days, performing "stations" that consisted of praying while walking and kneeling, immersing themselves in the icy lake waters, and walking on shards of rock, they would descend, with bloodied feet, into the dark cave. The prior of the grounds would shut the door and lock it, leaving the pilgrim to endure twenty-four hours of solitary confinement. Afterward, the pilgrim believed she was free from all sin. "The cave is a house of remedy for the ills of the soul. On leaving the cave the pilgrim discards his garment of sickness and is fully restored in the healing waters of the lake."[94] These practices had been forged within the climate of early medieval penitential theology, which supported the belief that penance had to be accomplished prior to death to be efficacious.

The particularly harsh penance was often accompanied by reports of tactile, miraculous phenomenon, best exemplified by the escapades of the knight Owen in the *Tractatus*. The *Tractatus* popularized the cave on the island and the pilgrimage. Within the context of the anchoritic tradition in Ireland, the pilgrimage became a place where non-anchorites could engage in their own spiritual battles and reap the rewards of temporary reclusion. Owen's story and records describing a penitent's journeys through the cave emphasize the connection between penance and spiritual warfare. The battleground was the penitent's body and psyche. Pilgrims fought back their natural sense of hunger as they starved for fifteen days, their need for warmth as they endured cold air and rain, their desire for comfort as they resisted sleep and walked and prayed on rock shards and then immersed themselves in the lake's icy waters. They battled their fears as they were enclosed and locked up in a small, dark cave for twenty-four hours. Through this ordeal they strengthened their will and gained spiritual weapons to be used in a moral battle against evil. The extreme physical experience was accompanied by encounters with demons, angels, and souls that pilgrims perceived to be real. The spiritual battle was generally not interpreted as metaphorical, as Irish and Europeans flocked to the cave in hope of experiencing the real fires of purgatory.

Contemporary historians of Lough Derg have pondered the curious visionary tradition that portrayed physical journeys through spiritual places, and historians have tended to sever the visionary tradition of Lough Derg from the penitential tradition. However, the earliest narratives suggest that penitents were not working within a worldview that severs spirit from matter. Through penance, practitioners accessed spiritual spaces, which were at once physical and spiritual. The problem of purgatory's materiality hadn't arrived on the historical scene yet.

Just before and certainly after its codification as a doctrine at the Second Council of Lyon, scholastic philosophers began to debate purgatory's status as either physical or spiritual, or somehow both. It would, indeed, become a problem. The purgatory in Ireland would be shut down several times, first by the Church, and then by the English government, motivating Aodh Mac Aingil to lament, in 1737, "God allows these schools of satisfaction, these retreats of penance, be banned to us, something which will result in thousands of us burning in the firelakes of hell."[95]

2

Lough Derg

NOT MORE THAN one hundred years after the monk H. of Saltrey wrote about the knight Owen's travels through the earthly purgatory at Lough Derg, scholastic philosopher and bishop William of Auvergne was working through the logistics of purgatory. He pondered, "If the place of purgation of souls, which is called purgatory, is a specific place, destined for the purgation of human souls, distinct from the earthly Paradise, from Hell, and from the place where we reside, then there is a problem."[1] The problem, according to William, was revealed by the many reports, some from reliable sources like popes and clergy, of souls from purgatory who were able to speak, eat, and leave physical evidence of their visits. The ability to manipulate physical objects, to William's mind, should be impossible for what he assumed to be incorporeal souls. Furthermore, William wondered about the location of purgatory. Was it a place on earth, or was it more ethereal, located somewhere below heaven, and not on earth at all? These were difficult questions, and William's important work was the creation of taxonomy of created things, called *De Universo*, or *The Universe of Creatures*. In this work he addressed the issue of spirit and matter and he differentiated ghosts from demons and legitimate souls in purgatory from pagan gods and goddesses, who, he argued, were trying to lead common people to engage in idolatry. He advocated punishments for those who did not adhere to his categorizations. People who either were not aware of his taxonomy or who defied it by engaging with souls from purgatory that might be demons were to be, as William advocated, run through by sword or burned by fire.

The problem of purgatory, for Auvergne and other scholastic theologians, was primarily the problem of its materiality—where did it exist, and how was it possible that souls from purgatory acted in ways that produced concrete, this-world effects? Many scholastic philosophers, William included, mostly adhered to a form of metaphysical dualism, or the belief in two substances— matter and spirit. However, there was much variation within this philosophical framework. Thomas Aquinas (1225–1274) proposed that spiritual matter and corporeal matter were distinct, and he privileged reason, which he thought was not corporeal, over matter. To Aquinas, angels, who were noncorporeal beings, were more perfect than humans, precisely for the reason that they were purely rational or not of material substance. He did not necessarily assume that spiritual substance was completely devoid of matter. Instead, Aquinas maintained that it was just a different substance. Regardless of the intricacies of debates about the substance of spirit, scholastic views about spirit and matter translated into an overall ethos, adopted by Church authorities, that advocated a framework that would impact beliefs about the physicality of purgatory. As James Bono writes, "A spirit-matter dichotomy became a dominant category for analyzing relationships among things."[2] By and large, for scholastic philosophers, matter was to be thought of as distinct from spirit, and souls are spirit by nature, "in short, the spiritual model of life, death and afterlife increasingly emphasized the incorporeality of the vital principle by contrast with the material nature of the body and the tangible world."[3] This "problem" of the commingling of spirit and matter that appeared to occur in connection with souls from purgatory vexed William and his fellow theologians throughout the "long twelfth century," roughly the time period between 1050 and 1215.[4]

This era also marked the genesis of purgatory as it would come to be defined by the Roman Catholic Church, as well as the consolidation of the system of church-approved associated practices and rituals. The Gregorian Church Reforms, instituted by Pope Gregory VII (1073–1085), established the Church as the principle authority in ecclesial and secular matters and attempted to restore, what was at the time, the embattled reputations of the clergy, by forbidding clerical marriage and preventing simony—the act of paying for or selling clerical positions or offices. The intention of the reformers was also to centralize the hierarchical structure of authority of the Church and to emphasize the importance of the priest to parishes and establish rules governing the sacraments and church attendance. The reforms were also prompted by the "great schism" in the eleventh century between the Greek Orthodox and the Roman Catholic churches that separated these into two separate political-ecclesial institutions. These factors informed interpretations of purgatory to varying degrees. Although theologians did not present a unified theory of purgatory, there was a gradual progression within official Catholic doctrine to codify purgatory as an afterlife state, not an earthly place, and to deemphasize its more sensual aspects. Jacques Le Goff notes that among the scholastics, "One senses a desire to rationalize Purgatory, to tidy it up, to control it—in a word, to purge it of its offensive popular trappings." These trappings included the "vulgar and superstitious piety," but more specifically things referring to "the senses."[5] In other words, the concrete aspects of purgatory became problematic for scholastic theologians, and hence the Church. However, even as the scholastics were crafting their theory of purgatory, pilgrims continued to journey to the purgatory cave at Lough Derg.

To be clear, there were many purgatories, or rather, many interpretations of purgatory that circulated during the era of the long twelfth century. Some theologians believed purgatory was on earth, and others believed that it was an invisible, afterlife state. Many people went to Ireland to journey through what they believed to be a real entrance to purgatory. Despite various conceptions, however, two clear interpretations of purgatory emerged that would endure. One interpretation arose from the metaphysical dualism of the scholastics. It also informed the official doctrine, which was codified along the lines of conceptualizing purgatory as a place without physical coordinates, non-concrete, non-spatial, and definitely without sensual attributes. Another version of purgatory is revealed through an examination of popular practices, including the penances at Lough Derg, as well as the myths associated with the Lough Derg purgatory and the anecdotes and reports of ghosts that haunted the cave. These ghosts defied the dualism of the scholastics by appearing in physical guise, and in some cases hitting pilgrims, rowing boats, and otherwise exhibiting all of the tactile attributes that defied William's metaphysics. This latter purgatory, linked to places, objects, and things, would prove to be problematic for the Church hierarchy, as official statements by Church officials about purgatory increasingly de-emphasized its physical aspects. The cave at Lough Derg was destroyed in 1497 by Pope Alexander VI, because "it being understood...that this was not the purgatory Patrick got from God, although they were, everyone, visiting it."[6] It was soon rebuilt by the Irish, and yet again destroyed in 1632 under the English-ruled government. Rebuilt shortly after this, it has remained a popular destination for centuries. Today the site receives approximately sixteen thousand pilgrims a year, of whom 99 percent are Catholic.[7]

Even as the material elements of purgatory presented a metaphysical problem for scholastics and Church theologians, it remained an

important component to the Lough Derg pilgrimage, as well as a persistent motif in narratives about purgatory. As scholastics worked out the
parameters of the problem of the place of purgatory, the narratives and
legends of Lough Derg shifted from representations of the purgatory as
a location at once spiritual and physical, to representations that still
embraced this aspect of purgatory—but qualified it considerably with
interpretation and explanation. This shift in the meaning of the purgatory cave at Lough Derg had no significant effect on its status as a sacred
destination, however.

The Problem with Purgatory: Scholastic Rationalism and Metaphysical Dualism

Although Europeans entertained a belief in physical entrances to purgatory, heaven and hell, these beliefs and practices competed with burgeoning theological doctrine that, not unlike world maps, de-emphasized the
physical aspects of these speculative locations. The scholastic movement
of the thirteenth century lent theological support to what would become
the official doctrine of purgatory. Scholasticism was an intellectual movement originating in the early medieval era, founded by Irish-born theologian and poet Johannes Scotus Eriugena (815–877), whose knowledge of
Greek set a standard for future university-trained theologians. Influenced
by the Greek philosophers Aristotle and Plato, Eriugena traveled to Paris
to run two universities and established the precedent of utilizing Greek
philosophy to inform Christian theology. Scholastic theologians were
known for developing a system of scriptural exegesis, or translation, using
principles of rationalism that they partly adopted from ancient Greek
philosophical texts. The emphasis on rationalism and logical coherence
presented unique problems, especially with respect to issues regarding
purgatory, as Scripture presented no direct information about it, having
never named it specifically. Yet if popular sentiment and reports of places
like St. Patrick's Purgatory suggested such a location, logic and rationalism compelled it. What was the fate of one who died in grace yet with
venial, or forgivable, sins? According to Aquinas, these souls *must* endure
some penance prior to going to heaven. This penance was purgatory. The
question remained however, where did the penance take place?

   Carl Watkins calls Paris in the 1100s a "crucible of innovative purgatorial and penitential thought."[8] The new penitential theology, which
promoted the possibility of afterlife penance, was spreading through the

work of scholastics like Peter Lombard, bishop of Paris in 1159, who maintained in his work *Sententiae* that venial sins could be dissolved by afterlife penance between death and the last judgment. Later, William determined that purgatory was an afterlife destination, but that souls actually performed their penance on earth. Therefore, purgatory was on earth, but was a place of purgation for the dead, not for the living. This innovation owed much to William's interpretation of Pope Gregory I's (Gregory the Great, 540–604) anecdote about a soul from purgatory, the Roman bathhouse ghost. H. of Saltrey, the Cistercian author of the *Tractatus*, also owed much to Gregory I.

Gregory I's legacy on the twelfth century is significant. The Gregorian Reform movement, while instigated by Gregory VII, was named for Gregory I. Much of Gregory I's works, such as the *Dialogues and the Rule for Pastors*, emphasized the supernatural nature of the church in secular affairs, and set the precedent for interpreting visions and sightings of apparitions. H. of Saltrey mentions Gregory I in his prologue and drew upon a literary convention that had been established by Gregory. Gregory participated in the transmission and the construction of ghost stories and can be credited with forging a literature of purgatorial realms possessing its own conventions and characteristics. Medieval iconography of Gregory portrays him hunched over a manuscript with a dove hovering near his head and dictating in his ear. The dove is a symbol of the Holy Spirit and reveals a direct link to the sacred that authorizes his writing as sacred truth. Whereas in the early medieval era the ecclesial culture for the most part rejected ghost stories as false or diabolical and pagan.[9] Gregory's work provided authority to later writings by monks and clerics dealing specifically with souls in purgatory.

Two types of stories about souls from purgatory eventually coalesced into two distinct traditions: the visionary literature for which Dante Alighieri was famous, and purgatory literature that focused on this-world visitations from souls. The first visions primarily occurred in dreams while the visionary was stationary. In his mind's eye or in a dream a visionary would travel to afterlife destinations or see souls in purgatory. The other type of story was location specific and could be characterized as a visitation, in that it featured a soul from purgatory haunting a place. Location haunting stories featured "this-world" elements like souls appearing in waking life, eating, or leaving behind physical evidence of their visits like scorched fingerprints. Gregory's account of the stories of haunted souls lays out a rudimentary framework for future otherworld journeys.[10]

The story of the Roman bathhouse ghost is typical of visitation lore.[11] In the sixth and seventh centuries, bishops and clerics regularly enjoyed public baths. As recounted by Pope Gregory in his *Dialogues*, one bishop frequently bathed in the waters in the town of Taurina and related a curious story. Each time the bishop visited the bath he encountered a kind and humble man. This man was a regular at the baths and attended to the bishop's needs with respect and a quiet demeanor. Wishing to repay the man for his services, the bishop offered him two loaves of bread. The man replied that he was, in fact, dead, and being a ghost he couldn't eat the bread. He continued by stating that he was simply atoning for his sins in the place where he had committed them, which was there, at the Taurina baths. As the bishop considered this uncanny scene, the ghost continued speaking. If the bishop wished to repay him, he said, he could offer the bread to God as that would lessen the time he would have to spend serving at the baths. After saying this, he vanished. Pope Gregory states, "The bishop reported that his man had appeared as flesh and blood."[12]

The account is told to Gregory secondhand, and he faithfully records it, thus distancing the himself from the actual tale, an element that will be repeated in later instances of Latin purgatory literature such as H. of Saltrey's *Tractatus*. Another element that will become formulaic is the appearance of the ghost as a real person going about her or his business as he or she had in his or her previous life and haunting the location at which he or she committed sin. The emphasis on the corporeal nature of the ghost is significant as it confers realism to the story that distinguishes it from a dream or a vision. It also functions as evidence of the reality of the purgatorial realm. Having "wakeful dreams" or apparitions helped to "reinforce the credibility of a tale."[13]

In his prologue to the *Tractatus*, H. of Saltrey credits Gregory with establishing how one is to interpret apparitions and, specifically, the location of purgatory. The issue of the materiality of the afterlife, and its overlap with everyday life, receives particular emphasis. H. of Saltrey references Pope Gregory I as his predecessor, in this regard:

> We have read that the blessed Pope Gregory has related many things about what happens to souls released from their earthly bonds. He says that souls taken away and returned to the body tell of visions and revelations made to them either of the torments of sinners or the joys of the just. However, everything mentioned in their tales is concrete or similar to material elements: rivers, flames, bridges, boats, houses, woodlands, fields, flowers.[14]

H. of Saltrey concludes that "physical punishments have been prepared by God, so it is also said that physical places have been arranged where these punishments can take place."[15] For H. of Saltrey, there are physical places where souls go to endure their penance, and these are likely on earth. H. of Saltrey is writing in the 1180s and would have been aware of the shifts in penitential theology taking place in Paris at the time.[16] His conception of purgatory appears to be a compromise between older penitential concepts, where penance had to be performed by the living on earth, and new ideas of penance that promoted an afterlife place where souls could expiate their sins after death. Watkins notes that "Owein entered the purgatory to perform a kind of 'super-satisfactory' penance for the great many sins he committed. But his assumptions were subverted on two counts as he wandered in the otherworld." Watkins notes that Owen is able to use divine grace to put the demons at bay, and he is "the odd man out" in the purgatory, as all the other souls are dead.[17] Thus, according to Watkins, this aspect of H.'s narrative of purgatory is a bridge between old notions of penance and the new notions that were gradually taking root.

Just a few years later, in the 1230s, William considered the material elements of purgatory in light of Gregory I's anecdote of the bathhouse ghost. For William, generally only demons, who were fallen angels and therefore incorporeal, were able to hold concrete objects and engage with material things. Yet here was an eminent Church father, Gregory I, writing about a ghost who acted like a demon. His analysis of the bathhouse ghost was unique in that it accounted for the problem while at the same time furthering the innovation of purgatory reflected in the *Tractatus*: under certain circumstances, generally when God allows for matters of instruction, matter and spirit can commingle. Informing his analysis were several assumptions, mostly gleaned from his interpretation of the philosophies of Plato, Aristotle, and newly translated Arabic texts, although Le Goff notes that some scholars suggest that William was hostile to the philosophy of Aristotle.[18] His understanding of philosophy suggests a normative pattern based on metaphysical dualism—souls are not bodies, and bodies are not like souls. Souls are immaterial and bodies are material.

However, according to William, souls can "appear" to people as a sign from God to warn them not to commit sins. In his analysis, purgatory was a place on earth where souls must do penance at the location where they committed their sin. In his treatment of Gregory's Roman bathhouse ghost, he notes that the sinner appeared to the bishop in the place where he had sinned, and that he gathered wood and tended to "the fire."[19] Earth is therefore the place where souls do their penance, because it is on earth where people committed their sins. With respect to the actions of the soul, according to William, under ordinary circumstances a soul would not be able to do the things that the bishop witnessed, and the living generally cannot see these souls. But in certain cases, the dead interact with the living, "by God's power."[20] Therefore William admits that God suspends the normal laws in certain cases, so that souls from purgatorial realms, who are doing penance at the place where they have done their sins, can be a warning to others.[21] William's purgatory was a place on earth, but was not accessible to the living, and souls doing their penance on earth were generally not visible, although there were exceptions to this rule. These exceptions included the apparitions of souls from purgatory who appeared to defy the laws of metaphysical dualism—that is, they were able to engage with concrete objects and things.

Another problem that William addressed was the fire of purgatory. If souls were incorporeal, how did they actually burn, and was the fire that burned them material? That souls suffered from fire in purgatory was, to William, not in doubt. There were too many accounts from people who had seen souls on fire to consider that this aspect of it could be wrong. However, the materiality of the fire was a vexing problem and William attempts to explain it by positing that it is perhaps not real: "Sometimes [people] dream that they are burning and are in fire and are being tormented intolerably, as if they were really burning. And therefore, since the truth and substance are not in them, but only the appearance of fire is in either their fantasy or their imagination, it is manifest that they suffer the torment of this type of fire merely from the appearance of fire."[22] Further, the Creator, according to William, can torture souls with fire or with any torment, "by means of the intellect alone." As much as this suggests that William is delineating a theory of spirit and matter whereby an incorporeal fire is able to burn an incorporeal soul, he later suggests quite the opposite, "[Fire] really corporeally torments bodies and souls too."[23]

Historians have interpreted William's apparent contradictions in divergent ways. Alan Bernstein, in an influential article about William's philosophy of purgatory and hell, argues that William articulates a theory of matter and spirit that is tailored toward two audiences: an unsophisticated laity, whom William believes require literalism to believe in the reality of the afterlife, and his fellow scholastic philosophers, who understand the intricacies of philosophy and can therefore tease out his emphasis on literalism for what it is—a rhetorical ploy not meant for them. Bernstein maintains that William's statements about the realism of purgatory on earth or with respect to the reality of its fire should be considered metaphoric. "[William] advocated the dissemination of a simple, literal view to the faithful, even while he elaborated an esoteric, metaphorical position of his own."[24] For Bernstein, William did not believe in the literal fire of purgatory. Le Goff's interpretation of William's contradictions is opposite of Bernstein's. Le Goff writes that William, more than many other scholastics, argued for the literalism of purgatory as a place with real flames. "Did anyone ever offer better or bolder arguments for the view that the theater of Purgatory is not a theater of shadows but a corporeal theater, in which souls suffer in their bodies from the bite of a material flame?"[25]

Most likely William was articulating something altogether different from what either Bernstein or Le Goff suggests. Although metaphysical dualism would come to frame the discourse of spiritual matters, and in particular that of spiritual beings, it does not appear as if William believed that he needed to adhere to a rigid metaphysical dualism. Like H. of Saltrey, who doesn't see a problem in narrating a tale of a living knight who walks through the land of the dead and returns with bruises to show for it, William was writing within a framework where the dead and the living interact and engage with each other through events that are charged with meaning. Attention to the meaning of the events shows that an important message presents itself at the juncture of spirit and matter. With regard to the Roman bathhouse ghost tale, when the bishop in Taurina finds out he is speaking with a soul from purgatory, the soul vanishes. The bishop is left with a meaningfully charged episode, which William interprets as a warning. William argues that incorporeal souls can appear and perform physical actions, when the results of these actions are meaningful events, or messages from the dead to the living. Despite the arguments of Bernstein and Le Goff, who attempt to interpret William as either arguing for or against the literalism of purgatory, attention to what happens, according to William, at the interface of spirit and matter reveals that it is precisely at this moment when a message is revealed. The warning or meaningfully charged event serves as a qualification or gateway for the spirit to engage with the material world. This aspect of William's theory plays out, in practical terms, at the location of Lough Derg, the sacred place where spirit and matter collide.

Another scholastic philosopher who grappled with the materiality of purgatory was Thomas Aquinas. Aquinas was a Dominican priest who became the regent master at the University of Paris twice, between 1245 and 1272. His works, including the *Summa Theologica* and his commentaries on Aristotle, were influential in aligning Christian principles with philosophical principles—mainly those of the Greeks, and they became the basis of the European university curriculum. In a work that was left unfinished, he treats the subject of ghosts or souls from purgatory who visit the living. Like William, Aquinas rejects the notion that God would allow souls from purgatory to wander back into the realm of the living, and notes that they must only do so on special reprieve, as a warning to the living. In this way, he also follows the precedent set by Gregory I:

> separated souls sometimes come forth from their abode and appear to men.... It is also credible that this may occur sometimes to the damned, and that for man's instruction and intimidation they be permitted to appear to the living; or again in order to seek our suffrages, as to those who are detained in purgatory.[26]

Aquinas goes on to further clarify a metaphysical dualism in which souls generally cannot defy natural laws and usually remain untethered to bodies. "It does not follow, although the dead be able to appear to the living as they will, that they appear as often as when living in the flesh: because when they are separated from the flesh, they are either wholly conformed to the divine will, so that they may do nothing but what they see to be agreeable with the Divine disposition, or else they are so overwhelmed by their punishments that their grief for their unhappiness surpasses their desire to appear to others."[27] As with William, Aquinas argues that souls from purgatory can defy metaphysical dualism for purposes of warning the living or for requesting suffrages, in other words, within the context of a meaningfully charged event. This requirement also had the consequence of narrowing the acceptable interpretations of apparitions of the dead.

The scholastics were influential in codifying beliefs about purgatory and in systematizing the ways apparitions should be interpreted. When purgatory was defined, at the Second Council of Lyon in 1274, Thomas Aquinas and other scholastics were invited to the Council. The first papal proclamations about purgatory were more politically expedient than philosophical. The problem of the schism between the Greek Orthodox Church and the Latin Church was at the forefront of discussions about purgatory. In the proclamations about purgatory, popes made no mention of the messy issue of the material aspects of the place of purgation. Theologians from the Eastern tradition recognized that prayers for the dead were inexplicable without the existence of an afterlife state of purgation, yet they never officially defined purgatory and much later, during the Council of Basel, Ferrara and Florence, they would refuse to define it as a literal fire. In an effort to encourage unity between the traditions, yet to establish doctrinal dominance, Pope Innocent IV (1243–1254), in a letter to the Roman delegate to Greece, called for the universal use of the term "purgatory" to refer to the beliefs and set of practices held by both traditions:

> It is said that the Greeks themselves unhesitatingly believe and maintain that the souls of those who do not perform a penance that they have received…are purified after death and can be helped by the prayers of the Church.
>
> Since the Greeks say that their Doctors have not given them a definite and proper name for the place of such purification, We, following the tradition and authority of the holy Fathers, call that place purgatory; and it is our will that the Greeks use that name in the future.[28]

A few years later, the doctrine of purgatory was defined in a council that was called by Pope Gregory X in an attempt to reconcile the Greek and Latin churches. Although he had been summoned to the council, Thomas Aquinas died en route. However, the influence of the scholastic theologians was in evidence. More than three hundred bishops were invited as well as a thousand representatives from European universities. At the Council, theologians defined purgatory as an afterlife realm where "souls are cleansed after death in purgatorial or cleansing punishments." They also stated that the "the suffrages of the faithful on earth can be of great help in relieving these punishments, as, for instance, the Sacrifice of the Mass, prayers, alms-giving, and other religious deeds which, in the manner of the Church, the faithful are accustomed to offer for others of the faithful."[29]

Within the declarations of purgatory, no mention was made of purgatory's earthly provenance. Was it a place or a condition? Were the punishments physical? Did they have to occur after death? Additionally, Church-related activities like Masses and indulgences were declared to be efficacious in moving souls through purgatory to heaven and an exchange system of suffrages, indulgences, and money gradually began to exist alongside local penitential customs. This was accomplished in several ways. Local practices of penance were subject to control, as evidenced by the pilgrimage at Lough Derg, which in 1180 was put under the control of Augustinian canons. As will be revealed, the Church destroyed the purgatory cave several times. Additionally, even as William acknowledged that souls, by the power of God and under certain circumstances, could become corporeal and perform concrete actions, he proposed severe penalties for people who engaged with these souls. In their efforts to appease these souls, Europeans engaged in practices such as leaving nighttime offerings on windowsills and attempting to converse with the apparitions to find out what they might want. For these unfortunate people, William advocated death.[30]

Meanwhile, on the Ground... the Myths of St. Patrick's Purgatory

Despite the declarations of the council in 1274, the purgatory on the island of Lough Derg continued to be a place believed to be an actual location of purgatory. It also continued to be a site where practitioners engaged in rituals intended to expiate their sins. The metaphysical dualism of the scholastics had not penetrated Irish localities or parishes. This was typical during the medieval era, as the theological fervor of members of the Parisian universities had yet to infiltrate England's Lincoln seminary, which provided priests for the local parishes. During the thirteenth century "some parish priests [were] still demanding rigorous, fully satisfactory penances" of their parishioners.[31] Pilgrims continued venturing to the cave they believed to be a real, physical location of purgatory, and the visions they reported defied dualist frameworks by featuring afterlife personages who spoke to, scratched, and on some occasions provided secret knowledge of current events to pilgrims.

The myths of Lough Derg are a stark counterpoint to the gradually developing metaphysical dualism of the scholastics, and they also illustrate the aspect of William's and Aquinas's theories that have been largely unexamined—the *qualifications* that allowed spirit and matter to commingle. This is the meaningfully charged event that William and Aquinas, and Gregory I before them, identified as the gateway for these spirits to enter the world of the living. According to them, God suspends normal laws of spirit and matter under circumstances where the living would be given spiritual messages and warnings. Additionally, the myths of Lough Derg, including narratives like the *Tractatus*, defy the dualism of matter and spirit. Yet the *Tractatus* is just the first and most popular of the many tales of ghostly apparitions that haunt the purgatory island and are contained within the thousands of tracts, poems, and histories about the place. Almost without exception, these narratives delve into the ghost stories and myths associated with the purgatory cave, opening a Pandora's box of unruly spirits and souls who do not neatly fit within William of Auvergne's tidy categorizations of spirit and matter. There are two main types of narratives: the myths of Lough Derg link pilgrims directly to the landmarks and environment on the island, and the reports of ghosts tell a tale of interactions between the living and the dead, solidified through rituals of penance.

The works of several scholars of medieval history who have focused on ghosts and apparitions provide a useful framework for understanding the social functions of these narratives. In his analysis of European medieval ghost stories, Jean-Claude Schmitt outlines a theoretical approach that he terms a "social history of the imaginary." He points out that tales of souls returning to speak to loved ones benefited "above all, the powerful," in that they helped promote the burgeoning liturgy of the dead and rituals associated with purgatory that ultimately proved economically advantageous to the Church.[32] However, he cautions against a facile reading that reduces these tales to propaganda, as for every tale that promoted the Church's doctrines, there were others that opposed them, as the case of the Lough Derg hauntings reveals.

Similar to Schmitt's analysis, Carl Watkins's work on the supernatural in the medieval era explores tales of ghosts and the miraculous. Rejecting the "linguistic turn" that contends that texts are social constructions that have no bearing on actual historical reality, his analysis of medieval chronicles and their emphasis on the supernatural yields "valuable information about customs and rituals of locality and region." He further states, "The miraculous, the demonic and more ambiguous manifestations of the supernatural are all depicted in chronicles as part of the fabric of local and immediate experience."[33] In other words, through attention to the telling and retelling of these stories and through noting repeated patterns, one might acquire an idea of how an experiential core informed the stories, and gain a more thorough understanding of religious belief in the medieval era. While Watkins explicitly rejects categorizing his work as a history of popular, folk, or lay religion, he seeks to formulate a history of medieval culture in its diversity.[34]

Taking a cue from Watkins's work, that is, attending to the myths, stories, and folklore of Lough Derg, reveals clues about how they functioned as gateways to the otherworld. The myths and ghost stories of Lough Derg established intimate ties between pilgrims, the site, and what they imagined was to be their afterlife. Like Owen, the characters in these dramas defied what William of Auvergne believed to be laws of nature by appearing in broad daylight, and as is the case with the serpent that haunts the lake around the island, leaving physical remnants of their bodies to be handled and considered by penitents. The stories of the site are recorded from the beginning of the written history of Lough Derg, although it is not known when they were first imagined or told. What is known is that the myths were first recorded when Lough Derg was at the nexus of political and social strife, and at the same time that St. Patrick became the main saint associated with the site.

Although written history of Lough Derg begins in the twelfth century, evidence from a nearby monastic settlement, Columcille in Iona, provides clues about the prehistory of Lough Derg. Like the settlement on Lough Derg, the Celtic monastery on Iona contained a church, a library, workshops, and buildings supporting a small settlement. Its inhabitants included a scribe, a lector, the prior, an anchorite, and cooks, most likely the same types of people who lived at Lough Derg. In 836 this settlement, and others like it, was destroyed in a series of invasions.[35] What happened at this site? Another monastic settlement at Lough Mahee provides insight as to the likely fate of the inhabitants of these Irish monastic settlements. The settlement on Mahee was sacked in the same series of invasions, in 974. Describing the ordeal and archaeological preservation of the site, Irish historian Alice Curtayne writes, "Some of the monks succeeded in escaping; all the members of the settlement who were caught were killed, and the buildings were either set on fire, or they caught fire during the sack. [Archaeologists at] Belfast Archeological Society at Nendrum have excavated with great care, writing tablets of slate found on the floor of this building just before the alarm had been given. They were able to identify a school-house, the designs on them [the tablets] clearly visible, a letter of the alphabet, a Celtic decoration design, and a humorous drawing of a horse half-seated."[36]

Documents written by the Celtic monks were destroyed during the invasions. Ironically, the earliest written accounts of the pilgrimage at Lough Derg were authored by Anglo-Norman clerics, H. of Saltrey and Gerald of Wales in the twelfth century, which was a time of rapid expansion of Anglo-Norman influence in Ireland. The Danish, and then, Anglo-Norman invasions and influence, along with the impetus of theological reform that was sweeping Europe, England, and Ireland, significantly impacted the organization of the pilgrimage site. Throughout the twelfth and thirteenth centuries, thirty-four Cistercian houses and 122 Augustinian foundations had settled throughout Ireland.[37] Authority over the site shifted from that of Celtic monks to Augustinian monks.

Between 1130 and 1134 Lough Derg was monitored by the Abbey of saints Peter and Paul in Armagh, and soon after that the Augustinian canons took control of it. Throughout the twelfth century Rome instigated the reform of the Irish Church. As part of the reforms, the Irish Church structure shifted from monasticism to parishes. The Cistercian Máel Máedóc Ua Morgair, or Malachy, a papal legate to Ireland, was responsible for much of this change. Malachy sought to cure monastic abuses and further Christianize the country, and sought Pope Innocent II's approval to institute the reforms.

The reforms targeted monastic orders with the intention of emphasizing austerity, although some authors have suggested that with the Augustinian adoption of Lough Derg, the penances that were practiced there were actually softened from the time it had been under the control of Celtic monks.[38] In any case Lough Derg, being a location that was already popular with indigenous Irish, would have been important to the Augustinians and Cistercians who would have utilized it to promote the reforms or to monitor local religious practices.

At the same time that the original settlement was transformed through Anglo-Norman contact, the island and surrounding territory was being hotly contested by several competing Irish bishops and kings. These battles often resulted in bloodshed. In 1152, two new archbishoprics were created, which moved Lough Derg to the Clogher diocese. The archbishop of Armagh, Giollag mac Liag, angry about this change, fought with the king of Airghialla, an ally of the competing archbishop.[39] Mac Liag was seriously wounded in the fight. Lough Derg was important enough to have been the subject of political strife, and at the same time its religious meaning was being transformed.

During the same century, several events transpired that likely solidified the connection between Lough Derg and St. Patrick, as well as with the surrounding northern Irish province of Armagh. As Peter Brown argues his influential book, *The Cult of Saints*, within hagiographic Christian literature Christian saints were often "revealed" to dominate a location of pagan worship, through the strategic placement of relics or other physical reminders of their lives. Previously, the cave had been associated with St. Davog (*Dabheog*), who was thought to be a disciple of St. Patrick and who, in contemporary oral tradition, is considered to be the first abbot of Lough Derg. The shift to St. Patrick most likely had to do with the Anglo-Norman invasions. The Anglo-Norman knight John D'Courcy had invaded and captured the southern part of the province of Armagh in 1177, where Lough Derg is situated. Ten years later D'Courcy directed the writing of *The Life of Saint Patrick* and funded the Ceremony for the Translation of the Relics of St. Patrick, St. Brigid and St. Colum Cille to the Cathedral of Down in the north. This latter ceremony involved placing the believed physical remnants of several saints beloved by the indigenous Irish in a place that would become a pilgrimage site. Although one can only guess at D'Courcy's motivations, the consequence was that the Irish flocked to pray at the site. It is significant also that D'Courcy was known to support the Cistercians and was responsible for building several abbeys for the order. It is an interesting coincidence that the *Tractatus*, authored by an Anglo-Norman Cistercian, which associates the cave with St. Patrick, was written within approximately the same time frame as D'Courcy's focus on St. Patrick. It is impossible to trace exactly when the purgatory cave became associated with St. Patrick, but most likely it was a consequence of the efforts of Cistercian and Augustinian monks, in conjunction with the Anglo Normans, to regulate and control the practices at the cave.

Scholars have drawn connections between the violence associated with Lough Derg's history and penance. Victor Turner and Edith Turner suggested that the pilgrimage was the locus of "penance and self-punishment for Irish cultural and political divisiveness" and as such functioned as a national totem of Ireland.[40] While violence and battles are a factor in the history of the site, they also remain thematic in another form of its prehistory, the ubiquitous myths about its creation.

There are many histories about Lough Derg, written by both advocates and polemicists, and none have excluded its myths and ghost stories. Founding myths and hauntings provide an interesting subtext to its official history and have been utilized to serve multiple agendas. Anti-Catholic polemicists tended to emphasize the superstitious nature of Catholic belief by focusing on the fantastic and unlikely nature of the stories. Charges of "superstition" and "pagan" abound in such tracts. Catholic authors, however, emphasized the intrigue and sacredness of the location. There are still other, more psychological functions of the myths, as Rev. Daniel O'Connor hints at in his late nineteenth-century history of Lough Derg.

"According to popular superstition, which prevailed amongst the peasantry of Ireland down to recent times, wherever a murder or other tragic event occurred, the spot where such murder was committed was supposed to be haunted by the ghost or spirit of the victim. Hence, such ghost-stories are generally the most reliable traditional evidence respecting the commission of certain dark deeds, even at a remote period, and often indicate the scene of such crimes with the greatest precision."[41]

Taking O'Connor's statement as a point of departure, an analysis of the founding myths of Lough Derg offers an insight into not only what is known of the actual history of the island, being an embattled location at the nexus of colonial and sectarian strife, but also about the pilgrim's relationship to this history. The myths of Lough Derg are violent, but beyond this they function in a way that has been overlooked. They connect the pilgrim to the island in very specific and concrete ways. For example, several large rocks are called "St. Brigid's Chair" and stones on the island are called "serpents' teeth." The myths go well beyond the neat categories specified by the scholastics, since they are stories directly linked to place, and they connect the pilgrim physically with the island, the lake, and the purgatory cave, as well as Ireland's archaic past.

In its most general sense, a myth is also a sacred history, or a history where meaning is emphasized over actual facts. Mircea Eliade, folklorist and scholar of religion, provided a useful framework for understanding myth's connection to concrete events and locations. For Eliade, folklore and myth are not stories told to explain the unknown, but are stories that overlay an empirical or experiential reality, which then becomes exaggerated over time.[42] In the case of Lough Derg, there are several ancient myths that are most often told together and in a variety of amalgamations. Each of these stories is not a story in the traditional sense of a narrative told about a past event, but instead is a story about a past event that conveys into the present, as concrete aspects of the story persist as they are present to pilgrims in the form of the rocks, stones, and other concrete objects on the island. These objects have persisted through a pre-Christian past until the present, and can be handled, sat upon, and prayed at. The myths function to connect the penitent physically to the pilgrimage site. They also provide an interpretive framework for this physical connection. The meanings of these foundational myths are accessible through attention to these recurring symbols: a Celtic warrior, a witch-mother, a Christian saint, and above all, a serpent.

The Serpent in the Lake

The most ubiquitous myth about Lough Derg is that of the serpent, whose blood gives the Red Lake, Lough Derg, its name. The story of the serpent

FIGURE 2-1 Serpent. Hibernia/British Library, London, UK/© British Library Board. All Rights Reserved/The Bridgeman Art Library.

is also one of Lough Derg's creation myths and circulated in several itera-tions that all share a common pattern. The most frequent of these, found in several lay histories of the purgatory, tells the tale of the legendary Celtic warrior Fin Mac Coul (English: Fin McCool) who wrestles a gigantic and deadly lake serpent. (See fig. 2-1.) Despite his heroism, it takes a Christian, St. Patrick, to actually render the serpent powerless as a demonstration of his faith and God's strength. Pictures of the serpent appear on medieval maps of Lough Derg, and Henry Jones records pilgrim's stories about the serpent, as well as their seeing its "teeth," in 1647. The following is recounted by nineteenth-century antiquarian Thomas Wright. The myth begins with an old witch who lives on the island with her son. Her son is a giant who devours people and spreads terror throughout the land. The local king calls upon the mighty Fin Mac Coul to rid the island of the witch.[43]

When Fin arrives he bravely fights the giant and dismembers the giant's mother, the witch. A warrior of Fin's party impetuously throws the bones of the witch into the lake, whereupon a worm escapes that "imme-diately rushed out [as] an enormous beast, so terrible, that all the party, heroes as they were, lost no time in hiding themselves from its fury." (See fig. 2-1.) The roving serpent then swallowed hundreds of the local towns-people "whole." Fin, recognizing a certain weak mole on the beast, was able to stab it and as it struggled, its blood leaked into the lake water, which then turned red. Wright concludes, "There the beast lay writhing and bellowing with pain, till St. Patrick came and found it, and, to show the power of the faith he was preaching, ordered it to go to the bottom of the lake, where he effectually secured it."[44]

The motif of a powerful female figure and her son, associated with an ocean or lake, is found in a variety of ancient creation stories including the Babylonian *Enuma Elish*, perhaps the most famous of this type. In this story, a warrior, Marduk, dismembers the evil goddess Tiamat to create the earth. Tiamat gives birth to serpents. More familiar to the Irish and English visitors to Lough Derg would be the story of *Beowulf*, which also features an evil mother and her cannibal son, who are killed by the hero Beowulf. The story also features a dragon/serpent. After he kills the mother and her son, Beowulf then slays a dragon.[45] With respect to geo-graphical locations and their myths, Eliade is helpful. He argued that cre-ation myths around geographical locations establish them as places at "the center of the world."[46] In the Lough Derg/Red Lake myth, two representa-tives of Ireland, the Celtic warrior Fin Mac Coul and St. Patrick, establish dominance over a place and subdue a serpent and a powerful but evil woman, the witch.

All of the elements of a creation myth are present—the powerful woman who is dismembered, the serpent and the hero, or, in this case, heroes. The Celtic warrior Mac Coul cannot entirely subdue the serpent and requires the help of St. Patrick. Each hero is a representative of Ireland, one a Celtic warrior, the other the later arriving Christian saint. Blood figures promi-nently in the myth. The serpent's blood colors the lake red, giving the lake its name, and the two islands subsequently float on a lake of blood. It is tempting to interpret this aspect of the myth as a blood sacrifice. At its most basic level, a blood sacrifice opens and solidifies a connection be-tween gods and humans. The continuation of the myth supports this link, as God opens the cave as a place where humans can literally peer into the afterlife and otherworld.

Another creation myth of Lough Derg relates how St. Patrick is having difficulty converting the Irish. Perplexed as to how to convince the inhabit-ants of the truth of Christianity, Patrick bends down and traces the ground with a stick, a scene strikingly reminiscent of the Gospel account of Jesus

and the woman adulterer. God allows Patrick to trace a hole in the ground
that opens a pit of fire, a direct link to purgatory and hell. When the people
witness the sputtering flames of hell and hear the wails of those being
tormented, it is said that they are readily converted.

Another iteration of this story recounts how God gives St. Patrick the
cave as a gift to the Irish, so that they can endure punishments on earth
in order to avoid them in the next life. In this version Jesus appears to
St. Patrick and shows him "a rounded pit, dark inside, and said to him that
whoever, being truly repentant and armed with true faith, would enter this
pit and remain for the duration of one day and one night, would be purged
of all the sins of his life. Moreover, while going through it, he would see
not only the torments of the wicked, but also, if he acted constantly according to the faith, the joys of the blessed."[47]

Yet another version of the myth has St. Patrick ridding the island of the
gods of the druids, which were also demons and haunted the island.[48] As
Patrick moved northward on his journey of conversion, the devils fled and
hid in the cave. The Irish were so frightened by the demons that they
wouldn't even look in the direction of the infested island. When Patrick
heard the tales of the demons' orgies and mischief, he marched toward the
island to rid it of the demons. Despite warnings from the inhabitants, he
spent twenty-four hours fighting the demons and finally vanquished them.
"This legend makes the Station Island the final site of the struggle between
Patrick and Druidical power.... Christian art represents the saint standing
on the head of a serpent, or with a serpent coiled around the foot of his cro-
zier, in allusion to the belief that he drove out from Ireland all of the snakes
and reptiles. The deed is supposed to actually have been performed on
Station Island."[49] The legend continues by telling how, having killed the
demons, Patrick then consecrated the island as a site of penance.

These legends reveal multiple meanings. The displacement of an earlier Celtic and Druidic religious tradition by Christianity is an obvious
motif, as Patrick "bests" the Celtic hero Fin Mac Coul by finally subduing
the lake serpent. Patrick also vanquishes the gods of the Druids, who are
also called "demons." In each case, Patrick's faith in the God of Christianity
is demonstrated as a means to conquer evil, and as a way to solicit conversions of the Irish. Myths of heroes slaying serpents are often interpreted
as indicating the replacement of an older religious tradition by a newer
tradition, which overlays its own saints over previous ones.[50]

Beyond this interpretation is another facet that illustrates how the
myths connect the pilgrim to concrete structures of the island. Returning

to Mircea Eliade's contention that myths often overlay an experiential core, the myths of Lough Derg connect the sacred history of the cave to the penitent's experience. The characters identified in the legends are associated with physical landmarks on the islands and in the lake. Interestingly, the penitential practices align penitents not with the vanquishers like St. Patrick, but with the vanquished. A closer look at the character of the serpent sheds light on this point.

In the polemical work "Saint Patrick's Purgatory: Containing the Description, Origin, Progress and Demolition of That Superstitious Place" (1647), Henry Jones, a Protestant bishop of Clogher (Church of Ireland), writes about how the concrete landmarks of the islands supplement the penitent's experience of their exercises and fortify their belief in the purgatory.[51] After having learned of how the lake attained its red hue, Jones remarks how, as if to confirm the legend, practitioners "showed a great, *knotty bone*, said to be one of the left joints of that serpents tale." Penitents pointed to several rocky protrusions that dot the lake that are referred to as the serpent's bones. Although Jones dismisses the penitent's association of physical artifacts as confirmation of the myths as "not suitable for serious discourse" he did find that it was a practice commonly invoked that provided a framework for the penitent's own interpretations of Lough Derg.

The serpent's bones dot the shoreline and its blood colors the water of the lake. Within a mythological framework that takes into account sacrificial symbols, the serpent and the mother of the giant whose body the serpent emerged from are the sacrificial victims whose blood consecrates the purgatory. The penitents make their stations over the rock shards that are said to be the broken teeth of the serpent, and throughout the modern era part of the serpent's bones were contained in the sanctuary on Saints Island, in a church called "Reglis." The bones were also displayed alongside other relics associated with St. Patrick, such as a bell that he was said to have carried. One part of the penance that remains today is that of making the stations while barefoot. Due to the rocky terrain, the penitents still suffer from punctured feet, which they soothe in the waters of the lake. The lake waters and stone structures called saint's beds help pilgrims recover as through sitting on the stones and putting their feet in the water they "are healed of the sores occasioned by their going barefoot on sharp rocks and stones."[52] The mixing of their blood with the blood of the lake, or the mythic blood, places them physically and symbolically in relationship to the vanquished serpent and mother. In this way the penitents reach beyond the tradition of St. Patrick to a pre-Christian past, and the myth functions as a "vertical shaft driven into the past, disclosing deep strata of ancient symbols, potent signifiers that reinforce nationalistic sentiments."[53] Their suffering also aligns them with that of the vanquished characters of the myth, the serpent and the mother. The fact that their real blood mixes with mythic blood is one way that the myths defy easy categorizations that posit text against place, and spirit versus matter.

Another way that pilgrims connect symbolically with their place-based history and heritage is through engaging with the large stones on the islands. The stones are associated with several Irish saints. The two islands on the Red Lake that are linked to the purgatory cave are Saints Island, which is two miles northwest of a smaller and rockier island, Station Island. Two large stones near Saints Island are associated with St. Patrick and are said to be a place where he "kneeled a third of the night," while the rest of the night he spent in the cave. In one of the stones there is a "print reported to be made of St. Patrick kneeling or standing thereupon"[54] There are other large stones that are incorporated into the penitential practices as stations and that are associated with St. Davog. There are actually two men, each named St. Davog, who are connected with Saints Island. The first St. Davog, as mentioned earlier, was a disciple of St. Patrick in the fifth century. The other was of Irish descent and lived in the seventh century. Both lived on Saints Island where there was a monastery established in the sixth century.[55] A large stone is called St. Davog's chair, while six circular stones are named after the Irish saints Brigid and Brendan. The saints are said to have utilized the stones in their stations and the stones are subsequently also used by pilgrims in a similar fashion.

The myths of Lough Derg form a significant part of its story and meaning. They tell of a violent creation to the cave, including the sacrifice of its demonized gatekeepers, a mother and her giant son, a sea serpent and, less often referenced, Druid priests. The violence of the myths correlates to an actual violent history, at least from the time of the Norman and Danish invasions in Ireland. The myths also come alive in the sense that elements from the stories, like the blood of the mother and the serpent, and the serpent's knotty bones, are an identifiable part of the landscape and are incorporated into the penitential exercises performed by pilgrims. The lake is red and named for the blood of the vanquished gatekeepers and the stones are the same stones that formed beds for the saints who also prayed near them. In these ways the myths are interwoven with Lough Derg's geography and help pilgrims engage with the place and its history.

Even today the pilgrimage is a physical experience that engages the senses. The fast has been shortened from fifteen days to just three, and the night vigil is spent in a church instead of a cave, yet it still serves to test the modern pilgrim's fortitude. Pilgrims' still stop at the stones as they make their way through their stations. Stained glass windows, created by Harry Clarke in the early twentieth century, provide an updated view into the otherworld and illustrate how important the landscape and material objects are to penitents. One modern pilgrim, Maeve, commented on this aspect of her experience:

> I felt strongly that I was sustained and motivated and inspired by the art in Lough Derg and there was no reference made to it. For example the hardest time for me was when the Basilica doors closed for the night vigil, I felt scared, regretful, trapped. So I looked at the Harry Clarke windows and the light was so beautiful on them. As we walked in circles all night I studied each one and they are all so delicate and intricate. I looked at them for hours and they change with light as he would have planned. It was my first time in Lough Derg and it was hard, and I did not know how to approach my pilgrimage with courage, so the work of Harry Clarke, the words of Patrick Kavanagh, and Seamus Heaney on Lough Derg, and the ancient, Saint's Chair, a kind of work of outdoor sculpture in itself, if you will were the objects of consolation and motivation for me.[56]

The medieval penitential context, where it was believed that a penance satisfactory to God could alter one's ultimate otherworld fate, is the most important framework for understanding how the purgatory functioned for medieval penitents and for how the purgatory cave became established as an actual location for Purgatory. It is this context that also explains why ghost tales and myths of Lough Derg, such as found in the *Tractatus*, incorporate elements that refer to *actual*, not visionary, journeys.

The Haunted Island: Ghosts that Row Boats and Secret Knowledge

As medieval pilgrims performed their penances at what they believed to be a portal to the otherworld, they reported encounters with souls, demons, and angels in purgatory. These tales are a common thread throughout the narratives about the location from the past and versions of ghost tales circulate even today. In the 1980s, Irish Nobel Laureate Seamus Heaney wrote *Station Island*, a poem inspired by his visits to Lough Derg. He writes about encounters with ghosts from his past. The ghosts who haunt him are innocent victims of the infamous "Troubles" in Northern Ireland, and part of *Station Island* is devoted to the ghost of a boyhood friend whom he describes as "the perfect victim." The specter appears to him, bloodied and disfigured from the violence of a bomb explosion. Heaney asks the ghost for forgiveness for his "indifference" to the violence and for his "circumspect involvement."[57] Among other things, *Station Island* is a record of Heaney's public penance.

Another modern pilgrim, John, discusses how during his pilgrimage he was overcome by the memory of his father's death:

> I realized I had never got over his passing. It was a tough, emotional pilgrimage for me. I sat on my own and will never forget the kindness of a second night pilgrim on talking to me before she went to bed. She smiled, touched my hand and told me my father would be with me all night. She had troubles way beyond my own. It gave me great courage for the night ahead. I left the island a happy-healed man.[58]

While today's ghosts remain safely within the "spiritual" category proposed by William of Auvergne, that is, they appear as memories within the minds of pilgrims, not as real, substantial presences that exhibit corporeal reality, the medieval and early modern ghosts of Lough Derg appeared and acted as if they were real. They rowed boats and yelled at pilgrims. Even the archangel Michael makes a very physical appearance in several of the narratives. During that era, the realism of the ghost stories solidified Lough Derg's reputation as a haunted island. William Butler Yeats's poem "The Pilgrim," written in 1909, illustrates the common perception: "All know that all the dead in the world about that place are stuck, / And that should mother seek her son she'd have but little luck / Because the fires of purgatory have ate their shapes away."[59] Tales of the physical nature of the ghosts and the journey through purgatory competed with the burgeoning scholastic understanding of the physical limits of the souls from purgatory. The ghosts of Lough Derg defied these limits and their excesses would cause the cave to be destroyed in 1497.

Histories of Lough Derg tend to demarcate the years between 1180 c.e. to 1500 c.e. as the era of "ghosts and visions." Commencing with the *Tractatus* in 1180 and ending with visions of the early 1500s, scholars generally agree that "from this time on, the association of Lough Derg with [realistic] visions of the next world virtually ceases."[60] Several factors contribute to this shift. Scholastic theology influenced the official idea of purgatory as an afterlife state that was becoming increasingly associated with spirit, rather than matter, and this called into question purgatory's possible placement on or in the earth, as revealed in Church documents and papal encyclicals. Coeval with this development was concern about simony and the sale of indulgences. Anything resembling a promise to secure an afterlife fate for money exchanged reeked of "abuse." However, during this period ghosts haunted the desolate island and its cave and provided evidence of their physical presence.

Ghosts of Lough Derg did not fit neatly into William's scholastic framework of only appearing physical as a warning to the living. If one draw of the island to pilgrims was that it allowed penitents to ameliorate their afterlife fate through the ascetic exercises, another was the promise that one could speak directly to the dead, who were thought to have secret knowledge, or at least greater knowledge than the living.

In 1353, the Hungarian knight Georgias Crissaphan made the journey to Lough Derg. Georgias was a young knight who had sinned greatly, and tales recorded about him state that he committed "two hundred and fifty murders, not to speak of other crimes, before he was twenty-four."[61] Georgias's pilgrimage, penance, and absolution are well documented and the story of his visions appear in several extant versions in German, Czech, and Latin from 1414 to 1896.[62] His journey bears striking similarities to the knight Owen's. As he enters the cave it expands into several fields and demons rush at him, attempting to thwart his journey. As he struggles to escape punishments, he calls out the name of Jesus Christ, just like Owen, which effectively subdues the demons and allows him to continue on his way. His account differs from Owen's however in that he encounters the archangel Michael, donning a green robe and shining as bright as the sun. Michael has important information that Georgias must deliver to significant public figures: Richard Fitzralph, the archbishop of Armagh (Ireland), who is told that he must remove the interdict on a state within his diocese; the King of England, Edward III, and the King of France, Jean le Bon, are told to make peace; and Pope Innocent VI, who is told to absolve a certain prince. Georgias asked Michael how these people could be sure that his message was divine, and the angel responded that he would have certain signs and secrets that only they would know, and this would therefore corroborate his knowledge.

Georgias's journey is conveyed as a real, concrete journey through afterlife realms where otherworld figures are presented as physically tangible. Not only is the archangel Michael presented as a real physical presence, he is witnessed by titled men, including the prior and his canons, and the king of the region who is also accompanied by nobility who had journeyed to meet the illustrious knight and to hear about his journey. No doubt aware of the intrigues of the cave, they came eager with anticipation. They weren't disappointed. As Canon O'Connor relates the story:

> As they stood in expectation he appeared in company with a beautiful youth, the latter clothed in gorgeous emerald robes, crowned with a diadem so richly begemmed that it outshone the mid-day sun, and bearing in his hand the golden cross. They recognized George, but as to the other they could not tell if he were man or angel. St Michael and the pilgrim stood conversing together for a certain space of time in the presence of them all.[63]

When Georgias finally emerges from the cave, the spectators are so overcome by the physicality of the experience they are moved to procure for themselves the only physical objects available that bear the qualities of the otherworld: Georgias's clothes. "As he stood in the midst of the admiring throng, all were overwhelmed by the ineffable odour of paradise that was given off from his garments, so much so, that seizing knives they cut and hacked at the 'femoralia' [breeches] in which he was clad, being desirous to keep the rags as relics, until at length they left him naked. Then they attempted to cut off his hair for the same purpose."[64] At this point, and having allowed the spectacle to continue long enough, the king intervened and provided Georgias with his own robe.

This tale clearly exceeds the frameworks established by William in *De Universo*. The archangel and the demons Georgias encounters are not incorporeal and without substance, since they talk, walk, and appear to others. The story relates that authorities—the prior and a king—are witness to the physical presence of Michael. The "odor of sanctity," or the lovely smell emanating from Georgias's clothes, is another indication that this is a physical experience. Most significant, however, is that Georgias is given secret knowledge that will presumably have real-world effects: a king must remove an interdiction and the pope must absolve a prince. While thirteenth-century theologians believed that angels, souls, and demons—who were generally thought to be invisible—could on occasion defy natural laws, this was rare and in most cases they believed this was the work of demons, not angels, especially if the appearance was not a means to warn or morally edify the observer. Therefore, Georgias's journey would have been suspect to orthodox theologians.

In 1412 Laurence Rathhold De Pasztho, a Hungarian who belonged to the court of King Sigismund of Hungary, made the pilgrimage to Lough Derg. He was accompanied by a "herald and a numerous retinue, as befitting his station." The story of his adventure, like Owen's and Georgias's, was very popular. However, two hundred years after the publication of Owen's journey and about fifty years after Georgias's famous pilgrimage, the tone of the pilgrimage story changes markedly. The question of whether or not the journey is physical, and not just a vision, frames the narrative and recurs through the end. Additionally, St. Michael the archangel, dressed in a green robe, just as he appears in Georgias's story, unambiguously defines purgatory. At one point in his travels through the cave, Laurence witnesses the disconcerting sight of his relatives, parents, and friends roasting in a fire. Troubled, he asks Michael, "What is the nature of this flame?" Michael answers, "My son, this is purgatory, in which are purified the souls of these destined for salvation, and there is no other purgatory." Further, Michael makes the point that "thou dost not behold me, nor the fire of purgatory, *in reality*, but only as God has seen fit to permit thee."[65] This directly correlates to William of Auvergne's condition that invisible beings are not actually physical, but "appear" physical, and only so by the grace of God.

James Yonge, the author of the account, asks Laurence to state his motivations for going into the cave, and also whether the experience was "in the body or in the spirit." Laurence's answers seemed tailored specifically to the questions raised earlier by the scholastics. He replied, "First and foremost, because I had heard and read that if anyone had any doubt with respect to the Catholic Faith he should enter the Purgatory in order to have that doubt resolved. I had grave doubts about the substance of the soul, and for this principal reason I entered the place of purgatory, and learnt the truth." Making a direct reference to the substance of the soul, and anticipating the issue of the physicality of it, he says, echoing St. Paul in the New Testament, "Whether I beheld the visions in the body or out of the body I cannot tell;

but it seems more probable that I was rapt in the body, because I lit, one after another, nine pieces of candle, and kept them lighting until I came out of the cave."[66] Even as the question arises about the physicality of the experience, Laurence seems to indicate it is "in the body," yet the archangel Michael indicates that it is not, and insists that these things are shown to him as permitted by God, but not "in reality." This point is further made more forcefully when Laurence asks to be shown the soul of his former beloved, and the pains of heaven and hell. To this, Michael responds that he cannot be shown these things because he is not dead. This supports the scholastic division of spirit and matter, where the dead are relegated to the spirit and cannot appear materially, or as physical substance.

Several aspects of Laurence's story are notable and reveal a shift from earlier "descent" narratives of Lough Derg. The emphasis on the question of the physicality of Laurence's experience is new and noted by later historians of Lough Derg like John D. Seymour, who writes with approval "that [the author] shews a decided tendency to soften down the crude materialism displayed in other visions described in this book."[67] The account also relates a specific definition of purgatory as an afterlife destination, and not a physical place. Additionally, Church-sponsored rituals are specifically endorsed by the authority of God's archangel Michael. Each of these innovations reflects that the scholastics' view of purgatory and souls from purgatory were in some manner making their way into the vision narratives. (See fig. 2-2.) The text confirms the scholastic message that souls could not encroach upon the experience of the living unless God permitted it, and he would not permit it unless there was a morally edifying reason, which mostly consisted in warning the living of their fate unless they changed their ways. Ironically, Laurence's own testimony also undercuts the messages that were made so strongly by Michael, as he says that he was probably "in the body" as his candles remained lit throughout his journey. This account provides contradictory ways of viewing purgatory and the journey through the cave—on the one hand it is physical, and on the other hand, it is not. Significantly, this contradiction permeates the narrative and is never resolved. The document, one of the last testimonies involving a vigorous physical journey through a real purgatory that includes meeting souls and spiritual beings like Michael, reflects the tensions between two interpretations: is the cave a real portal to purgatory? Or is it a pilgrimage like other locations in Ireland, simply a place where one can journey to absolve sins, but not where one can enter the real place of purgatory?

FIGURE 2-2 King of France has vision of punishment of the damned from manuscript of Voyage of King or Saint Louis IX of France into Purgatory of St. Patrick. Italian. 14th Century. Museo Correr Venice. Alfredo Dagli Orti/The Art Archive at Art Resource, NY.

Seventy years after Laurence's descent into the purgatory, a Canon Regular of St. Augustine, from Holland, journeyed to the island to endure the penance (1494). His journey, however, did not result in visions in the body or out of it. He fully expected to journey into purgatory and see spiritual beings and souls. He was so disappointed with his experience, or lack of it, that he complained to the pope, Alexander VI, who consequently had the cave

completely destroyed. The reasons cited for the closure reveal that the scholastics' frameworks for categorizing the souls from purgatory were influencing policy, and that the Lough Derg pilgrimage was in the direct line of fire.

The monk, who has never been named, went through the regular process
of obtaining the bishop's permission to enter the cave and securing further
permission from the prior of the island. At each juncture the authorities
demanded that he pay alms, or fees, which he found to be excessive. After his
visit to the cave, "he came out wondering greatly that he had neither seen,
heard, nor undergone any of the visions and other experiences with which so
many others were said to have been privileged. Disappointed and chagrined
he went straightaway to Rome and laid a prejudicial report of the pilgrimage
before the sovereign Pontiff, Alexander VI."[68] At the time, foment against the
selling of indulgences to release souls from purgatory was reaching an extreme pitch, and only a few years later in 1517, on the night of All Hallows
Eve, which is followed by All Saints' Day and then All Souls' Day, the holy day
dedicated to the souls in purgatory, Martin Luther nailed his 95 theses to the
door of Castle Church in Wittenberg. Indulgences, the selling of prayers and
alms for the release of souls in purgatory, were often accompanied by certifi-
cates, and the Dutch monk was no doubt alerted to the similarity of the pilgrimage and its protocols with other pilgrimages that were at the time
coming under fire for their link to indulgences like the Crusades and abuses
of simony. Martin Luther specifically criticized the popular refrain against
the seller of indulgences, Johann Tetzel: "As soon as the coin in the coffer
rings, a soul from purgatory into heaven springs." The social climate was
ripe for suspicion of alms for penance, and the Dutch monk's report found
fertile ground with the pope and his cohorts.

Hundreds of years later, in his sermon on purgatory, Pope Benedict
XIII cites several reasons for Alexander's closing of the cave, one being the
abuse of selling indulgences, and the other deriving directly from scholastic theology. "It remains for me to answer the third question, viz., if at
the present time there exists such a Purgatory. It will suffice to relate what
happened to a Canon Regular from Holland in 1494. This man repaired
to Ireland, and having heard great things concerning the Purgatory of
St. Patrick, with a lively faith and with the desire of satisfying divine justice, asked leave of the Prior of the Monastery to descend into the cave. He
did go down; and the trembling Canon every moment expected to see,
hear, and perhaps also suffer the horrible things which had been mentioned of the place, but after remaining an entire day and night without
experiencing the slightest suffering, he was taken out the following day.

He thus proved by experience that the story was all fiction on the part of the custodians of the place, who had spread these reports for the simple purpose of collecting alms from the too-credulous people."[69]

Benedict never disputes that the purgatory cave of St. Patrick's existed and that the Irish did see the sufferings of souls in purgatory, but these happened during Patrick's life, and not afterward. These visions were of the past, and according to Benedict, do not happen anymore. Referencing scholastic theologian Thomas Aquinas, Benedict explains that because the current visions do not conform to the manner in which souls from purgatory should appear, that is, as warnings or to inspire conversion, they cannot be real. "If God, through the merits of St. Patrick, and during the Saint's lifetime, performed the miracles of rendering visible to the people what faith teaches us of the punishments and rewards reserved for us in the next life, the miracle ceased after the conversion of the people to the faith, since the motive for it had ceased."[70] Benedict then cites Aquinas's Supplement 72 to bolster his point.

The early modern stage was set for the regulation of not just the purgatory cave but also of the stories, visions, and tales regarding purgatory and souls who appeared from purgatory. Speaking non-specifically, yet addressing stories and tales similar to those inspired by Lough Derg, Pope Pius IV, at the twenty-fifth session of the Council of Trent (1563) promoted restraint in representing purgatory: "While those things which tend to a certain kind of curiosity or superstition, or which savour of filthy lucre, let them prohibit as scandals and stumbling-blocks of the faithful." He also suggested that, with regard to purgatory literature "the more difficult and subtle questions, and which tend not to edification, and from which for the most part there is no increase of piety, [should] be excluded from popular discourses before the uneducated multitude."[71]

As for the Irish documents that cite reasons for the closure of the cave, the Annals of Ulster state that the reason for the closure was that the particular cave in question was not the one granted to St. Patrick: "this was not the Purgatory Patrick got from God."[72]

The Cave Is Destroyed ... Maybe

The cave was destroyed, under the watchful eyes of Catholic authorities, on St. Patrick's Day, 1497. Then, ironically, after the closure of the cave, two appeared: the cave on Station Island, which had been moved to Saints Island, and then had apparently been moved back to Station Island in the early 1500s. What was the cause of the move, and of the creation of another cave? Alice Curtayne speculates that the Irish caretakers created a false cave and then stood by silently as they observed it being destroyed, without alerting the authorities that the real cave was still in existence. She suggests, "For some reason that cannot be easily determined, the pilgrimage authorities, previous to the Dutch monk's visit, had ceased to take pilgrims over to Station Island for the vigil, but had opened for that purpose a cave of their own within the monastery enclosure on Saints Island. This explains perfectly why the Papal Order had been so rapidly carried out. The cave that had been filled in was only a substitute cave on Saints' Island and the primate and the Bishop looked on at its destruction with equanimity."[73] Despite the closure, pilgrimage to the cave continued to the new location, and it shifted from a situation of the solitary confinement of one pilgrim in the cave to a group endeavor where multiple pilgrims entered a cave, and separate caves were demarcated by sex.[74]

However, the era of the hauntings and ghost tales had peaked. In his history of the pilgrimage, John D. Seymour noted the growing skepticism toward the ghost stories:

That a spirit of scepticism with respect to the wonders to be seen within St. Patrick's Purgatory was commencing to spread abroad is shewn by the foregoing paragraphs. It also manifested itself in another way, i.e., through the medium of literature. From allusions in books it can plainly be observed that the belief was commencing to lose its hold on the world in general; Though in order of time they occur after the actual closing of the cave in 1497, yet they are indicative of the feeling that was abroad at the end of the fifteenth century and the commencement of the sixteenth. The celebrated Albert Krantz (who died in 1517), in his posthumous work Daniae, Sueciae, Norvegiae Chronica says: "The Irish remember a Purgatory of a sometime saint called Patrick, but such dreams and flitting phantoms, mere old women's tales, I did not think proper to insert in a history of real transactions." Erasmus in his Adagia (pub. in 1500) considers that the legend was derived from the classical cave of Trophonius, and adds: "Nevertheless there are many who descend into the cave at the present day, but they are first exhausted by a three-days fast lest they should enter it with a clear brain. As for those who descend it is said that ever after they have no desire to laugh.[75]

Alice Curtayne connects the demise of the visions with the beginning of early modernity: "The tale of visions, however, had run its course even before the visit of the censorious Dutch monk. It was over. The world had altered now and popular taste had changed."[76] Despite this, she is not settled on the conclusion that the era of visions was solely attributable to a medieval worldview. Writing about the ubiquity of the visions, she questions, "What is one to make of it? To dismiss the whole thing as imagination is the easiest way to be rid of it, but the puzzle is not so easily solved. The universality and the persistence of the testimony that visions occurred at Lough Derg is disturbing to the most determined commonsense. It went on for so long, for four hundred years, and the witnesses came from every walk of life and from so many countries."[77]

The tales would come to enjoy a second life, as the fodder for poems, plays, and novels throughout the modern period in the plays of Shakespeare, the Spanish playwright Pedro Calderon de la Barca, and many others. Despite this, the pilgrimage site did retain its function as a "real purgatory" where practitioners performed penance for one's sin. Meanwhile, theologians continued to write about purgatory. The new technology of printing shifted the medium and periodicals became the new venue for purgatory narratives.

3

Exile from Ireland

BISHOP JOHN ENGLAND'S REPUBLICAN
APOLOGETICS OF PURGATORY

IN 1827, THE Reverend Caesar Otway (Church of Ireland), wrote, "Ireland is such an unfashionable country, that to travel out of it seems the pursuit of everyone who is not forced by poverty to stay at home."[1] Among those who left was John England, who was ordained a Roman Catholic priest in 1809 in County Cork and, due to his affiliation with Irish nationalist Daniel O'Connell, was promoted out of Ireland by the Catholic Church and sent to the United States as a bishop in 1820. He loved his new country, but he sorely missed Ireland. For England, the revolutionary fervor that was sweeping Europe and the Americas was providential. It augured a new future, free from religious persecution. England's biographer, Patrick Carey, notes, "The French Revolution, among other things, put the European Catholic Church in competition with the principles and practices of religious liberty, separation of church and state, voluntaryism, and republicanism. During the late eighteenth and early nineteenth centuries the Catholic Churches in Ireland and the United States evolved in a different direction."[2] John England's fervent adoption of the tenets of the French Revolution, and its philosophical support—Enlightenment ideals such as the privileging of reason—influenced his understanding of purgatory and the afterlife. England promoted his views through tracts, pamphlets, and a weekly periodical. The power of the press, for England, was supreme. It was a witness to injustice and a means to educate non-Catholics and Catholics about the faith. He combated nativism and hoped to establish a new Catholicism, one forged in the crucible of revolution. His adoption

This chapter has been adapted from my article "The Eagle and the Dove: Constructing Catholic Identity through Word and Image in Early American Catholic Popular Literature," in *Material Religion: The Journal of Arts, Objects and Belief* (Oxford: Berg, 2008). Used with permission.

of Enlightenment values may have been expedient, but it had an encompassing impact on his interpretation of purgatory and the afterlife. England's case is illustrative of the effects that the Enlightenment had on modern conceptions of purgatory, and the purgatory cave at Lough Derg.

Lough Derg: That Place of Superstition

In 1840, Bishop John England was adamant in his assessment of the pilgrimage to Lough Derg, stating that if there were superstitions and fables associated with the location, it was not the fault of the Irish or of the Roman Catholic Church. According to England, the fables were caused by one thing: English colonization. From the initial suppression of the cave in Lough Derg in 1497 until England's writings in the early nineteenth century, Ireland had undergone a series of wars and rebellions. Irish Catholics were subject to harsh laws that inhibited the practice of their religion as well as their cultural traditions. Not surprisingly, sources about the pilgrimage to Lough Derg are scant during this time period, other than what is known from Irish bardic poetry and English references to various suppressions of the cave. What can be pieced together is that throughout the eighteenth century, pilgrims still journeyed to the site, and bardic poetry indicates that they still interpreted the site as being a place of purgatory—that is, as a school of satisfaction where penitents were able to absolve their sins through extreme penance.[3]

By the early nineteenth century, during John England's formation and education as a young priest, pilgrimage to the site experienced an upswing, and the nineteenth century would see numbers of pilgrims exceed previous eras. Pilgrimages also gained papal favor in 1870 when Pius IX granted pilgrims a plenary indulgence for completing the pilgrimage. However, the nineteenth century also witnessed a definitive shift in how the pilgrimage site, and purgatory, would be viewed. John England's assessment of purgatory and its relationship to the pilgrimage site is representative of this shift. The fables of Lough Derg would no longer be tolerated, and the association of the cave with an earthly entrance to an otherworld purgatory would be severed forever. In England's case, this was due to his adoption of values gleaned from the European Enlightenment, and, specifically, that of reason as the ultimate guide to revelation. England recast purgatory to conform to Enlightenment reason. Instead of focusing on souls in purgatory, England revealed how rituals of memory for the dead, as occur for Catholics on November 2, All Souls' Day, were natural inclinations mirrored in the practices of non-Catholics as well, such as that of the observance of George Washington's birthday. In other words, England naturalized the rituals of purgatory. This development emerged directly from his experience as a Catholic in Ireland.

John England was born at the end of the "Penal Times." Roughly spanning 1607 through 1778, the Penal Times composed the era in Irish history characterized by severe oppression resulting from the colonialist practices of the English government. Ireland was an English colony. Catholics were subject to English laws that effectively barred them from owning land, wealth, or guns, and prevented them from holding public office. Catholics could not practice their religion freely and without harassment, and the primary ritual of Catholicism, the Mass, was forbidden.

John England's childhood memories during the rebellion of the Irish and French against British forces in 1798 formed his political conscience. The brutality of the English armed forces against the clergy and unarmed peasants impressed many young people, including England and future archbishop John Mac Hale, both of whom later credited these episodes as being formative to their decision to become priests. As children they watched when Fr. John Murphy, in County Wexford, was forced to fight the British after they burned his house down. He was later captured on July 2, 1798, and brought before a military tribunal that found him guilty of treason against the British Crown. He was publicly flogged, decapitated, and burned in a barrel of tar. His head was placed on a spike as a warning to other revolutionaries. Another public hanging of a beloved priest, Fr. Conroy of Addergoole, is credited with gaining rebel troops and creating future nationalists. Mac Hale was seven years old at the time of the hanging. He later wrote of the experience as singularly transformative, stating that he "was then and there resolved, that if given life, ability and position, [I] would expose the misdeeds of those who ruled Ireland."[4] At the time of Addergoole's hanging, John England was twelve years old.

In the early eighteenth century, British authorities viewed the connection between land ownership and the practice of Catholicism as inextricable. The penal laws were a tour de force of colonial ideology, enacted by the British government to effectively dispossess the Catholic majority from owning land or weapons or holding political power or office. *The Act to Prevent the Further Growth of Popery* (1704) forbade Catholics from buying land, leasing it for more than thirty-one years, or inheriting land from Protestants. It is estimated that the amount of Catholic-owned land declined from 90 percent in 1603 to 5 percent in 1778.[5] The penal laws effectively dispossessed the Irish of their land, but they were also intended to eradicate the practice of Irish Catholicism. Clergy were singled out for specific oppressive restrictions intended to create divisiveness and break the bonds between the people and their religious representatives: the priests. Large yearly stipends were offered to priests who converted to the Church of Ireland. These "apostate" priests were also allowed to conduct their liturgies in Irish, which other Catholics were forbidden to teach or speak. The laws also created favorable inheritance benefits for Catholic sons and wives who similarly converted and who were then given rights to their Catholic ancestors' lands.

The Bishops' Banishment Act (1697) required all priests and bishops exercising ecclesiastical jurisdiction to leave Ireland by 1698.[6] Lower-level priests were allowed to remain but had to register with the Irish Parliament and take an "oath of abjuration"[7] that most priests refused.[8] Ironically, in the minds of some of the British authorities, the oath was actually intended to create an outlaw class of priests, as "the least conscientious priests would be registered and the most conscientious excluded."[9] Unregistered priests, in a dark irony, those who were the most "conscientious" as described by the English lawmakers, became outlaws who conducted church services at night and in secret, under constant threat of jail, deportation, or worse, death. Due to the fact that there were no bishops, there were no ordinations of new priests and this had the effect of eroding away the ranks of priests. However, letters written from Irish Anglican bishops to local magistrates reveal that unregistered priests continued their duties as clergy. "The insolence of our popish clergy is unspeakable. Our law makes it death for any of them not qualified or licensed as the Act of Parliament directs by taking the Oath of Abjuration, to officiate. But I am abundantly assured that very lately in my own diocese four or five masses were openly said by many different priests."[10] In another irony, the extreme oppression bound Irish Catholics to their priests more strongly; in other words, it had the opposite effect than what the English had hoped. "The statutes created an experience of persecution for both the laity and the clergy, cementing them in a common bond which continued into the twentieth century."[11]

Throughout most of the eighteenth century, the British government paid people to identify and capture priests who did not take the oath of abjuration. These people were dubbed "priest catchers," and they "added a new terror to the code."[12] Large bounties were offered to men who informed on and captured unregistered priests.[13] Although this was an abhorrent practice to most of the Catholic population, some were driven to it through poverty as "the rewards offered by the law and often increased by proclamation, gave a great stimulus to the pursuit."[14] A priest hunter was paid "fifty pounds for every archbishop and twenty pounds for every regular priest" and often much more. In a petition to a local magistrate, one priest hunter mentions his "greate want and poverty" as well as his two children and wife who are in danger of starvation, as motivations for his desire to catch priests.[15]

Unregistered priests celebrated Mass in a variety of ways in order to avoid detection. They celebrated under the cloak of darkness at night, wore veils so as not to be recognized, and often celebrated through a hole in a rock edifice so that if celebrants were asked by authorities who it was that officiated the ceremony they could answer truthfully that they didn't know. The Catholic majority protected the identities of their clergy. The penal laws failed to extinguish the popular practice of Catholicism, and in many ways made it stronger, motivating one nineteenth-century historian to note that "while the code in so far as it was meant to pauperize and degrade was completely successful, it was a single failure in its main purpose of Protestantising the mass of the people. Nay, even it had the very opposite effect."[16] For Irish Catholics, merely practicing their religion was a form of resistance to English oppression.

Fortunately for John England, the late eighteenth century proved to be a period of brief respite from continuous poverty. The continued cultivation of the potato crop brought about an agricultural boom. Food was widely distributed and money from exports helped foster a Catholic mercantile class or "strong farmers." This in turn caused a significant rise in population, which, between the years 1779 and 1841 increased by more than 170 percent.[17] England came of age during a period where there was also a shift in the attitudes of the Protestant elite minority and the Catholic majority, a confluence of events that brought them together in an uneasy relationship under the auspices of a "united Ireland." At the same time the Protestant Irish began to resent the claims that the English government made on the Irish economy and in the Irish Parliament. In 1793 the Irish Parliament passed laws allowing Catholics with some property to vote (albeit this concession only amounted to only a small number of Catholics). The Anglican minority began to view the Catholics as allies against the British and appealed to their sense of unjust treatment by the government. Anglican nationalist Theobald Wolfe Tone published a pamphlet in 1791 called "An Argument on Behalf of the Catholics of Ireland" that argued persuasively for the union of the Protestants and Catholics against the British.

Wolfe Tone's pamphlet and other revolutionary publications were most likely read by or read aloud to the Catholic majority and stoked the embers of hope for the recovery of their lost land. Contrary to the assessments of eighteenth-century English, the Irish peasantry was not uneducated and illiterate.[18] Against the backdrop of the penal laws that forbade education of Catholic children and punished schoolmasters, independent, secret schools flourished. These were called "hedge schools" because they were held behind hedges, in barns or in other inconspicuous places (John England's father was threatened with deportation to the West Indies for teaching a hedge school). These schools produced a "relatively" high literacy rate, although "an inability to read was not necessarily a barrier to knowledge of contemporary events."[19] As historian Marianne Elliot has observed, a mobile class of domestic workers, farmhands, dairymen, and canal work served to bridge rural and urban communities and facilitated a freeway of communication. Catholics across Ireland were exposed to the works of Thomas Paine and French Enlightenment philosophers through the workings of these groups, some of whose members consolidated into voluntary societies with names that evoked the American and French revolutions, such as "The Liberty Boys" and "Friends of Freedom."[20]

The distribution of pamphlets, news books, and other periodicals aroused widespread revolutionary sentiment.[21] Additionally, the novel alliance between the non-Anglican Protestants (the Dissenters), disenfranchised Catholics, and the Anglican Irish led to a series of attempted rebellions and brutal British reprisals throughout the 1790s, culminating in the rebellion of 1798. Emboldened by the success of the American and French revolutions, Wolfe Tone, the new leader of a formative nationalist movement called The United Irishmen, traveled to France to enlist help in an attempted revolution against the British. The attempted revolt failed, but it revealed a new, irrepressible resolve among the Irish under British rule. Elliot, writing about this development, stated that "the courage and the ferocity with which the rebel forces had repeatedly attacked the well-armed and disciplined [British] troops displayed an almost suicidal element in the rebel campaign."[22]

Although the British defeated the French and the Irish revolutionary forces, Wolfe Tone's anti-imperialist sentiments resonated with Irishmen and Irishwomen, Catholic and dissenter alike, who were aptly called the "men of no property." This sentiment is summarized well by the anonymous pamphlet that had a wide distribution, "The Poor Man's Catechism": "I believe in a revolution founded on the rights of man, in the natural and imprescriptable right of all citizens to all the land.... As the land and its produce was intended for the use of man 'tis unfair for fifty or a hundred men to possess what is for the subsistence of near five millions."[23]

John England's political views were formed within this revolutionary context. To England, Enlightenment ideals offered freedom from religious oppression, and the successful revolutions of France and the United States provided hope that Ireland could also successfully break free from English rule. He embraced the revolutionary zeal of his new country, the young republic of the United States. His view, shared by most Irish Catholics, was that "the cause of American freedom was Ireland's as well."[24] In Ireland today John England is remembered along with his friend, the "great liberator" Daniel O'Connell, for their efforts in promoting Catholic emancipation.[25] Once in the United States England forged successful alliances with other influential American Catholics of Irish decent such as Bishop John Carroll. He was as popular in the United States as he was in Ireland, and was invited to be the first Catholic to preach to the Congress of the United States.

John England's tenure as bishop of Georgia and the Carolinas coincided with the first waves of Irish Catholic immigration from Ireland (1820–1842) to the United States, and his death in 1842 occurred during the darkest decade of Irish history, the peak of the "Great Hunger," *an Gorta Mor*. England could not have known what was to befall his countrymen and countrywomen in the years following his death. During the decade of the 1850s, more than 12 percent of Ireland's population would arrive at the shores of New York. More than a million would die from conditions of starvation and disease at home in Ireland, a million would emigrate, and hundreds of thousands more would not survive the trip across the Atlantic Ocean in boats called "coffin ships."[26] In the meantime, England was planting the seeds of tolerance through the pages of the periodical he self-published, *The Catholic Miscellany*, readying the republic for its newest members from the shores of Ireland.

Purgatory in the Pages of The Catholic Miscellany

John England waged his writing campaign with the intention of promoting a new Catholic identity that he interpreted as anti-imperialist and informed by the values of the European Enlightenment. Throughout the 1820s and 1830s, England used his influential post as bishop to become a one-man publishing house.[27] He wrote much of the content in *The Miscellany*, sometimes as himself and often under pseudonymous names. Like fellow American

Catholics such as John Carroll, who also espoused Enlightenment values, England believed the United States provided a unique opportunity for Catholics—it would be a land rich with opportunity and a haven from religious persecution. He also linked his newspaper with the growing tide of Protestant publications that provided a forum for education and news. In the first issues of *The Miscellany*, England articulated its mission: "The object of this publication is to provide and supply an apparent want in the United States of North America.... Almost every division of Christianity here has its peculiar publication, for the exposition of its doctrines, the communication of facts and when necessary, the vindication of its tenets."[28] *The Miscellany* shares the distinction with *Tabernacle and Purgatory* as being among the oldest Catholic publications in the United States.[29]

He specifically addressed two other aims of the periodical: to unify the faithful and to correct misperceptions of Catholicism:

> By its means [the paper] the thousands of Roman Catholics spread through these states, from Maine to Florida and from Kansas to the Atlantic may hold constant communion; by its means they may also learn the state of their brethren in communion with them in other parts of the globe; by its means those persons who have been misled into erroneous opinions of the principles of their neighbors, will be enabled to judge correctly of their tenets and to form rational opinions of their practices.[30]

Purgatory and the rituals and practices associated with it was one of the most maligned of Catholic doctrines, so it is not surprising that England devoted a large portion of *The Miscellany* to defending it and correcting what he perceived to be its misrepresentation. Fables and references to its material manifestations, including knowledge about who was in purgatory or soon to be released from purgatory, were not acceptable considerations, in England's view. Instead, he refocused attention on the material aspects of purgatory, but recast these in fundamental ways.

In 1840, John England published an article titled "On Certain Superstitions Imputed to Catholics: Concerning the Fable of St. Patrick's Purgatory, and Some Other Foolish Inventions of the Protestant Press."[31] In the article England describes the fables and stories associated with the Lough Derg cave superstitions. He blames the development of the superstitious aspects of Lough Derg on two things: the Protestant press and religious oppression. He also states that the living do not possess knowledge of the afterlife, as ordained by God. "A dark curtain divides us from the world of spirits. Our mighty Father could shoot the beam of knowledge through the immense mass of clouds if He would; but He does not."[32] His reference to clouds, clearly just an aside, does provide an illustration of purgatory in the sky, and not on earth. Hundreds of years earlier Thomas Aquinas argued that good things were associated with air and spirit, and bad things with the depths and matter.

Although England called the superstitions surrounding Lough Derg "fables," he forcefully advocated for the pilgrimage. Irish Catholics were "excited to devotion, [and] pray there and in the vicinity with sincere piety."[33] England maintained that Lough Derg was an important place of worship for Irish Catholics. He attributes the superstitious elements associated with Lough Derg to the effects of English colonization, and suggests that the tenacity with which Catholics clung to their practices, amid severe repression and almost a complete lack of catechesis, was a laudable form of resistance. In this way, the pilgrimage of Lough Derg took on a more specific, nationalist meaning. England paints a picture of the pilgrimage site and its pilgrimage as an important place where Irish Catholics asserted their heritage amid powerful forces of oppression.

For England, the superstitious elements associated with Lough Derg, among the Irish at least, are attributable to "the effects of British cruelty, rapine, and perfidy." Speaking specifically about the Irish Catholic clergy, he noted that it "was impossible for a hunted, persecuted and almost exterminated hierarchy to enforce restrictive discipline upon a race who, for their attachment to the Faith, endured worse than Egyptian bondage." England maintains that English oppression created a climate where superstition thrived. Superstition "was introduced in days of that ruinous oppression and unprincipled confiscation which destroyed religion in the ravages of civil strife." England maintains that poverty also contributed to the breakdown of the Catholic religion, and therefore if the fables of Lough Derg took hold of the Irish imagination it was because of the poverty caused by the English. "Be it remembered that if the Irish Catholic is poor, his poverty has been caused by the confiscation of the possessions of his ancestors, for their adherence to that faith which they received from their fathers, and by the testimony of their reason. If this peasantry be ignorant; be it remembered that such ignorance was forced upon them by the men who enacted that if any person of their own church dared to give them instruction, or offered them a little learning except at the price of their creed, he should be treated as a felon. Can any conduct be more shameful than this?"[34] England was reacting to his immediate circumstances, but also to a larger context of prejudice toward Irish Catholics. England was not just being reactionary, as esteemed newspapers at the time, like *The Times* (London) made perfectly clear how Irish Catholics were perceived by non-Catholics, as this 1849 quote illustrates: "in a few more years a Celtic Irishman will be as rare in Connemara as is the Red Indian on the shores of Manhattan."[35]

Even while England excoriated the fables of Lough Derg, he advocated the site as a place of devotion. This was in part due to Lough Derg's status as an important destination for the Irish, whose religious practices were altered by the penal laws. Lough Derg and other places of pilgrimage became significant as destinations where practitioners could assert their religion and their Irish Catholicism. Religious practices occurred outside of the confines of traditional ecclesiastical structures, thus "popular religion" in pre-famine Ireland was the dominant form of religion in which most priests, being unregistered and working in secret, were intimately involved. Most Catholics did not attend Mass, because it was outlawed, but engaged in pilgrimages to holy wells and sacred sites and attended open-air Masses officiated by non-registered priests.[36] Lough Derg and other pilgrimage sites, including *Cairrag An Aiffrin*, or Mass rocks, which were stones upon which priests officiated mass, were important places of worship.

England was clear that with respect to what Catholics ought to believe about purgatory, the questions about who was there, or who was released, were not to be entertained, because they couldn't be answered. He referenced the "general doctrine," and suggested that all questions and considerations that didn't fall under the "general doctrine" were superfluous. "We believe the souls in purgatory do need our aid, and may be assisted. But though we know this general doctrine, we cannot know the fact that a particular individual is in purgatory, nor what special quantity of prayer or other suffrage would be adequate to full relief. It is true that God does know, and may inform us if he will, but he has not done so, and we are not in every case to expect a special revelation of the fact. Such a revelation would be an extraordinary interference."[37] Although England seems to offer the possibility that an extraordinary interference, or a miracle, could offer this information, he later indicates that this hasn't happened, and will not be forthcoming.

> [God's] voice has penetrated through the chaos, and by the words of revelation he has taught us the general doctrine, he has exhorted us to the charity of aiding those who suffer, and taught us that our prayer will avail, but he has not informed us to what extent. We then,

with eyes suffused with tears, yet lifted in hope, and hands stretched out in supplication, offer for our departed friends the suffrage of our prayers, of our works, of our piety, and through the merits of Christ we beseech for them a speedy release from the house of bondage.

However, he reminds his readers that there is "no certainty of release."[38]

In Defense of Purgatory—A Catholic Republican Apologetics

As stated in its manifesto, *The Miscellany* was to provide a justification or apology of Catholicism as well as a means to educate Catholics and non-Catholics about basic doctrines of the faith. Additionally, it was to be a forum—a public sphere for Catholics, a textual community whereby Catholics could learn about one another, whether they lived as far away as other countries or as near as neighboring counties. England was strategic in his rhetoric. Knowing he would have to appeal to Catholics who knew little about their faith yet needed to defend it within an often hostile environment, and also to non-Catholics who were ready to believe the worst about Catholics, he identified a common language with which each could identify. This common language was that of the republic—the language and symbols of liberty, democracy, and freedom. England clothed the ritual aspects of Catholicism, particularly aspects relating to purgatory and the communion of saints, with the language and symbols of the American republic. He also revealed the ways in which non-Catholics engaged in similar activities, thus naturalizing these doctrines and making them seem less alien to readers. England's purgatory apologetics was framed with the language and symbols of the New Republic. As a consequence, within *The Miscellany* he eradicated the supernatural-materiality of purgatory, the belief that purgatory was in Ireland, and the belief that souls from purgatory left evidence of their hauntings.

The banner of *The Miscellany*, displayed as an image and as text, was also the most prominent symbol in the newspaper. It was the establishment clause from the First Amendment of the United States Constitution, and it literally framed every issue of the paper. It was not the only image on the paper, however, as it was accompanied by the image of an eagle, clothed with the American flag and clutching a cross and a Eucharistic chalice. This text and image fused the American symbols of freedom and liberty with ritual symbols from the Catholic Mass, thus creating a new symbol with multiple meanings and associations. As the head banner, it acted like a gateway to the contents of the periodical and framed the narratives within. The clause, which read, "Congress shall make no law respecting an establishment of religion, or prohibiting the free exercise thereof," functioned as a statement of liberation. This is made clear by a narrative mainstay on the front page that spoke directly to the issue of religious persecution. "In these states perfect freedom of conscience exists; thus, men of various religions have fled hither as to seek asylum from the persecutions of the dominant sects of other countries."[39] In image and rhetoric, England linked national symbols with Catholic ritual symbols, thus constructing a Catholic identity that was simultaneously American and Catholic, and that emphasized Enlightenment values of religious freedom and democracy.

Purgatory, as well as the practices of honoring the dead such as the veneration of saints' relics, was perhaps the most alien Catholic belief to non-Catholics. England naturalized these doctrines and rituals by associating them with the civic ceremonies of ordinary Americans, rituals that Americans took for granted like saluting and honoring the flag, keeping and memorializing objects of deceased military heroes, and observing national holidays in honor of those who died in the service of their country. One of *The Miscellany*'s major themes is precisely this analogy—the veneration of saint's relics with the veneration accorded to national symbols by Americans. This took a variety of forms in the periodical, as short anecdotes, poetry and images, and as apologetic narrative.

One anecdote relates how Martha Washington, widow of the first president of the United States, presented the American flag to a company of soldiers. It had been previously flown at the Battle of Eutaw Springs, and it was now to be venerated as a symbol of freedom and peace. The brief narrative is entitled "A Relic":

Colonel, permit me to offer to you, for the service of the Washington Light Infantry this banner, which has been unfurled on the field of battle on some memorable occasions, particularly at Eutaw.

Forty years and more have rolled away since it floated on the field of battle for the last time. During that period no hostile foot has dared pollute the soil in this section of our beloved country. Long may we enjoy the blessings of peace, but should the storm of war arise, I trust that the association connected with this banner will heighten the flame of patriotism in the breasts of those over whose heads it is now destined to wave.

I feel assured that I place it under the guardianship of a band of
Citizen Soldiers, who, on no occasion, will suffer its purity or lustre
to be tarnished.[40]

A poem in the same issue explains how the memorial impulse that all
people feel toward their deceased loves ones is also at the basis for the
Catholic practice.

Relic
The gem deck'd star—the warrior's plume—The poet's lyre—
    the sage's pen—What re they?
Relics from the tomb, Snatched by the loftier sons of men!
Then smile not, if the pilgrim draws
Heart-treasured relics from the shrine;
He but obeys the general laws,
Which rule, in different forms, in thine![41]

Oftentimes, short narratives remind readers that American civil practices
are suspiciously akin to the veneration of relics. One issue cites a North
Carolina law, enacted in 1821, that makes it a state offense to "knowingly
spit upon, or in any way stain or designedly injure, or in any way deface
the Statue of General Washington, erected by the General Assembly of
this State." After citing the law, the narrative goes on to state: "Thus family
pictures and images are memorials which naturally create a claim upon the
affections."[42] This is embedded within a larger section defending prayers
to saints' images and prayers to the souls in purgatory. Narratives like
these—long apologies on purgatory, and prayers for the holy souls and to
saints—occupy more space than any other single topic in the approximately
eight-page weekly. A typical issue devotes roughly one-third or more space
to these issues.

Another way in which England used national themes as a defense of
doctrines like purgatory was by shaming non-Catholic Americans for their
unjust treatment of Catholic Americans and for breaching republican ideals like religious toleration. England sought to hold American citizens
to their new rules of religious toleration. He often noted that the new
American Catholic and the common American had fought a common
enemy: England. He critiqued the American Episcopal Church for its
seemingly friendly reception of tracts from the English Anglican Church
that contained direct attacks on the issue of purgatory and prayers for the

dead. "The people of America on all other subjects appear to be extremely cautious how they receive testimony reported from England, why not manifest the same circumspection in receiving evidence upon the religion and characters of a people, whom England insulted, degraded, calumniated, and punished at home?"[43] The specific offenses regard the doctrine of purgatory as well as the practice of indulgences. England reprints the offensive declarations: "In page 13, the article CIV, is the following: of Purgatory—the Romish doctrine concerning purgatory, pardon, worshipping, and adoration, as well of images as of relics, and also invocations of saints, is a fond thing, vainly invented, and grounded upon no warrant of Scripture, but repugnant to the word of God."[44] England goes on to report that others from the Baptist faith added their own assessments of purgatory too. To Baptists, purgatory was not only repugnant to Scripture, but to "common sense and reason," and as such has "lead to all manner of gross idolaters." England points to a double standard with respect to civil disagreement within the public sphere. "Had a Catholic dared to have been the Author of such libels as these upon any of his dissenting brethren, what a clamour would immediately be raised against him!!!" He adds that the Catholic would instantly be proclaimed "a malicious defamer, a dangerous character, and a person not fit to be allowed into society!"[45]

The dual purpose of *The Miscellany*, to "exhibit to our Dissenting Brethren the reasons and evidence of our faith and practice," while at the same time "to instruct our Catholic Brethren" was particularly evident regarding devotions to the souls in purgatory and its associated practices. Several times a year, but especially during the month of November—the time in the Western church devoted to remembering souls of the faithful departed—England devoted entire issues to purgatory, its history in the Jewish and early Christian church, and to the necessity of engaging in devotions meant to aid those who were in purgatory. In these instances England strayed from his usual republican apologetics, preferring to appeal to the ties that bind, memory and love. "Is there a Catholic possessed of the least feeling of gratitude for the parent who gave him birth, who nursed and cherished him, . . . and will not now in the day of need make some grateful return to his relation?" This return was to take the form of prayers, petitions, and Masses said for those mourned. Regarding the one in mourning, England stated that "the generous impulse of his heart influences him, the dictates of his faith not only permit but require him to supplicate the Divine Mercy in behalf of his afflicted friend, and thus impart the only assistance in his power to him who has passed the threshold of death, on whom the night has closed and surrounded with darkness, that he cannot labour for himself."[46] It was an obligation of the living to pray for the souls of the departed.

Wresting Purgatory from the Revolutionaries

In July 1824, an article appeared in the mainstream and widely read periodical *The North American Review*. Written by Venezuelan diplomat Luis Mendez, it concerned the various South American revolutions and emancipatory movements from Spain. In the article Mendez provided a detailed and bone-chilling account of Spanish colonization of the Americas. Like England, Mendez believed it was his moral duty to provide written witness, through the venue of the periodical, to the devastating effects of colonization. He believed his article was a means to preserve the witness of "sixteen millions of people, who suffered under a burden of oppression, which had for three centuries crushed their ancestors into the earth."[47] Significantly, Mendez signaled out purgatory as the doctrine that was most widely utilized by corrupt clergy to subjugate and disenfranchise peasants. For Mendez, purgatory was the best example of a religious doctrine that was used by both a government, in this case Spain, and a religious institution, the Catholic Church, as a tool of imperialism.

The article infuriated England, who published a refutation. At stake were several issues. First was the status of purgatory as it had been popularly characterized by non-Catholics from the time period of Martin Luther's Reformation to Voltaire's Enlightenment, as a fable meant to deceive and impoverish unwitting Catholics. England had been working hard to refute this characterization. More at issue, and most likely what most infuriated England, was Mendez's equation of Catholicism, and purgatory, with imperialism. This struck at the very heart of England's campaign to reimagine a new American Catholic identity. According to England, Catholics, especially Irish and American Catholics, were full participants in the new world of democracy, equality, and liberty. They were revolutionary citizens of a new world. But according to Mendez, Catholics were enemies of the new world and of progressive governments founded upon democracy. England's revolutionary credentials were impeccable. If there was anyone who could combat Mendez's version of purgatory, it was England. It was important that he do this, as well, as in every way he and other Irish Catholics fit in perfectly with the revolutionary ethos of the new American republic—in every way, that is, except for being Catholic.

Founded in 1815, *The North American Review* was, at the time, the most influential magazine published in the United States. It was known as a forum for important cultural discussions concerning global issues. It is still the oldest literary magazine in the United States. The intention of its first editor, William Tudor, was to create a forum whereby influential Americans would be able to discuss matters of importance pertaining to the new republic and thus improve American society. The table of contents for the volume in which Mendez's article, called "South America," was published included other articles that suggest a readership of progressives. William Somerville authored "Somerville's Letters on France: Letters from Paris, on the Causes and Consequences of the French Revolution" and Thaddeus Mason Harris wrote "Natural History of the Bible." Thomas Jefferson had been a subscriber.

Mendez's article was a survey of the revolutionary movements in Spanish South America from 1800 through 1820, which saw the formation of the new countries of Venezuela, Colombia, and Ecuador. Mendez had been imprisoned for his revolutionary efforts. In his article he calls the movements for independence some of the most important developments in the history of humanity. His motivation for writing the article was to inform people in the United States of the status of their neighbors, and to expose the "nature of the Spanish colonial government," including "its ecclesiastical establishments." He wished to unveil the "conspiracies of crowned heads to rob men of their rights."[48] According to Mendez, it was never the intent of the Spanish royalty to uplift or establish justice, peace, or dignity to the inhabitants of the colonies. Instead, he described a situation of wanton and callous exploitation. In the minds of the Spanish royalty, the colonies existed to benefit Spain economically and the clerics were the petty bureaucrats willing to enact their program. "The prosperity of America was a thing never meditated in the system by which Spain governed her colonies." Rather, he claimed it was their intention to "oppress the Americans in every possible manner, and extract from them every possible advantage; to enforce labor, impose slavery, extort tribute, and draw from the sinews and sufferings of an immense population the means of supporting the pride and luxury of a few titled despots."[49] For Mendez, Catholicism was the right hand of Spanish imperialism.

Mendez singled out the clergy as being particularly effective in carrying out the oppressive policies of the Spanish government. "The spiritual guides of the people were the worst enemies to their peace and happiness."[50] Clergy utilized the doctrine of purgatory and its associated practices, such as indulgences for the deceased, because they appealed to the emotional ties that bound the living to the dead. "Bulls," which were specific indulgences, were usually purchased by people when they were grieving. "The most extraordinary imposition was the tax levied through the instrumentality of the Church. The bull of the dead was indispensible to rescue departed souls from purgatory. It was bought by the relations of a deceased person, as soon as possible after death; and poor people were thrown in agonies of grief and lamentation, if they were not able to purchase this passport for the spirit suffering the miseries of purgatory."[51]

The bull of the dead was part of a series of indulgences issued from the popes yet were administered through the Spanish government. All the revenue from the bulls returned to the monarchy of Spain. They included the "bull of the dead," which released souls from purgatory, the "bull of composition," which released those who had stolen property from others from having to return it to its original owners, the "bull for eating milk and eggs during Lent," which was reserved for the clergy, and the "bull for the living," which exonerated a person who purchased it of all crimes except heresy.[52] Of the bull of composition, Mendez added that "the price of these bulls depended on the amount of goods stolen; but it is just to add, that only fifty of them could be taken by a single person in a year."[53] Mendez noted that the most lucrative day for the church, and thus Spain, was November 2, All Souls' Day, which was a day to memorialize and pray for the souls in purgatory. Mendez quotes a native Peruvian, who describes the common practice of securing prayers for the dead:

> The second of November in every year is the day appointed by the Romish church for that festivity. On that day hundreds of monks and priests inundate all the cities, villages and towns and country chapels, in search of responsos, which are "Pater Nosters," Said to liberate souls from purgatory. This service, which occupies but a moment, costs six pence, and although the price is so trifling, it is a source of large income to the priests, as the people universally order responsos for their deceased relatives and friends.[54]

Beyond the monetary benefit to the clergy that was a consequence of such practices, Mendez also emphasized its emotional costs to the native Peruvians, especially when they were taxed for the funeral solemnities that assured that their deceased loved one's soul would be prayed for in purgatory:

The tax levied upon [funeral] solemnities is most painful to the Indians, and the most barbarous avarice is displayed in its action. The sum which the Indian is obliged to pay is in proportion to his wealth, varying from $5–100. His property is narrowly investigated, and the violence I have seen the poor Indian weep till his heart was well nigh broken at the levying of this unjust contribution. But the European *Curas*, whose hearts are harder than the gold they covet, turn a deaf ear to the wailing of the widow, whose children are taken from her to pay this tax. A religion so abused, and transformed into a systematic mode of thieving and robbery, is a calamity more dreadful than a pestilence.[55]

By linking practices of purgatory to Spanish imperialism, Mendez cast his argument within the framework of the American and French revolutions and thus situated his claims within a larger narrative of emancipation from Catholic powers and governments, one that was by 1824 commonly invoked.[56] He claimed that it was "the example of other nations and the progress of knowledge" that motivated the people of South America to finally throw off the tyranny of Spain and the Catholic Church. He also charged that the emancipation of South America from Spain was more akin to the American Revolution than the French Revolution. "The changes that have occurred in South America, the establishment of political institutions, the advancement of civil culture and knowledge, and the progressive emancipation of a whole continent, are destined to have an incalculably more important bearing on the future condition of the human race, than the great and dazzling scenes which have been exhibited on the theatre in Europe."[57] Part of the logic of Mendez's framework was an assumption that the providential history that began with the Reformation cast the new world, America, as "separating from and seeking to purify Europe."[58] The "purification" of which he writes is explicitly related to Catholicism. The Americas would provide a new opportunity to inaugurate the advancement of humankind, which was thought to be inevitable.

The inevitable advancement of which Mendez wrote was part of a dominant European conception of the place of religion within civil society, derived from the developments consequential to the Enlightenment. In the eighteenth century, philosophers such as Immanuel Kant and literary figures like Voltaire argued that humankind was progressing into a more rational, "enlightened" stage of development, and religions that emphasized ritual and dogma were part of the past, and as such were archaic.

This assumption involved a teleological framework in which Europe was thought to be progressing into a modern, civil era and leaving behind old, superstitious frameworks for more advanced ones, based on reason, as opposed to those based on revelation or dogma. Proponents of this worldview advocated a moral system of reason-based ethics over against ritual-based religions. Catholicism, associated with ritual and dogma, was characterized as superstitious and irrational, and Voltaire and Kant thought that ritual-based religions would eventually be replaced by more enlightened religious forms such as Deism.[59] The new religious framework contained political overtones. The rhetoric of Protestant enlightened reason was expedient for those in France who wished to replace a Catholic government. It equated Catholicism with the past and humanism with the future.

The Enlightenment influenced Americans like Benjamin Franklin and Thomas Jefferson, and Mendez placed his own interpretation of the Colombian and Peruvian revolutions within the framework of "reason" advocated by Jefferson. Mendez wrote, "The revolution was not the explosion of a moment; but the gradual development of principles which make every mind conscious of its right to freedom and self government."[60] This logic naturalized Deism and the new Protestant religious movements, constructing them as the natural extensions of a reasonable society or at least as the worldviews of the most reasonable of citizens of the eighteenth and early nineteenth centuries. Catholicism was coded as superstitious and archaic.

Of the myriad Catholic rituals and practices, Mendez focused on the dogma of purgatory and its associated devotions and specifically linked these to political oppression and colonization. He argued that the selling of indulgences and the levying of taxes linked to the fate of the deceased was a political strategy that promoted superstition and also caused a financial burden on the common people. Beyond the normal taxation meant to maintain temporal order, a spiritual taxation would "wring from them the little that remained after the torturing engine of taxation had done its heaviest work; this tax corrupted the morals of the people at the same time that it picked their pockets."[61] Although Mendez did grant that the claims of Catholicism regarding purgatory were not in themselves abusive, they were open to be abused, and this was the problem. For Mendez, the hereafter was unknown territory, a region far more exploitable than the terrestrial frontiers of the new world. The danger inherent in such a frontier was too much to bear, and Mendez argued powerfully to remove it from the conceptual map.

John England was furious that the article appeared in the *North American Review*, a revered and respectable forum for American intellectuals. He was angry that a public forum that claimed to represent the people of the new republic would provide a voice for anti-Catholicism. England wrote that Mendez was "a deliberate and wanton libeler of the largest Christian body in the universe."[62] More diplomatically, he assumed that the criticism was the consequence of faulty knowledge about the dogma of purgatory rather than intentional calumny. "Now, the writer of the Review did not understand the Catholic doctrine, and yet he has most majestically condemned what he did not take the trouble to study. I prefer this to the other side of the alternative; for if he did know the Catholic doctrine, I should be reluctantly compelled to think most unfavorably of his moral feelings."[63] Part of the problem that England had with Mendez's account of the emancipation was that it did not conform to his own assessment of what being Irish Catholic, and American Catholic, meant.

Mendez's version of being Catholic was as antithetical to England's as two versions could get, yet each was based on lived histories and testimonies. These versions were not just different, but competing, for Mendez painted Catholicism in the same way that England painted the country of England—as the great oppressor. The mistake each author made was to assume a universal Catholic religion, devoid of regional contexts.

Mendez's article equated anti-Catholicism with intellectualism and the progress of knowledge, and it criticized Catholicism for mixing political and economic factors with spiritual matters, especially those that pertained to the afterlife. His revolutionary citizen was one who kept the otherworld and afterlife an "unknown," separate from political and economic matters in the interest of progress. England's American revolutionary, on the other hand, was accompanied by all of the members of the Catholic religion that came before him, and, contemporaneously, with him, in purgatory and in heaven. England's revolutionary mixed the spiritual and the temporal worlds, and in his view, these would never be separate. However, the Enlightenment framework that allowed England to forge an American Catholic identity that espoused religious freedom also motivated him to carve out a specific framework for interpreting purgatory. Lough Derg, and the tales of ghosts and visions, was not a part of this framework at all, and England's advocacy of the Church's "general doctrine" did not leave room for speculation regarding visitations from spirits or journeys through a purgatory of the senses. England's revolutionary fervor, which served him well as an Irish immigrant to the early republic, also contributed to an interpretative framework that privileged spirit, or reason, over matter. England went further than just relegating purgatory to spirit; he recast it as being analogous to American civil ceremonies. In this way, its super-natural aspects were completely erased.

England's philosophical commitments inspired him to condemn what he termed "the superstitions" of Lough Derg. Addressing the charge of superstition with regard to the pilgrimage, made in a non-Catholic period-ical called *The Gospel Messenger*, England distanced Church authorities from the legends about the site that circulated. "In Venice, in the year 1522, before the existence of an English protestant, when all Ireland was Catholic, an edition of the breviary was printed by Antonio de Giunta, in which leg-ends commendatory of this pilgrimage were inserted—they were erased by the Pope's orders, and two years after, the same de Giunta published his edition revised without them; and an order was made at Rome, prohibiting any republication of the suppressed legendary." In this statement, which England approves, the pope literally erases the references to the supernat-ural associated with Lough Derg. England also referenced the closing of the cave by Pope Alexander VI, whom he noted died well before "Luther began to dogmatize at a period where all England and Irish were Catholic." England specifically cites the reason for the closing: "because of the fables, and the superstitions practiced there." Although England doesn't spe-cifically refer to what superstitions were practiced, his emphasis on an abstract, nonmaterial version so evident in his writings would suggest that he is referring to the belief that the cave was a real purgatory where peni-tents could absolve their sins and avoid punishment in the afterlife and where they often came into contact with the deceased. He insisted that the official doctrine of purgatory should not in any way be associated with the heresies at Lough Derg. "Thus it is clear that Rome is not accountable for these superstitions if they still exist."[64]

Conclusion

John England's version of purgatory was forged in the crucible of revolu-tionary fervor, at a time when Enlightenment values like liberty, democ-racy, and the separation of church and state offered hope to beleaguered Irish Catholics. The Catholic context in Ireland was different from other European Catholic contexts. The French Enlightenment had stirred revo-lutionary hopes for the Irish and seemed to point to a way out of religious oppression. At the same time, however, the same values were espoused by members of the French Revolution, and resulted in severe religious oppression for Catholics in France subject to the tragic consequences of the Reign of Terror in 1793. At the same time that French Catholics were being persecuted by their government, Irish Catholics viewed these same revolutionary governments as potentially helpful to their cause. England's adoption of a rationalist interpretive framework for purgatory was a consequence of his fervent acceptance of ideals gleaned from the Enlightenment, of which he was an advocate. He espoused the separation of church and state, reason over revelation, as well as the fallibility of the pope. This set him apart from his non-Irish, Catholic contemporaries, but he did share these views with other Irish, English, and American Catholics like John Carroll and Daniel Carroll. Most of the churchmen of the French and Italian Catholic Church, however, were critics of the French and American revolutions. Famous revolutionaries like Thomas Jefferson, Thomas Paine, and celebrated European intellectuals such as Voltaire espoused deism and considered the Catholic Church to be antiquarian and an enemy to reason. Contrary to the European Catholic Church, the political and social contexts of Ireland and the early republic of the United States produced a form of Catholicism that incorporated many ideals espoused by the revolutionaries such as democratic rule, the separation of church and state, and reason as a guide to faith. A Catholic Enlightenment prevailed in England, Ireland, and North America during the late eighteenth and early nineteenth centuries. Using a purely rationalist framework, England recast purgatory, unmooring it from its Irish soil and placing it firmly in an abstract home. He naturalized the rituals associated with these practices hoping to make them palpable to non-Catholics.

England's apologetics was an answer to the specific streams of Enlightenment thought that equated ritual aspects of religions with the past, as superstitious, and as antithetical to reason. England maintained that one could be abstract and rational, *and* embrace the rituals of one's religion. In other words, one could be Catholic and fully invested in Enlightenment principles. England and Carroll's Enlightenment Catholicism incorporated ritual and the belief that the sacred could be revealed through matter, and described a subjectivity that was at once inwardly directed and outwardly focused. While anti-Catholic sentiment caused various French governments to remove the material culture of Catholicism, including outward signs of rituals such as Church bells, grottos, and statues, English and American Catholics defended rituals and devotions with the language of reason. Perhaps it was a benefit that American revolutionaries weren't fighting against a Catholic government since this provided a space for American Catholics like England to challenge an anti-ritual version of the Enlightenment.

After the 1830s, with the increasing arrival of European immigrants, an anti-ritual discourse became the prevailing framework of an elite, Protestant class, who employed it to distinguish themselves from lower-class Catholics. What had been a useful ideology for French humanists seeking a new government became the predominate lens through which non-Catholic Americans viewed Catholics in the nineteenth-century United States. However, American Catholics like England were forging their own Enlightenment at the center of which was an emphasis on devotions, particularly those for the souls in purgatory. England's erasure of the supernatural elements of purgatory was representative of the works of theologians and intellectuals (who were mostly converts) of the nineteenth century. This is evidenced by many sources, and is the subject of the following chapters. This development is also revealed in discourse about Lough Derg. In an article published in the *Irish Ecclesiastical Record* in 1865, an Irish priest notes that "on the dawn of the so-called Reformation, Protestant writers seized on these poetic fables as if they were matters of sober fact, and availed themselves of the fictions of romance to cast ridicule on the practices of Catholic piety and devotion."[65] England's recasting of purgatory was part of a trend that did eventually play out in the publications read by the Irish diaspora, and by other European American Catholics of the nineteenth century. His efforts reflect a definite shift in representations of purgatory, all of which take on a distinctly apologetic tone. Like England, Catholic intellectuals and theologians adopted reason as a framework for interpreting purgatory with the consequence of de-emphasizing purgatory's material elements. A more abstract, spiritual version of purgatory will come to replace the more spatial, place-based, and material representations. Additionally, publications that embraced a place-centered version of purgatory would eventually, like Lough Derg, receive regulation and suppression from the Church, and ridicule by non-Catholics.

4

That Sensible Neighborhood to Hell

FIERY APOLOGETICS: PROVIDENCE AND MATERIALITY
WITHIN THE PERIODICAL (1830–1920)

JOHN ENGLAND'S RHETORIC about purgatory was distinctly apologetic.
He attempted to counter nativism and he was eager to present Catholics as
enlightened subjects of the new republic. His inclination to de-emphasize
the material aspects of purgatory followed the same trajectory as most
of the scholastic philosophers five hundred years earlier. In this sense he
is representative of those at the higher rungs of Church leadership, who
also emphasized purgatory's association with spirit rather than with matter.
This was not the case for others who wrote about and concerned themselves
with purgatory, however. Historian Guillaume Cuchet, in *Le Crepuscule
du Purgatoire*, reveals that there was a revival in devotions and belief in
purgatory in the mid-nineteenth-century France. Competing with other
forms of the cult of the dead, like spiritualism, the doctrine of purgatory
received a renewed emphasis. By the end of the First World War, Cuchet
argues, devotions to purgatory dropped off, signaling its eventual end, or
near end, in the twentieth century.

Cuchet's study of purgatory in nineteenth-century France is helpful in
providing an overview of nineteenth-century American Catholic devotional
practices and beliefs for several reasons. First, the effects of the French
Enlightenment created a zeitgeist of secularism, that is, it promoted the
value of the separation of church and state and the privatization of religion
in France and in the United States. Although the nineteenth century was
not completely "the century of secularization," as scholars have previously
maintained, the ethos of secularization motivated religious innovation. For
historians, "the question is to understand how religiosity continued within
and around a rhetoric (and a reality) of increasing hostility to the Church."[1]
Catechesis, regulated by the French school system in the eighteenth century, was now a private affair to be accomplished by churches without the

support of the state. The resurgence of belief and devotions to purgatory of which Cuchet writes is part of a larger context of religious innovation. Spiritualism, the nineteenth-century movement that spanned Europe and the United States, provided a new framework of interaction with the dead. Purgatory, which had been for centuries the institutional framework for regulating interactions between Catholics and their deceased loved ones, adapted to the times as practitioners adopted the practice of direct communication with the souls in purgatory, who often interceded in miraculous ways in their lives. Cuchet traces the formation of this innovation, and it is also a prominent feature of purgatory narratives published in English that circulated in the United States.

Catholic immigrants in the United States maintained their own literary cultures, but they also shared a common literature with Europeans that included devotional works like pamphlets, books, and periodicals. The nineteenth century witnessed a massive influx of European Catholic immigration. In 1850 Roman Catholics composed 5 percent of the population of the United States. By 1906, this statistic rose to 17 percent.[2] Certain authors, like theologian and convert Frederick William Faber, translated French devotional literature about purgatory into English that met with an enthusiastic reception. Polemical diatribes appeared in English Protestant periodicals ridiculing articles about purgatory in French Catholic periodicals. Periodical titles contained words like "miscellany" or "world," and promised readers news from around the world, instilling the perception that they were linked to the communities from which they were geographically severed, as well as providing information from other cultures.

In addition to Cuchet's treatment of the revival of purgatory in France, historians Emmet Larkin and Ann Taves have shown that there was a revival in devotional practices among mid-nineteenth-century Irish and American Catholics.[3] This revival is attributable to a number of developments. The ubiquity of the printing press contributed to the spread of devotional literature. In Ireland, and in particular after the famine and with the consolidation of the Irish Catholic Church, attendance at Mass rose to an all-time high and catechesis was no longer a punishable offense. In the United States, the Irish continued to participate in an Irish diaspora that included a rich literary culture of periodicals, pamphlets, and newspapers. Although Taves cautions against assuming a homogenous subculture of Irish Americans, within the mid- to late nineteenth century, as earlier, Irish Catholics viewed their Catholicism through a nationalist lens, and hardly separated their Irish identities from their Catholicism.[4]

Within the context of a general revival in Catholic devotions, recorded devotions to the souls in purgatory in prayer books in the United States increased after 1840.[5] In France, nun Eugenie Smet founded an order, the Helpers of the Holy Souls, in 1854 to address the need to pray for the "Church suffering," or for those who were deceased and languishing in purgatory. It is perhaps no coincidence that amid widespread immigration, devotions related to the doctrine of Church Suffering would flourish. The doctrine, part of the Communion of Saints, extends the Roman Catholic community from those on earth, called the Church Militant, to those in heaven, called the Church Triumphant, including those in purgatory, who are the Church Suffering. Devotions to this extended Catholic community would reinforce the perception of belonging to a greater community of Catholics, even as one was separated, in physical distance, from one's community of origin. As part of the revival, authors commented on and republished texts about purgatory from foregone eras, such as fifteenth-century saint Catherine of Genoa's *Treatise on Purgatory*. Other, new manifestations of belief in purgatory arose, particularly fictional and nonfictional narratives about interactions between people and souls in purgatory. These are found in the plethora of periodicals published in the mid- to late nineteenth century, the audience of which mostly included women and children, and focused on the family.

In the variety of sources focused on belief in purgatory, including periodicals, pamphlets, prayer books, and catechisms, a persistent theme emerges: the "reality" of the material elements of purgatory is a theme that is tackled directly, resulting in the appearance of two versions of purgatory, one that focuses on purgatory formulated in the language of materiality and another represented as a more abstract "pain of loss," with little reference made to its spatial, material features. Additionally, authors invoke Providence as an explanatory framework for understanding the relationships between the living and the holy souls. The souls contact the living and the living actively solicit the help of the souls, and real events are interpreted as confirming this interaction—Smet took the religious name Sister Mary of Providence as an affirmation of this interpretation. Often, a purgatory narrative ends with words evoking the providential world of meaning over a random one of meaningless events. Thus the focus on purgatory and its real-world effects acts as a rhetorical strategy to bolster belief in the doctrine and to confirm a Catholic worldview.

The problem of purgatory's materiality becomes more pressing in the nineteenth century than it had been in previous centuries, as belief in a

terrestrial purgatory becomes fodder for anti-Catholic polemicists. Even
as Church authorities and anti-Catholic writers acted in concert (though
not working together) to suppress this belief, periodicals devoted to the
subject of purgatory published narratives of embodied souls from purgatory who appeared to the living and left physical evidence of their visits.
Therefore, on the one hand, through the works of elite Catholic converts
such as Frederick William Faber and John Henry Newman, purgatory's
link to earth was completely severed, and on the other hand, tales told in
regional periodicals and publications recorded visits from embodied holy
souls and these reinforced the interpretation of purgatory as "a sensible
neighbor to Hell."[6]

Purgatory and Polemics

At the same time that John England was downplaying the superstitions
associated with Lough Derg, several attacks on the doctrine of purgatory
appeared in the English press that focused on the terrestrial aspects of
purgatory. Polemical literature was often published in the form of tracts.
A reassessment of purgatory, and subsequent polemical attacks on the doctrine, was in part motivated by the success of tracts published by Anglicans
who were revisiting, and in some cases adopting, the doctrine. Two Catholic
converts brought renewed attention to the doctrine. In many ways, even
as they conferred legitimacy on the maligned doctrine by their attention,
they also focused on its conceptual, rather than material, aspects. In England,
John Henry Newman inspired a movement of Anglicans who readdressed
several traditional Catholic beliefs that had been discarded by the Protestant reformers. *The Oxford Movement* also motivated several very prominent Anglicans to convert to Roman Catholicism. Newman is perhaps
the most famous of the members to convert. Faber was another convert
whose writings were popular, particularly on the subject of purgatory. In
1835 Newman delivered a lecture about purgatory, called "The Intermediate
State." In this lecture he said that there was scriptural evidence for such a
state of purgation.[7] The members of the movement were well known for
publishing tracts, and the movement became known as the *Tractarian
Movement*. The tracts were widely circulated between 1833 and 1841. In
Tract 79, called "On Purgatory: Against Romanism," Newman argued, before his conversion to Catholicism, the "mere letter" regarding purgatory,
articulated in the documents of the Council of Trent, was not objection-
able.[8] "Purgatory is not spoken of at all of as a place of pain; it need only

mean, as its name implies, a place of purification."[9] The problem with the doctrine of purgatory was that it was based on the supernatural or "the popular stories of apparitions witnessing to it."[10] Newman cites Bishop Jeremy Taylor (Church of England), with whom he agrees, that "We do not think that the wise men in the Church of Rome believe these narratives; for if they did, they were not wise; but this we know, that by such stories the people were brought into a belief of it."[11] Later, in *An Essay on the Development of Christian Doctrine*, he writes that, according to the early Church regarding purgatory, "there were two schools of opinion: the Greek, which contemplated a trial of fire on the last day for which all were to pass, and the African, resembling more nearly the present doctrine of the Roman Church."[12] The mention of two traditions would become more frequent by theologians and authors of tracts and pamphlets about purgatory. In any case, Newman wrote about purgatory well before his reception into the Roman Catholic Church, in 1845.[13]

The response of English non-Catholics to Newman's renewed interest in purgatory and other Catholic doctrines was negative. Many considered Newman, and other members of *The Oxford Movement*, to be secret agents of the pope. In response to these accusations Newman published *Apologia Pro Vita Sua* (A Defense of the Author's Life), which outlined the reasons for his eventual conversion. Newman argued forcefully that his conversion was motivated by reason and scriptural analysis. Significantly, in his writings about purgatory, Newman deemphasized its material aspects and distanced his own position on purgatory from the history of its legends and private revelations, in other words, from its material representations. Newman's version of purgatory was conceptual. It was derived from Scripture, but whether or not it had substance, Newman would not state.

Newman was not the only *Oxford Movement* theologian to bring attention to purgatory. Faber also wrote popular tracts and books that addressed the doctrine, some of which are still being published. He had been ordained as an Anglican priest in 1839 and was received as a Roman Catholic priest in 1847, after an illness nearly took his life.[14] Faber emulated John Henry Newman and founded a monastic community whose members expressed a devotion to the Virgin Mary. His writings were popular among all Catholics, so much so that Faber "was indeed a household word for many English-speaking Catholics."[15] Many of his works were translated into several languages and sold widely throughout Europe. His book *All for Jesus* was published in 1853 and was so popular that it was translated into Flemish, French, German, Italian, and Polish and sold in the United States.[16] He translated St. Louis de Montfort's *True Devotion to Mary* into English, and his subsequent writing about Mary Queen of Purgatory, which he committed to song, was popular until the 1960s. Many of his works, especially those about purgatory, are still being published, and he is the subject of a recent biography.[17]

Faber, more than Newman, identified two historically distinct versions of purgatory, and privileged one above the other: "There have always been two views of purgatory prevailing in the Church." He elaborated on the differences between each version and subsequently made the problem of purgatory, which is its materiality, the focus of his discussions. The "material version" of purgatory, in Faber's writings, is also equated with hell, which he feels is probably wrong. Although he doesn't blatantly reject representations of purgatory that focus on sense and concrete experience, he leaves no doubt in the reader's mind to which "view" of purgatory he subscribes, and which is his preferred version. The view of purgatory that is based on sense, the version that renders purgatory "that sensible neighbor to hell," is associated with "violence, confusion, wailing, and horror." He argues that this view "dwells, and truly, on the terribleness of the pain of sense." Along with the scholastic philosophers before him, he wonders how "the soul is mysteriously permitted to endure" these sensible atrocities. In this respect his argument rests on an assumption of substance dualism, in that the soul is spiritual and is not made of matter and therefore the commingling of these substances should be impossible. According to Faber, the soul is devoid of matter, and its potential contamination with matter is part of what makes the sensible purgatory so off-putting: "There is a special and indefinable horror to the unbodied soul in becoming prey of this material agony." To complicate matters for Faber, in the material versions of purgatory, angels, whom he believes to be messengers of God, "are represented as active executioners of God's awful justice."[18] Additionally, "The fire is the same fire as that of hell, created for the single and express purpose of giving torture." For Faber, the material representation of purgatory is portrayed as a less eternal version of hell. Also, part of the problem with this version is that an immaterial spirit, or soul, appears to be subject to sensible torments.

For all of the confusing elements that Faber lists—the apparent vengeance of God, the confusion of placing an "unbodied soul" in a situation that seems to suggest that the soul is corporeal—he cannot deny that this version of purgatory dominates the Catholic tradition. He notes that many saints witnessed these visions, and they have "been borne out in its minutest details by the conclusions of scholastic theologians." He notes that even as some of the saints attempted to soften this version of purgatory, they were warned against doing so: "It is remarkable also that when the Blessed Henry Suso, through increased familiarity and love of God, began to think comparatively lightly of the pains of purgatory, our Lord warned him that this was very displeasing to him." Through his research of the history of purgatory, Faber acknowledges that purgatory has mostly been portrayed as a sensible place, and he admits to the ferocity of these representations, but he does not accept it. "This then, is a true view of purgatory, but it is not a complete one."[19] Instead of rejecting the "sensible" portrayal of purgatory, which he cannot, he instead elaborates another version.

Faber's additions to completing the view of purgatory rely mostly on the *Treatise on Purgatory* by St. Catherine of Genoa, whose work was first published in 1551 in Italy. Her work enjoyed renewed popularity during the mid-nineteenth century as several members of *The Oxford Movement*, as well some within the Catholic community, published tracts and commentaries on her *Treatise*. Among those who addressed her work on purgatory were Newman, Henry Edward Manning, whose commentary on her *Treatise* was published in 1858, and Faber. While Faber's assessment of what he calls the sensible purgatory tradition relies on multiple sources, his "other version" relies on the work of Catherine of Genoa and one other vision of purgatory, that of the thirteenth-century nun St. Gertrude. From their works he is able to construct a nonmaterial version of purgatory. He argues that the "spirit of this view is love."

Although Faber avoids disparaging the sensible view of purgatory, he does place it *out of sight*: "The other view of purgatory does not deny any one of the features of the preceding view, but it almost puts them out of sight." In his version, the soul is not corporeal and "there need no angels to convey it thither." Faber chooses adjectives to describe the soul that convey concepts, instead of places or things. Purgatory is "purely of souls." As a soul stands in front of God, Faber describes it as "clothed and adorned with charity." Air is another term that Faber uses to connote spirit, and not matter: "There are revelations too which tell of multitudes who are in no local prison, but abide their purification in the air, or by their graves, or in the rooms of those who pray for them." There is punishment in this purgatory, but it does not consist of fire. Instead, punishment consists in "the unbroken union with God."

Along with John Henry Newman, Faber de-emphasized the material features of representations of purgatory and replaced them with abstract terms and references. In doing so, they were participating in a reconceptualization of the afterlife that was taking place throughout the nineteenth century, but particularly in the later half, in England, Ireland, and the United States, as well as in Europe.[20] Scholars have documented the development, reflected in sermons and theological tracts, of how representations of hell shifted from conveying punitive images of torture to portrayals that featured hell as an eternal exile from God. What was once represented as a literal place filled with fire and brimstone gradually gave way to characterizations of hell as a state of regret. Progressives on each side of the Atlantic preached a softer, more conceptual version of hell, like Congregationalist Henry Ward Beecher, who claimed that "hell as a place of fire and brimstone" was a relic of the past.[21] Guillaume Cuchet, in his analysis of the revival of purgatory during the nineteenth century in France, argues that this trend informed conceptions of purgatory, in that they provided an alternative way of conceiving of punishment: "the signs of a decline in hellfire preaching in the second half of the nineteenth century were numerous and mutually confirming." The latter part of the nineteenth century witnessed "the gradual passage from the picture…of a just, awe-inspiring and vengeful god to the picture of a God of love, understanding, and forgiveness."[22] This development played out in the publications of Faber and Newman.

Despite Faber's efforts to void purgatory of its "terribleness" and replace it with a more acceptable "spirit of love," non-Catholic polemicists were more than happy to focus on what Faber called the "hell" tradition of purgatory. The polemicists published popular tracts about purgatory, and without exception they attacked purgatory's status as a material, literal place of punishment. The Reverend (Church of Ireland) Samuel Edgar's *The Variations of Popery* was first published in 1831 and enjoyed several printings. It was printed in the United States until 1848. Like Faber, Edgar provides an analysis of the narratives of purgatory handed down by saints and theologians, and he focuses on the most literal and concrete expressions. Unlike Faber, he doesn't offer another version of purgatory. Additionally, he utilizes these examples to ridicule them and to reveal, in an age that is post-Enlightenment, the absurdity, in his view, of maintaining belief in purgatory.

Edgar is conscious of his role as a polemicist: "The polemical pen, which in the British dominions, had slept in inactivity, has resumed its labors." He notes that "Ireland in particular manner, has become a field of noisy disputation," and he decried the view, held by John England, that Catholicism is "rejected only when misunderstood." Against John England's version of purgatory as a form of civil religion, Edgar reveals the long history of purgatory as conceived of as a place. He makes clear that he will be focusing on the material representations of purgatory, and he acknowledges that there have been some who have de-emphasized these aspects of the doctrine: "Augustine, according to Bellermine and Aquinas, divested this intermediate mansion of all material locality, and characterized it as a spiritual residence for spiritual souls."[23] However, he believes that this was a minority view within the tradition. For the polemicist, the materiality of purgatory is its mockery.

The primary problem with purgatory, according to Edgar, is that it has long been thought to be on earth, which wouldn't be so bad had it been associated with just one place, but it has been identified as being in several places, and for some, even in the middle of the earth. According to Edgar, this wouldn't be such a problem except that men of learning, theologians, people whom Edgar believes should know better, promulgated these beliefs: "the majority make this earth the scene of posthumous expiation." Another problem, he finds, is that they cannot agree. "Gregory and Damian, with glaring inconsistency, lay the scene in different parts of the world." Gregory's "infallibility considered the volcanic eruptions of Vesuvius, Aetna and Hecla as flames from purgatory," while others thought it was in the Southern Hemisphere.[24] The diversity of location presents a problem, as Edgar maintains that if there is one purgatory, it should have been found in one place, not several.

Edgar also points out that there have been diverse ways of describing souls in purgatory, and this is also a problem. Souls were to be found "in icy streams, a warm bath, a flaming cavern, or a burning mountain." He also notes that, in many accounts, hell and purgatory are adjacent, "in the same neighborhood." Edgar addresses the mode of punishment and critiques its materiality as well as its variety, "the medium of punishment is uncertain as the situation of the place. The general opinion, however favors the agency of fire." However, "many have represented water, accompanied by darkness, tempest, whirlwind, snow, ice, frost, hail and rain."[25]

The main problem with these representations, according to Edgar, is that they are not coherent regarding purgatory's place or its medium of punishment. As a polemicist his strategy is to utilize the variety of descriptions as a way to show that they cannot all be describing the same, objective reality. "These accounts have been authenticated by travellers who visited the subterranean empire," who reported seeing "a sulphurous well,

emitting flame and stench, which threw up men like sparkling scintilla-
tions, into the air, and again received them falling into its burning mouth."
After pages of these descriptions, revealing them in all of their variety, he
then attacks the legitimacy of the authors. "Dreams of this kind are peculiar to the faithful friends of a middle state of expiation."[26]

By suggesting that these representations are dreams, Edgar aligns
himself with several other opponents of purgatory who not only criticize
the variety of its characterizations but also its status as "private revelation."
In *The Doctrine of Purgatory and the Practice of Praying for the Dead as
Maintained by the Romish Church*, Rev. (Church of England) William John
Hall also criticized the variety of purgatory's manifestations, but also the
reticence of the Church authorities to comment on the specifics of the
place of purgatory: "The Council of Trent expresses itself on the subject in
a manner vague and ambiguous."[27] He goes on to state that any Christian
who then wants to know about the doctrine must rely on the various
descriptions about it, which seem to have no coherence. "'What is purgatory, where is it placed, who are its inhabitants, what are the punishments there inflicted—what is the duration, and what the result?' These
are questions that must be answered with respect to private revelation.
However, when these questions are answered by private revelation, church
authorities distance themselves from the answers," to which Hall notes
that "it is not unfair to conclude that [these narratives] contain doctrines of
the Romish Church, and not merely the *opinions* of private men."[28]

The issue of private revelation came to a head in the 1880s, when a
popular French periodical *Liberateur des Ames: Reveue Mensuelle des bonnes
Oeuvres de l'Eglise Militante et des Moyens de Soulager l'Eglise Souffrante*
(Liberator of Souls: Monthly Review of the Good Works of the Church
Militant and Ways to End the Sufferings of the Church Suffering) was
shut down by Bishop Guibert of Orlean. The bishop's reason for silencing
the periodical was that it included "private, non-Church accepted visions."[29]
The *Liberateur* had been continuously published for more than twenty
years, from 1863 through 1884. During this time it had published visions
of purgatory that were mostly written by nuns and clerics for an audience
that consisted of women and clerics. The view of purgatory presented in
the pages of the *Liberateur* confirmed what Faber would characterize as an
old version of purgatory, in other words, the sufferings of the souls were
evidenced in the flames that engulfed them as well as in other material
tortures. The editor of the periodical, abbe Celestin Cloquet, "cited Saint
Thomas' view of the fires as corporeal, although admitting that some (few)

authors imply it is metaphorical."³⁰ Cloquet also described purgatory's specific location in the earth.

In a series of articles that attacked the Copernican view of the universe, which places the sun at the center of a solar system of which earth and other planets orbit, Cloquet placed purgatory, with hell, in the center of the earth. The notion that the sun is the center of universe, according to Cloquet, was "l'idea la plus absurd, la plus diabolique." Cloquet cited revelation and scholarship to support his view. He referenced the seventeenth-century Jesuit and professor of astronomy Giovanni Batista Riccioli, who taught the non-rotation of the earth. Cloquet wrote that Riccioli's view was supported by the revelations of twelfth-century St. Hildegarde and seventeenth-century St. Mary of Agreda. He also stated that Galileo's views, which supported the Copernican solar system, were judged heretical in 1633, and were still heretical in 1880. He further recommended to the readers of the *Liberateur* that they take their children out of schools that taught the theories of Galileo. "It is the duty of parents to hinder their children from reading or studying such books; and they ought, even at the greatest sacrifice, to withdraw them from any school where such books are introduced." He recommended that parish priests follow suit. "And parish priests must not forget that they have the charge of souls, and are bound to exercise an active surveillance over the instruction given to the children."³¹

The controversy over the closure of the *Liberateur* garnered the attention of an eminent theologian of Trinity College, Dublin. Reverend George Salmon was a respected mathematician and theologian. He held a joint appointment in the departments of mathematics and divinity, and from 1888 until his death in 1904 he was the provost of Trinity College. In 1853 he published *Cautions of the Times*, which was a response to the tracts published by the members of *The Oxford Movement*. He was highly critical of the conversions by members of his own Church, the Anglican Church, to Roman Catholicism. Most of his criticisms of the Roman Catholic Church centered on the status of private revelations, which he called dreams, to support doctrines like purgatory. In critiquing private revelations, Salmon most often cited the belief that purgatory has an earthly location as being untenable and ludicrous to common sense. When the *Liberateur* was shut down, Salmon took the opportunity to congratulate Bishop Guibert in an article published in 1883, in two widely read journals, *The Contemporary Review* and *The Eclectic Magazine of Foreign Literature, Science, and Art*. In the essay "Purgatory and Modern Revelation," he argued that since private revelations revealed that purgatory was in the midst of the earth, and modern science revealed that the earth rotated around the sun, this placed these two in conflict. Because science is verified empirically, and private revelation is not, private revelation must be discarded. He utilized his knowledge of science to attack the idea that purgatory was a physical place, and he then suggested that the Roman Catholic Church hierarchy reject private revelation as a means to understand theological truths. He also noted that the periodical, *Le Liberateur*, which made frequent mention of purgatory's location on earth, was "blessed by Pope Pius IX, is still received at the Vatican, and is read by numerous savants and by priests of all degrees of the hierarchy."[32]

Salmon argued that "all revelations concerning hell and purgatory agree in placing them in the center of the earth."[33] He wrote that if people accepted this notion, and also accepted the tenets of modern science that reveal that the earth rotates, then one cannot help coming to the disturbing conclusion that "all the souls in hell and purgatory within, who, in the earth's vertiginous double motion, must roll about like grains of coffee in a grocer's mill."[34] He argued a similar point in the series of lectures he gave at Trinity College in 1888 called "Modern Revelations," and further castigated Church authorities for allowing private revelation to inspire new devotional forms. Lecturing about the relationship between private revelations and the official proclamations and dogmas of the Church, he stated: "No one can take up modern popular books of Roman Catholic devotion without seeing that their teaching differs as much from that of the Council of Trent, as the teaching of that Council differs from that of the Church of England."[35] The danger that this entails, he maintained, was that devotional Catholicism, based on private revelation, is a different religion from orthodox Catholicism, and that the Roman Catholic laity were being led astray by priests and bishops who privileged the enthusiasm that arose from revelations over historical veracity. Characterizing this, he stated that the pope "gives a kind of ambiguous approval, he honors the recipients of the alleged revelations, canonizes them as saints, encourages his children to ask their intercession, now that they are dead: but if questioned: Did these men when they were alive deceive the people by teaching them their own fancies as if they were divine revelations, he declares this a question outside his commission to answer." Salmon also admonishes Anglicans, including Faber, who converted to Catholicism: "Never, I believe, have any people been more cheated in their bargain than those who have left the Church of England for the Church of Rome, under the idea that in the latter communion they should be taught with more certainty what they were to believe."[36]

Anti-Catholic polemical literature repeated this strategy: it attacked the tradition of placing purgatory on earth as well as the variety of locations in which it was placed, linked these with private revelation, and then discredited private revelation. The issue of revelation, public and private, was already at the forefront of theological debate throughout the nineteenth century, within and without the Catholic Church. The Church maintained that public revelation, revealed by the Scriptures, was given to humans by God and it was believed to be historically specific to the era of the first apostles. Private revelation, on the other hand, was given by God to an individual, was subject to analysis by church authorities, and Catholics were not obligated to believe in it. This criterion, which was still in process, had been articulated by Pope Urban VIII in the 1625 papal bull *Sanctissimus Dominus Noster*.[37] Urban wrote that, in order to "prevent fraud," "opinions," "events," and "miracles" of holy and pious people should be directed to the Ordinary and then reported to the Apostolic See.[38] Reference to Urban's decree was used as a common disclaimer in a majority of the purgatory manuals, tracts, and periodicals: "In obedience to the decrees of Urban the Eighth, I declare that I have no intention of attributing any other than a purely human authority to the miracles, revelations, favours, and particular cases recorded in this book, and the same as regards the titles of Saints and Blessed applied to servants of God not yet canonized, except in those cases which have been confirmed by the Holy Roman Catholic Church and the Apostolic See, of which I declare myself to be an obedient son; and therefore I submit myself and all that I have written in this book to her judgment."[39]

Within the Church, the issue of revelation was divisive for Catholics. Modernist-leaning Catholics, those who espoused the historical method of exegesis, as well as those who questioned papal infallibility, were either ex-communicated or given severe warnings by Pope Pius IX in 1864. He articulated the problems of modernism in his *Syllabus of Errors*, which was a list of errors that, in Pius's estimation, were a threat to the Catholic Church and to papal authority. Listing the errors was his attempt to rout out Catholic proponents of the values widely espoused after the Enlightenment, which privileged reason and particularly its connection to revelation. John England, who had questioned the doctrine of papal infallibility and, as revealed in chapter 3, proposed reason as a guide to revelation, would most surely have been subject to Pius's warning. The subject "Revelation" is listed in the Syllabus as number five, and the error associated with it is "Divine revelation is imperfect, and therefore subject to a continual and indefinite progress, corresponding with the advancement of human reason."[40] Pius refutes the modernist belief that with increasing knowledge, gained through empirical study, people can reassess revelation and subject it to reason.

However, subjecting private revelation to scrutiny and reason was precisely what Catholics were doing. In the Dublin periodical *The Catholic Layman*, in an essay titled "Rival Revelations," the editors described the competing revelations of Saint Catherine of Siena and the Swedish Saint Brigit. Each had revelations about the Immaculate Conception of Mary, whereby Mary is believed to have been conceived in her mother's womb without original sin. Catherine determines, in a vision, that Mary proceeds from the seed of Adam. Brigit's vision reveals that Mary is untainted, and therefore free of original sin. Yet the editor points out that each revelation, though contradictory, is considered worthy of belief. To the editors, this contradiction points to "serious disputes within the Roman Catholic Church, touching alleged revelations," such that they decry "Roman Catholic unity, so often boasted of, so seldom realized."[41] Pope Pius IX comes under fire for his suggestion that the Immaculate Conception of Mary "had been revealed by God himself," as the editor notes that he relies on private revelations for the formation of this doctrine, which was decreed December 8, 1854.

At least with respect to private revelation, anti-Catholic polemicists and modernist Catholics, including converts, regarded it with suspicion. Each group discredited private revelation, specifically as it pertained to purgatory, as it tended to support a variety of interpretations that placed purgatory in various earthly locations. Faber and Newman were writing about purgatory in abstract terms and de-emphasizing its association with hell. Yet at the same time, other Catholics were working to establish purgatory as an actual, physical place, and as a place of suffering by real, not metaphoric, fire. In other words, they were keeping alive the material version of purgatory, precisely the version that Faber discounted. One such Catholic was Fr. Victor Jouet, a French priest and member of the Association of the Missionaries of the Sacred Heart of Jesus. He founded a church in 1894 called the *Sacro Cuore del Suffragio*, devoted to the souls in purgatory, and built it in a neo-Gothic style.[42] After a fire exposed what, to Fr. Jouet's mind, was the image of a soul suffering in purgatory, he traveled to Belgium, France, Germany, and Italy to gather physical evidence of souls from purgatory. Soon after he founded the church, Fr. Jouet built a museum to house the relics he collected from his travels. The museum, which is still open today, is steps from the Vatican, at 12 Lungotevere Prati, in Rome.[43] The contents of the museum include more than twenty objects, all of which display relics intended to document the physical features of purgatory and the souls detained there. These include books with handprints burned into the pages, clothes with clear handprints burned into sleeves and shoulders, pieces of furniture that have been handled by fiery hands, and accompanying documentation that included the testimonies of the priests, bishops, and other religious authorities who verified the relics. The purpose of the museum, according to an American author who interviewed Fr. Jouet, was to prove the material existence of purgatory as a location, and to prove that it was a place of "literal fire."

FIGURE 4-1 Mary as Queen of Purgatory. Juda Tadeas Supper, Virgin with Infant Jesus and St. Laurence, around 1750. Chornice (Czech Republic, Moravia), St. Laurence Church. Reprinted with the permission of the Department of Art History, Faculty of Arts, Masaryk University Brno, photo Tomasz Zwyrtek.

The museum caught the attention of a columnist from the American weekly newspaper, *The Star and Sentinel* (1867–1965), who then published a story about it in the column "Letter from Abroad." The author, W. B. Seabrook, was touring Rome when he came across a compelling invitation to "tour purgatory." The ad promised that the tour would be personally conducted by Fr. Jouet. "I thought it must be a joke-book, but no: it was a sincere, albeit friendly, invitation to go to Hell: and I went." Seabrook, a non-Catholic, explained that Fr. Jouet hoped that his relics would inspire belief in "purgatory as a definite geographical spot," as well as the belief that "the souls therein live literally in a lake of fire." Before embarking on the tour, Fr. Jouet explained how he was motivated to start the museum by a miraculous occurrence related to a fire that burned the chapel. A fire erupted in the church one night, while the chapel was empty. Thankfully, it had not spread far and the damage was confined to just one part of the wall, which was burned. As Fr. Jouet and the other priests of the order were cleaning up the ashes, there appeared on the wall, which the flames had destroyed, the picture of a man. In fact, it appeared as though "the flame had traced the picture on the wall." Father Jouet showed Seabrook the wall. Seabrook relates that "there was no shadowy smoke-effect requiring an effort of the imagination to discern, but a human face and figure outlined as clearly as it was depicted by the painter's brush." The man was dressed in red, wearing on his head a bishop's miter, and standing waist deep in flames.

When Fr. Jouet discovered the picture, he cried, "A soul in purgatory!" To which other priests, standing behind him, responded in whispers, "And a bishop!"

The next day, Fr. Jouet reported the incident to the pope, Leo XIII. Accordingly, the pope assigned several artists to examine the picture.

The artists determined that the picture was indeed well done, and they offered their reasonable explanation: it was a fresco that had been covered by plaster and had become exposed by the heat of the fire. Father Jouet, however, explained that this could not be true, because he had the wall made two years earlier, and the plaster was ordinary lime and mortar, and the workman lived down the street and could corroborate the fact. In other words, Fr. Jouet identified this as a miracle. The news of the miracle picture spread, and soon people were coming to the church to pray for their deceased. Seabrook writes, "I saw the mysterious picture with my own eyes. It is an awe-inspiring visage, a nightmare of a face, which haunts the imagination for hours afterwards. It is no accident or freak of nature. It was executed by a master's hand—whether man or spirit." Sometime after the fire, Fr. Jouet was paid a visit from his friend, an eminent Church historian from Piedmont. He showed the historian the image. "Scarcely had his eyes rested upon the features when he turned pale as death and gasped in Father Jouet's ears, 'My God man! Don't you know? That face! It is cardinal XXX!' And he mentioned the name of a great prelate, who had been dead for more than a quarter of a century."[44]

Soon after this incident, Fr. Jouet embarked on his trip through Europe to gather as much physical evidence and testimonies of visits from the souls in purgatory. The documents he sought to include, because of their effect in inspiring belief, were physical objects tinged by the fires of purgatory, books that had been touched and burned by souls, and testimonial evidence, including official church documents, signed by the priests and bishops whose task it was to confer legitimacy on private revelations, as well as witness to the events. The earliest of these documents and objects is from 1696, and several are from the eighteenth century. Some of the objects were stained with blood, which was not left by the souls in purgatory, but was evidence of the practices of scourging endured by the living for the intention of releasing their loved ones from the purgatorial fires. Although generally, late-nineteenth-century narratives about purgatory did not recommend scourging as penance for the souls in purgatory, the blood on the objects generated a sense of urgency and emphasized the vital role that the living played in the ultimate fate of their deceased loved ones. Novenas; thirty days of prayer; Masses; short, spontaneous prayers; and acts of good will were all recommended as ways that the living could aid the souls in purgatory.

Seabrook ends his article with a reference to the blood. Father Jouet related the story of a child novitiate to an Ursuline convent in the 1880s. Sister Maria, a youth with "zeal," had nightly visits from a "flame that would float above" her prayer stool in her cell. She reported this to a priest, to no effect, and finally to the mother superior of the convent, who sat up with her one night. While they were awake they witnessed an apparition of a nun who had recently passed away. The next day, the mother superior requested that all of the members of the convent pray for the soul of the deceased nun. That night, however, the nun reappeared and requested a special penance of Maria: she was to fast for nine days and scourge herself mercilessly. Father Jouet said that she inflicted "upon herself severe bodily pains. When midnight of the last day came, the devoted girl lay prostrate on the floor of her cell, half unconscious, so weakened by her fasting and self-inflicted tortures that she was unable to drag herself to bed." Then, the voice of the soul spoke to her and told her that it was soon to be released, and that it could see, from afar, the opening of the gates of paradise. Seabrook writes, "I bent to examine with breathless interest Sister Maria's scorched sleeve. There, indeed, in blackened outlines, was the unmistakable imprint of a woman's hand.

'And the drops of blood?' I asked.

'A scourge with leaden pellets,' replied the priest."[45]

Seabrook's travel to the museum and experience there in many ways reflected the cultural trends of the late nineteenth century. Seabrook, an educated non-Catholic, at first believed that the museum and its tour was a joke. Like modernist Catholics and most non-Catholics, the idea that purgatory was a place, and that its fires were real, was associated with beliefs of past eras. Father Jouet, and others like him, who were insisting on the materiality and reality of purgatory were fighting a trend in representation. Faber and Newman were at the forefront of the shift to recast purgatory in abstract terms. Narratives and places like Jouet's museum, which focused on the materiality of purgatory, were articulating a defensive rhetoric that took on greater urgency during this time, and in many ways reflects a position of retreat. The more the material aspects of purgatory came under attack, the more specific became the strategy to bolster these aspects. Jouet's strategy was three-pronged, in that he focused on procuring physical evidence; he collected confirming testimony from experts; and finally, he gathered testimonies from pious witnesses. This approach was repeated in narrative form in periodicals devoted to purgatory. Interestingly, Seabrook left the museum convinced by the relics. "No one who has been to the collection can harbor the suspicion that the fiery fingerprints have been fraudulently fabricated with the deliberate intention to deceive, that they have been 'faked,' to use an American slang expression."[46]

The Purgatory Periodicals: Providence—the New Materiality

Across the Atlantic, in Canada and the United States, the late-nineteenth-century influx of Catholic immigrants from Europe and Ireland supported several periodicals devoted to purgatory. On the one hand, periodicals such as *The Poor Soul's Advocate* incorporated the Faberian version of purgatory as an abstract place of loss. They also introduced a new concept of purgatory as reflecting "Divine Providence," which on the one hand appears to be abstract, but actually reveals God's actions in the lives of individuals and reinforces the interactions between the living and the dead, mediated by devotions and prayer. On the other hand, "The Consolations of Purgatory" and other pamphlets published narratives of purgatory that supported a version of purgatory as a concrete place. The evidence compiled by Fr. Jouet was repeated in narrative form in the pages of these latter periodicals and pamphlets. The editors of these magazines took care to insert the now-standard disclosure about private revelation that was a nod to Pope Urban VIII, and they also added the justification, elaborated in the thirteenth century by William of Auvergne, that God permits apparitions of souls from purgatory as warnings to the living. "God permits souls to come and excite our compassion, for their relief and to make us understand for ourselves the terrible rigors of His justice."[47] Or, stated another way, "Sometimes the souls of the departed are permitted by the wisdom of God to appear to men on earth."[48] This framing invoked tradition to confer legitimacy but to also provide the appearance of conformity to Church doctrine. However, predominantly, the warnings, manifested as apparitions and visits of souls, continued the tradition of purgatory as corporeal punishment, and not the Faberian idea of purgatory as the abstract pain of loss. Elements of corporeal punishment are the focal point of many of the narratives and are accompanied by explanations that address the apparent matter/spirit dilemma that these apparitions pose. In all of the periodicals, when physical evidence of souls' visits are presented, they are always presented as proof of the reality of the private revelations about purgatory.

The following narrative related in a pamphlet, "L'Echo du Purgatoire," published in Ontario, Canada, is typical:

> The event occurred November 16, 1859 in Foligno near Assisi, Italy. It is established as the undeniable truth. A sister Theresa was born in Bastia, Corsica, 1797, and entered in monastery in February 1826. She was a model of devotion. She died on November 1, 1859 of a sudden "apoplexy lightning." Twelve days later, on November 16th, Sister Anna-Felicia rose and went to the locker room to enter, when she heard groans coming from inside the room. A little frightened, she hastened to open the door, but there was nobody. But new groans were heard, and despite her usual courage, she felt overwhelmed by fear. *Jesus! Marie!* She cried, *what is that?* Then she

heard a plaintive voice accompany this painful sigh: "Oh! my God, I suffer!" Stunned, Sister Anna immediately recognized the voice of the poor sister Theresa. Then all the room filled with thick smoke, and a shadow. Sister Theresa appeared, heading toward the door, slipping along the wall. Sister Theresa cried, "Here is a testimony to God!" Having said these words, she knocked on the door, and left there a handprint of her right hand burned into the wood, as if it had been burned by a hot iron, and then she disappeared. Sister Anna was half-dead with fright. She began to scream and call for help. Her companions ran to see what had happened, and the whole community came and were surprised by the smell of burning wood. Sister Anna-Felicia recounted her story and showed them the door and the terrible impression. They also acknowledged that the impression of the hand was small, and that Sister Therese had been remarkably small.[49]

The community then spent the night praying for Sister Therese. The pamphlet reports that news spread of the incident, and many others from the local communities came to pray for Sister Therese's soul. The prayers, apparently, worked, for when Sister Anna went to her cell that night to sleep, she heard the voice of Sister Therese. Her voice now was cheerful, not frightening: "It is Friday, I go to glory! Be strong to carry the cross, be courageous in your suffering." Then she added, "Adieu, Adieu, adieu! And she transfigured into a dazzling white cloud, flew to the sky and disappeared." After relating the story, the author of the pamphlet provides corroborating evidence that the hand burned into the door was also the hand of the deceased Sister Therese. "In the presence of a large number of witnesses, they opened the tomb of Sister Therese. The burned imprint on the door matched exactly the hand of the deceased. The handprint on the door, added the Bishop Segur, is kept in the convent. The Mother Abbess, a witness to the fact, showed me the imprint, knowing that I was confirming these details, as reported by Bishop de Segur. I wrote to the bishop of Foligno, told him the stories were confirmed, and I sent him a facsimile of the imprint and the hand." The author adds, "Therefore, Divine justice punishes the slightest faults."[50]

Narratives of firsthand accounts of people who witnessed souls in purgatory are generally interspersed with recommended devotions and prayers for the souls in purgatory, mimicking the fashion of other nineteenth-century periodicals that feature a *miscellany* of content. In narratives where materiality is most invoked, for instance, where souls appear to be flesh-like and leave physical evidence of their visits, commentary on the nature of spirit and matter is interspersed with the story plot. In the tract *The Consolations of Purgatory*, a nun reports her experience of seeing a recently deceased colleague burning in fire and asking for prayers. "We read in the Life of the Venerable Mother Agnes of Jesus that while she was praying by the grave of one of her nuns, who had died a few days before, the deceased Sister suddenly appeared before her, clothed in her habit, and the reverend Mother felt as if her face were scorched by fire. The nun addressed her in tones of deep grief: 'Oh, my Mother, if men only knew how intense are the pains of purgatory, they would be always on the watch to avoid them.'" The explanation of how the nun, who is assumed to be a spirit, could appear physical occupies more space in the narrative than the report of the appearance. It begins with the question of the location of purgatory, "Although the soul after death is no longer united to the body, of which it is the substantial form and motive principle, St. Thomas and many others declare that there is a special place set apart for the punishment of the souls in purgatory, and that this place is not heaven, nor hell, but some intermediate place not far from hell."[51]

The explanation focuses on the issue of spirit and matter and the nature of the pains: "The fire of purgatory is an intelligent fire. It affects the intelligence, the memory, the sensibility, the whole soul. All the faculties of the soul are invaded and penetrated by the avenging fire; for the fire of purgatory has this peculiarity: that it is not, like the material fire of the earth, a gift of the wisdom and goodness of God, but the instrument of His avenging justice, destined to correct and purify whatever in man has been soiled by sin. The souls in purgatory suffer in their thoughts painful and distressing visions and imaginations; in their memories, poignant remorse and regret for the past; in all their senses, different tortures, corresponding to the nature of the sins committed and the degree of culpability contracted in each sin." For the author reporting this private revelation, the materiality of purgatory is conveyed together with less concrete elements like memory and thoughts. The explanation, which follows the narrative about a spirit who appears, incorporates abstract elements with references to locality and materiality and appears to combine the physically punitive version of purgatory and the new, Faberian version. Finally, in contrast to the description provided, the author ends his discourse with a disclaimer: "The Church, as a learned theologian observes, has not defined anything to be believed as of faith in respect of the duration or nature of the pains, or of the place of purgatory (F. Perrone, Tract. De Deo Creator e, p. iii., c. vi.)."[52]

In other periodicals, the principle of Divine Providence mediated between a version of purgatory that focused on literal fire and punishment, and an abstract, Faberian version that focused on the less concrete punishment of loss. Divine Providence offered a way for individuals to witness the direct intervention of God in the world and events, without recourse to direct physical evidence like scorched shirts or bloodstained garments and doors. Divine Providence, as articulated by John Newman and William Faber, was the principle whereby God acted in particular situations, most often as a response to prayer and devotion. Although the events of Providence were not obvious to individuals as they occur, upon reflection individuals could determine the principle working in their lives.

Divine Providence, in the Catholic tradition, was articulated by Thomas Aquinas in the *Summa Theologica* as a refutation of the belief that it was through chance that the universe and the things in it emerged, a position held by Greek philosophers Democritus and Epicurius. Instead, Aquinas maintained that God governed the universe and created things for a purpose. Through observation of human events and the natural world one can surmise a divine plan, or Providence. In the nineteenth century, Protestant and Catholic theologians revisited debates regarding Providence versus random chance, as empiricism and the theory of natural selection seemed to indicate that chance played a significant role in the creation of the natural world.[53]

The theology of the eighteenth-century French priest Louis de Montfort (1673–1716) was very influential for nineteenth-century Catholic theologians who wrote about Divine Providence. Montfort's works and life were very popular, and Pope Leo XIII beatified him in 1888. His books were translated and read widely throughout Europe and North America, and William Faber published a popular translation of his book *A Treatise on the True Devotion to the Blessed Virgin Mary*. Between 1839 and 1887 there were published no less than four biographies about Montfort, most of which focused on the work of Providence in his life.[54] During his life, he wrote more than one hundred hymns and Providence figured prominently in many of them.[55] His definition of Providence reflected Aquinas's in that he believed that events reflected a divine order and arrangement. At the First Vatican Council (1869–1870), Divine Providence was promoted to counter a Deistic interpretation of God who rules the world and then retreats. Instead, "all that God has created, he watches over and governs by his Providence." For Catholics, Providence was a principle that addressed God's actions and interventions in the world, and the person's unique, individual place within this plan.

The Poor Souls Advocate was a monthly periodical published by Fr. Francis B. Luebbermann and "an association of priests" between 1888 and 1907. Francis Luebbermann was ordained in 1880. He became a parish priest in Mount Vernon, Ohio, and continued there as priest for the rest of his life. He devoted himself to several publications. Along with *The Poor Soul's Advocate*, Luebbermann also published the German equivalent, "Der Armen Seelen Freund" (The Poor Soul's Friend) between 1888 and 1893.[56] The focus of these journals adhered mostly to a Faberian view of purgatory and a *new materiality* focused on Divine Providence as a manifestation of the reality of purgatory, rather than the manifestations of souls engulfed in flames. For the most part, *The Poor Souls Advocate* portrayed a version of purgatory where souls and the living mediated their relationship through church-sanctioned devotions, and, as a result, the living were able to witness the reality of purgatory and their relationship to the dead through acts of Providence. Additionally, the periodical referenced confraternities and other religious organizations in Canada and Europe devoted to the holy souls in purgatory. In this way, it presented itself as a cosmopolitan forum for American Catholics that bound them in a web of connection to the global Church Militant and the Church Suffering.

In line with establishing itself as a publication in conformity with official Church doctrine, Luebbermann references the church officials who have granted their approbation to the periodical. "'The Poor Soul's Advocate' has the approbation of the Rt. Rev. F.S. Chatard, D.D., Bishop of Vincennes, and of the Rt. Rev. M. Marty, D.D., Bishop I.P.I. and Vicar Apostolic of Dakota; and no doubt will received the warm approbation of all Archbishops and Bishops of the country."[57] He also, however, offers a warning about devotions to the souls in purgatory: "All devotions must be based on the firm ground of Catholic teaching. Otherwise, they will soon develop into vague and dreamy sentimentalism and finally into fanaticism and superstition." Luebbermann invokes post-Enlightenment terminology, as did John England in the *Catholic Miscellany*, to frame the periodical, "Thus only will our devotion be rational, enlightened and pleasing to God." With reference to the legends and narratives about the intervention of souls from purgatory, of which England never wrote but which fills the pages of Luebbermann's periodical, he writes, "The most approved legends will be culled from authentic sources for the interest and edification of the readers."[58]

In the first issue of the periodical Luebbermann explains that the principle of Divine Providence was at work in the establishment of the magazine. Invoking the global Catholic experience of the closing Sunday of the
Jubilee year of Pope Pius XIII, Luebbermann notes that all priests around
the world were enjoined to offer the Mass of the Requiem for the Souls
Departed. "This grand and unique occurrence in the history of the holy
church is the proximate occasion of publishing this periodical." After establishing this connection, he continues with an explanation of how an association of priests came together in an unlikely way to found the magazine.
"For a long time several priests in southern Indiana had contemplated
a publication in the interests and for the benefit of the suffering souls in
Purgatory. At a meeting, seemingly very accidental, they gladly surprised one
another with the expression of this idea, and at once banded together to
put it into execution."[59] The legends that were offered to edify readers
revealed that individuals were in direct communication with the souls in
purgatory, and by paying attention to events one would detect the workings
of Divine Providence.

Despite Fr. Luebbermann's earlier statement that he would provide
"approved legends from the most authentic sources" of the tradition, many
new and contemporary anecdotes about the holy souls in purgatory filled
the pages of *The Advocate*. Additionally, whereas other periodicals devoted
to purgatory featured the stories of nuns, *The Advocate* printed stories
about priests who interacted with souls in purgatory, though certainly
visions of nuns were included. By focusing on anecdotes from priests, *The
Advocate* differed from what had become normative within pamphlets,
periodicals, and devotional manuals focusing on purgatory. "A Wreck on
the Banks of the Delaware" is a typical legend. Instead of focusing on a
saint from tradition, the tale is told by an American priest, who recorded
his experience expressly for *The Advocate*. The tale reveals how Divine
Providence is used as an interpretive framework for understanding the
relationship between the living and the souls in purgatory. Through prayer
to the holy souls, a priest comes to understand that he was placed in a situation purposely to help others, and thus is shown how the invisible machi-
nations of Divine Providence are made visible in retrospect.

Despite being a contemporary tale from real life, the priest's story is
dramatic and chilling. "B." describes how, one Sunday evening, as he
was riding in a sleeping coach on a train, he became suddenly aware of
"a strange and unaccountable feeling of uneasiness." He felt, in fact, "that on
this trip I was going to meet my death. I had said the Itinerarium (clergyman's

prayer for a journey) with more than usual attention." Feeling worse, he "drew forth my Rosary and as I resolved years ago always to recite it for the Souls Departed, I now commended them to God and myself in turn to them." Unfortunately, his premonition proved correct. During the night, after a series of violent jolts, he and several passengers stepped outside of their coach rooms to witness a horrifying sight—most of the other train cars in the Delaware River. "Down a deep terrible embankment in the shallow water of the river we beheld our own engine and six cars upturned, splintered and already enveloped in flames. Trainmen and passengers immediately devoted their whole self to the work of rescue." One trainman, who was unfortunately wedged into a corner of the wrecked engine, was, horribly, "abandoned to his dreadful fate," even though "a hundred hands were ready to do anything for his rescue." The priest at once helped the injured, and in some cases provided the Sacrament of Absolution from sin, where there was no hope left. "One wealthy young man, a Catholic from New York, attributed the wonderful preservation of so many passengers to the presence of a priest among them. I myself thanked the poor souls in Purgatory for my narrowest of all escapes, and, then and there, resolved to make a public acknowledgement of thanks at the first opportunity, and ever to invoke their protection on any future journey."[60]

Another anecdote about a monk of the Society of Jesus reveals the intimate connection between the living and the dead, mediated through the Mass. While working as a porter in the Novitiate of St. Andrew in Rome, the monk "C." used his position to ask rich and influential persons for money to conduct Masses for the holy souls. He kept a garden of great beauty near the house and promised, in exchange for a gift for the holy souls, that he would create a flower garden or beautiful hedge named for the benefactors. He was able to acquire enough money to have Masses done continuously. "When the hour of his own death came, souls that he had helped stood visibly near him, and remained with him to the end to the great consolation of those surrounding the bed."[61] The index of works represents a focus on purgatory as less of a place of corporeal punishment than a doctrine that underscores the connections between the living and the dead that reveals the work of Divine Providence. Faber's works figure prominently in the periodical, including his poetry "The Queen of Purgatory" and "The Memory of the Dead."

Another North American periodical published at the same time as *The Advocate* was *Tabernacle and Purgatory*, which is still being published today as *Spirit and Life*. The periodical was published by the Benedictine Sisters

of Perpetual Adoration, in Clyde, Missouri, under the direction of Rev.
P. Lucas, O. S. B. In 1874, the Benedictine Sisters traveled from Switzerland
to help minister to the German population of immigrants who had settled in Missouri. They brought their periodicals with them, one of which
was the German *Tabernacle and Purgatory: Manual of the Confraternity of
the Perpetual Adoration of the Blessed Sacrament All under the Protection of
St. B. Benedict to Rescue the Poor Souls in Purgatory, the 3rd Order of St. Benedict
and St. Benedict's Association for Priests.*[62] The publication had been published in Germany in the 1880s, and the archconfraternity was founded in
1877 under Pius IX in Austria. Once it was transferred to North America
in 1893 under Leo XIII, in 1910, under the pontificate of Pius X, it received
the right of extension throughout the entire world.[63] Like *The Advocate*,
Tabernacle and Purgatory was published in English and German. It was a
quarterly that focused on devotions for the holy souls in purgatory, with
miscellany including anecdotes, church doctrine, and poetry.

As with other periodicals devoted to the souls in purgatory, the editors
of *Tabernacle and Purgatory* published the approbations of church authorities. "Reverend Dear Mother, I beg to say that your periodical of the Blessed
Sacrament 'Tabernacle and Purgatory' has my hearty approval and recom-
mendation. Wishing the Association of the Perpetual Adoration every success and blessing. I remain, with great regard, Very sincerely yours in
Christ, M.F. Burke, Bishop of St. Joseph."[64] They also took care to publish
remarks about private revelation attributed to Pope Urban VIII, "according to the decree of Pope Urban VIII in the year 1634 and 1641, in so far as
the Church has not decided upon them, claim only human credence."[65]

The anecdotes and legends reported in *Tabernacle and Purgatory*, which
include the visions of nuns of the past and present, as well as visions of
saints from tradition, reinforce the nineteenth-century trend in progressive theology that diminishes afterlife punishments. Several of the reports
specifically reinforce substance dualism, which privileges spirit over matter, as spirits are characterized as being of entirely different substance
than matter. Many of the representations of purgatory found in *Tabernacle
and Purgatory* go far beyond Faber's version in that within these anecdotes
even the damned are given a second chance of salvation, and purgatory is
represented as a place of joy.

A short essay from the May issue of 1905, titled "True Happiness of the
Poor Souls," reveals a version of purgatory that emphasizes its pleasures
as opposed to its pains. After conceding that traditional portrayals of purgatory paint it as a place of "indescribable suffering and unspeakable pain,"

the author offers a corrective, stating that purgatory "still has its joys." The "true joys" of purgatory are not sensible, but affect the soul. "*True joys* penetrating into the innermost part of the soul and in comparison with which all earthly happiness is truly nothing." The author ends her essay with a quotation from Faber: "I prefer the least and last place in purgatory to all the deceitful pleasures of this world." The author's further remarks suggest that she understands that she might offend readers with this version of purgatory, so she addresses this possibility: "Perhaps one or the other of our readers may think that what P. Faber says is somewhat strange. And still, his view concerning the choice between the pleasures of this life and the torments of purgatory, is perfectly correct."[66]

Other anecdotes about visitations from souls in purgatory specifically reference spirit and matter. A woman from France named Huguette Boy encounters the apparition of her wealthy aunt and claims that the souls in purgatory do not partake in the substance of matter, because they are ethereal, and, more surprisingly still, souls who are damned are given a second chance of salvation. Boy was near death with a bleeding wound when one morning a young, beautiful, white-robed maiden entered her room and offered to care for her. "But as soon as she had touched the patient, the latter found that her wound had been immediately healed." All who heard about the healing were amazed, and during the following night Boy again saw the apparition. This time, the apparition explained that she was Boy's aunt, dead for seventeen years. She had died suddenly, with mortal sin and had been condemned to hell. "I would have been eternally lost, had not Mary obtained for me the grace of true contrition. The abyss of hell was thus closed under my feet, but for seventeen years I have languished in purgatory." Boy protested and reminded the apparition that her aunt was quite old and ugly, yet the apparition was beautiful. The apparition replied, "Remember my daughter, that thou dost not see my former body, which rests in the grave and will rise only on the last day. I have an ethereal body that I may be able to speak to thee."[67]

Representations such as this present an obvious break from the tradition of purgatory as a sensible place and form the preponderance of the anecdotes in *Tabernacle and Purgatory*. However, there are a few short essays that delve into the material aspects of purgatory. These tend to portray purgatory as a place where there are two pains in purgatory, the pain of loss and the more traditional, material pains associated with fire. In "The Three Great Divisions of Purgatory," which describes the geography of purgatory according to St. Frances of Rome (1384–1440), a higher level of purgatory is contrasted with two lower levels. In the higher levels, souls who are only partially tainted by sin suffer the pain of loss, and in the middle regions "those souls are confined that have to atone for greater faults, principally by the pain of the senses." The lowest region is situated near hell, and is filled "with luminous fire."[68] The hierarchy of purgatory aligns with Aquinas's regarding matter and spirit. Spirit is privileged as a more perfect state, whereas matter is associated with being lower and less perfect, along with the senses. The lower region is reserved for the most sinful souls.

The success and longevity of *Tabernacle and Purgatory* are attributable to its acclimation to the cultural developments that witnessed the shifting nature of representations of hell in which its punitive aspects were downplayed. Other publications about purgatory also enjoyed similar longevity. Like the *Liberateur*, *The Echo du Purgatoire* was a French periodical published in the mid-nineteenth century, although it had a longer run and it enjoyed the approbation of Church authorities, including a bishop, who gave it his imprimatur from its first publication. "*L' Echo du Purgatoire* ran from 1865–1921 without interruption except for the Franco-Prussian War, then began again in 1923 and continued until 1940."[69] It featured stories of souls from purgatory and the visions of nuns, and had a largely female readership. Whereas the *Liberateur* was shut down amid scandal, *L'Echo* enjoyed much success and approbation. What accounted for the difference in reception? The editor of the *L'Echo du Purgatoire*, R. P. Francois Gay of the Society of Mary, wrote that the monthly magazine was intended "to increase the charity with respect to the souls in purgatory, and to bring knowledge of the events and works to increase the piety of their faithful devotees."[70] Part of the reason for the respectability accorded *L'Echo du Purgatoire* was that its editor took pains to confine the visions of purgatory, and private revelations, to those that conformed strictly to Church doctrine.[71] The visions, usually related by nuns who witnessed souls in purgatory, advocated purgatory as a place of loss, rather than a place where souls agonized in pits of fire in the middle of the earth. In other words, the visions were more in line with the Faberian version of purgatory as an abstract place of loss. Like its counterparts in North America, the version of purgatory in *L'Echo* aligned with the signs of the times. The visions de-emphasized the materiality of purgatory, provided a new version of devotions of purgatory as a means to participate in Divine Providence, downplayed punishment, and reinforced substance dualism that privileged spirit over matter.

Conclusion

In the 1940s, the content of the Benedictine publication *Tabernacle and Purgatory* reflected developments within Catholic culture that focused more on "Catholic action" and less on devotions and narratives about purgatory. Writing today about this shift in emphasis, the editors note, "In the 1940's the publication began to reflect shifts in theology, focusing more on Catholic action, the sacraments and catechesis, and less on devotions. The name change to *Spirit and Life* in 1965 reflected broader spiritual focus and the views of Vatican II."[72] The members of the religious order "The Society of the Helpers of the Holy Souls in Purgatory," founded by Eugenie Smet, or Sister Mary of Providence in 1856 changed the name of their order to "The Society of Helpers." Their reasoning was the same as that of the Benedictine sisters, although they were more explicit in distancing their order from a nineteenth century devotional framework. "The language and the images of Purgatory in the 19th century spoke of purifying, fiery prisons, of souls languishing there because they had not paid off the debt of their sins. In today's language, 150 years later, it may seem somewhat quaint and dated as a title but the fundamental thrust of the foundation is still there. Purgatory, purification, is an ongoing process in our lives. How often have we heard the phrase about someone who endures great suffering: 'She has done her Purgatory here.'"[73]

The gradual shift from conceiving purgatory as a place to its status as a spiritual condition was, for the most part, thoroughly accomplished by the mid-twentieth century. What had been common within mid-nineteenth-century pamphlets about purgatory—references to the physical presence of souls appearing to the living, revelations of the real fire of purgatory, and other references to its physical nature—gradually gave way to narratives of interactions with the souls in purgatory that appear as miraculous events occurring within a framework of Divine Providence. Within periodicals devoted to purgatory, such as *Tabernacle and Purgatory*, the narratives of Divine Providence and holy souls give way to narratives focusing on Catholic action in the world. The theme of purgatory would eventually be replaced completely.

5

The Ghosts of Vatican II

PURGATORY APOSTOLATES AND THE LEXICON
OF THE SUPERNATURAL

APPROXIMATELY SIXTY YEARS after the Society of the Helpers of the Holy Souls changed its name to the Society of Helpers, Catholics Mike Humphrey and Brian Bagley started an Internet apostolate devoted to spreading information about purgatory, which, they state on their website, has been "overlooked for *way too long*."[1] They chose to name their apostolate after the *Society of Helpers*, but they reinstated the old name and reference to the holy souls, so they are officially called The Helpers of the Holy Souls. On their website they feature a picture and short history of the founder of the religious order, Eugenie Smet, Sister Mary of Providence (1825–1871). (See fig. 5-1.) The average visitor count to their website in 2012 was 14,300 visitors per month, which has increased at an astonishing rate. Between January 2013 and March 2013, visitors to their site grew by 20,000.[2] Mike and Brian's effort to bring attention to purgatory and to devotions to the holy souls is typical of a small group of Catholics who are not affiliated with religious orders. The purgatory apostolates, most of which contain the approbation of bishops, take the form of publications and websites. A lay apostolate is a ministry organized by the laity in conformity with the magisterium of the Church, intended to facilitate a specific goal, such as alleviating hunger, ministering to the poor, or educating about a doctrine or devotion. Purgatory apostolates are created with the goals of educating Catholics about the doctrine of purgatory and creating prayer groups to alleviate the suffering of souls in purgatory. The websites feature old books about purgatory and devotions to the holy souls, published between 1400 and 1920. With an occasional rare exception, they do not publish new revelations about purgatory. The publications about purgatory, some of which are best sellers, contain copious anecdotes from medieval, early modern, and nineteenth-century purgatory narratives. They

Helpers of the Holy Souls - Apostolate of Purgatory
Sitemap - Search

Blessed Mary of Providence in the original habit of her Society

Mission

Helpers of the Holy Souls is inspired by Blessed Mary of Providence and the original mission of the Order she founded in 1856, Society of Helpers of the Holy Souls. Our presence on the web is a combined effort of Brian Bagley and a more computer-literate colleague and long-time friend, Mike Humphrey.

Mike also has managed and maintained his own apologetics web site AskACatholic.com since July 1996 when our Apologetics group was first founded. In all probably it was the very first Catholic Apologetics support group in the New England area, if not, the Eastern Coast.

Both Brain and I think the work of praying for the Holy Souls in Purgatory has been overlooked **for way too long.**

Our mission, one of mercy, is to relieve and gain release for the suffering souls in Purgatory who can no longer help themselves. We do this by monthly donations, collecting loose change and returning redeemable cans and bottles. All funds collected are used to place Holy Masses for all the Holy Souls in Purgatory.
We also fulfill our mission by holding a Holy Hour for the Holy Souls every Tuesday night immediately following the 7:00pm Holy Sacrifice of the Mass at the Fatima Shrine Chapel on Route 126 in Holliston, MA. All are welcome.

FIGURE 5-1 Helpers of the Holy Souls Website Mission, accessed January 24, 2014. Reprinted with the permission of Mike Humphrey and Brian Bagley.

focus on visits from souls who are tortured by fire and other forms of material punishments. By and large, they do not feature the abstract, Faberian version of purgatory as a condition or state of loss.

The apostolate movement spans the political spectrum from progressive to conservative; the leaders of the apostolates, as well as those who visit the websites and buy books and pamphlets about purgatory, are young, middle-age, and old. Through interviews, online surveys, and discussions, a picture emerges that illustrates that this small-scale movement is part of a larger context that includes reactions to the changes consequent to the Second Vatican Council. Although many of the leaders of the movement emphatically align themselves with the magisterium of the Church and the decisions of its hierarchy, they voice an implicit, and often explicit, criticism of Vatican II. As one purgatory apostolate editor said, "They didn't mean to, but when the changes [of Vatican II] happened they changed people's understanding of what happens after you die. Now people just think that you either go to heaven or hell. Well, it doesn't happen that way. Plus, now all the souls in purgatory have been completely forgotten. I know they didn't mean that to happen, but it happened."[3] This man was seven years old during the Second Vatican Council. On the popular website About.com, Catholicism expert Scott P. Richert notes that "indeed, many Catholics believe that Purgatory was tossed out with Vatican II, and since no one wants to believe that someone he knows has gone to Hell, we naturally

tend to think that everyone who dies goes straight to Heaven."[4] Regarding
the association of Vatican II with a loss of knowledge about purgatory,
historians of Catholic history appear to agree with the assessments of the
laity. Charles R. Morris notes that "after Vatican II, notions of Hell, damnation, and mortal sin, almost overnight, virtually disappeared from the
American Church—another example of 'spirit of the council' prevailing
over the texts."[5]

Scratching the surface of the criticisms reveals dissatisfaction not only
with the Church's silence about purgatory but also the ways in which the
contemporary Church, in its rare instances where leaders do speak of the
doctrine, utilize what one practitioner called "watered down language."[6]
Citing the dearth of contemporary works about purgatory, editors and apostolate leaders say that referencing old works and making them available on
their websites is necessary in order to educate Catholics about purgatory
and to keep the prayers alive for the souls languishing there. As one editor
said, "There are no more classics of purgatory. That's why we put the old
books up on our site. In order for people to know about purgatory, they
need to read these books. How else will they know about it?"[7] The choice
of old books placed on the websites and available as "classics of purgatory"
is revealing. The physicality of purgatory is thematic in all of the publications of the apostolates. One cleric, writing about contemporary views
about purgatory, suggested that the lack of discussion among Church leaders about purgatory as a physical place is a form of denial that it exists.[8]

The leadership of the Church is not the only institutional body that is
silent regarding purgatory. Within the last twenty years there have been
important sociological studies of American Catholics.[9] None of these studies references purgatory or its associated devotions. Guillaume Cuchet's
important historical work *The Twilight of Purgatory* provides evidence that
the devotion declined in France demonstrably after the First World War.
A review of Catholic popular periodicals suggests that this is the also the
case in the United States, as narratives about purgatory are sparse or nonexistent in most of the fiction in Catholic periodicals between 1930 and
1950.[10] After the Second Vatican Council, the decline in devotions associated with purgatory is noticeable in several ways. The material support for
devotions to the holy souls was removed from worship services. Statues of
saints were removed from churches and elements of the former Roman
Rite, including many within the Requiem Mass (the Mass for the Dead),
were changed completely and forbidden in most instances. In the old
Requiem Mass the catafalque, which is the structure that supports a coffin

and serves as the visible sign of the invisible presence of the deceased, was removed from the liturgy. Traditional hymns were removed also, such as the "Dies Irae" (Day of Wrath), which was a medieval Latin hymn about the Day of Judgment. Finally, as is the case with Sister Mary mentioned in the introduction, interviews with Catholics, lay and religious, reveals that most Catholics today have little knowledge about purgatory.

This chapter explores the efforts of editors and publishers of purgatory apostolates to recover and spread knowledge about purgatory and to create "prayer" groups, online and within churches, to alleviate the suffering of souls in purgatory. Through interviews with the leaders of the apostolates and the authors of contemporary books about purgatory, as well as through an exploration of the published content of the authors and web-aposto-lates, I will explore the motivations that inspire this work. At issue are feelings of loss and nostalgia, and most significantly the desire to establish a church-approved connection to the supernatural that apostolate minis-ters feel was lost during the years after the Second Vatican Council.

Contemporary spokespersons of purgatory reveal shared motives and hopes, the most significant of which is their desire to embrace the empir-ical aspects of purgatory, which is forcefully asserted in the discussions and stories they choose to pass on. Why focus on purgatory as a physical place, especially as, historically, the "real fire" of purgatory and its status as a location has become associated with superstition and has become rele-gated to the periphery of official discourse? Purgatory narratives of mate-riality are important in that they provide practitioners with what they perceive to be the means to access the supernatural and knowledge of the otherworld. The physical status of purgatory, for these Catholics and their audience, lends credence to its reality, but more important, the stories and anecdotes about souls visiting from purgatory and about the visits of saints to the otherworld provide a geography, spiritual map, and a lexicon of the otherworld. Time and again the stories are accompanied by refer-ences to imprimaturs (albeit from pre-Vatican II eras) and other forms of authority, thus assuring contemporary Catholics that their curiosity and desire to know about the otherworld is sanctioned, if not by contemporary society or the Church, at least by Church tradition.

Catholics Today: What Sociologists Tell Us

When I first undertook this study I believed that what I would find was that those who were publishing old books about purgatory and spreading their devotions would be conservative Catholics who were part of the pre-Vatican II cohort, or those who were adults during the Second Vatican Council. I believed that they would have been very vocal opponents to the changes brought about by the Second Vatican Council. I believed this because I had interpreted the impetus to revive old purgatory stories as nostalgic, or in other words, as a desire to return to the past. I was wrong. While I did find that some of the editors of purgatory apostolates certainly fit this description, most did not. The diversity of people who are actively involved in reviving devotions to souls in purgatory reflects the diversity among American Catholics generally. Distinctive among the leaders of the purgatory apostolates, however, is the belief that after the Second Vatican Council the language and stories of purgatory were lost, and that it is up to them to revive them.

In a recent analysis of American Catholics, sociologists William V. D'Antonio, Dean Hoge, James Davidson and Mary Gautier surveyed beliefs and attitudes among generational cohorts and compared results between studies from the 1980s until 2005.[11] Cohorts were divided into four categories according to birth: a pre-Vatican II cohort was born before 1940, a Vatican II cohort was born between 1941 and 1960, the post-Vatican II cohort was born between 1961 and 1978, and Millennial Catholics were born between 1979 and 1987. At the time of the study, 2005, American Catholics were divided among these cohorts as follows: post-Vatican II Catholics made up the greater portion of Catholics in the United States, at 40 percent. Millennial Catholics were 9 percent of the Catholic population, and Vatican II Catholics constituted 35 percent. Pre-Vatican II Catholics constituted 17 percent of the population. While each category is diverse and spans the spectrum of conservative to progressive, the pre-Vatican II cohort is distinctive in that its members display a greater association of Catholic identity with an adherence to external Church authority. In the 1980s sociologist Eugene Kennedy proposed the "two cultures model of American Catholicism," which argued that there were two distinct cultures of Catholics in the United States.[12] Culture I relied on external authority and valued obedience to Church teachings and identified as conservative, while Culture II adherents viewed many Church teachings as being open to interpretation and their reliance on external authority was less prominent than Culture I Catholics. In the 1990s sociologists tested this hypothesis by using "confession" as the test case for determining adherence within each cohort.[13] Confession is a sacrament that typifies reliance on external authority, as a person going to confession reports a sin to an external authority that has the institutional authority to have the sin absolved. This study faulted Kennedy's model for being too extreme in its conclusion that these communities, or cultures, are polarized, yet it also revealed that within the pre-Vatican II cohort most Catholics tend toward or are definitely within Culture I. Within the Vatican II cohort, 75 percent tend toward or espouse the tenets of Culture II. This trend continues with 79 percent of Catholics within the post-Vatican II generation either tending toward or being a part of Culture II. Today, the two cultures model of Catholicism is being used as a way to speak of the pluralism of belief within American Catholicism, with each culture representing the poles, from conservative to progressive.

In his 2009 address to an audience at the Catholic University of America, sociologist James D. Davidson utilized Kennedy's approach to brainstorm ways to bring about unity among American Catholics. Acknowledging the shift in orientation from a culture of obedience to external authority to a more personalized, internalized interpretation of faith, he suggested that both cultures should be understood as historically situated, "both cultures [are] legitimate expressions of the faith, with one being a more appropriate emphasis than the other at certain times, in certain places, and for some groups more than others." Before the 1950s, when Catholics were struggling financially and were immersed within extended urban communities of faith, the tenets of Culture I—obedience to authority, conformity to faith, and attendance at public devotions—made sense. As Catholics moved to the suburbs and left their extended families and communities of faith, attended universities, and became financially successful, they adopted the tenets of Culture II. As Davidson concludes, "The shift can be viewed as a movement from one culture that made sense under the circumstances at that time, to another culture that seems to fit a new set of circumstances."[14]

While these studies do not directly address purgatory, they identify a correlation between afterlife beliefs and participation in religious practices. The belief in a punitive afterlife corresponds to a more active participation in sacraments like baptism and confession, as occurred in the 1950s. "That [1950s] faith included an image of God as a stern judge and a view of the laity as people who were prone to sin. As a result, laypeople believed that the road to heaven was narrow and that the road to hell was wide. They turned to the Church for help, both socially and spiritually. These conditions gave rise to very high levels of sacramental participation."[15] These Catholics baptized their children very young to ensure that they "would go to heaven (and not limbo)."[16] In describing the declining participation of the sacraments from the 1950s onward, the authors cite the growing wealth and declining birthrate of Catholics, and the change from "the image of God as a harsh judge" to that of "an image of God as an unconditional lover. As a consequence, the laity now believes that its access to heaven has increased and that the likelihood of going to hell has diminished. These conditions have led to lower rates of participation in most sacraments."[17]

The Purgatory Apostolates

These findings correlate differing images of God with levels of participation in sacraments, and suggest that the view of purgatory as a place of punishment would also correlate to a higher degree of sacramental participation. Taking the findings of the sociologists into consideration, one would expect that the leaders of contemporary purgatory apostolates, who advocate attending the sacrament of the Mass to relieve the suffering of the souls in purgatory, would be among the pre-Vatican II and Vatican II cohorts, as they are heirs to an image of God characteristic of the 1950s and prior. I examined eighteen purgatory apostolates, six of which are organized by Catholics who are part of the Vatican II cohort, that is, who were born between 1941 and 1960. The remaining twelve included members whose ages span all of the cohort groups. In terms of placing the apostolate members within either Culture I or Culture II, the leaders of two apostolates were firmly members of Culture I. They stated that Catholics must obey Church authorities, yet they also believed that the leaders of the Catholic Church, since the Second Vatican Council, were guilty of the heresy of modernism in their efforts toward ecumenism and their position on limbo and silence regarding the doctrine of purgatory. The rest of the apostolate leaders were firm in their assertions that they supported the current magisterium and were not sedevacantists (i.e., they did not believe that the Seat of Peter, the Pope's Chair, was empty). They appeared to be part of Culture II in that they expressed a view that people can still be identified as Catholics if their beliefs differed from the magisterium on some issues. To them, what mattered most was that Catholics maintained what they believed were core beliefs: that Jesus is present in the Eucharist, and that Mary is the mother of God. However, all members, whether a part of Culture I or Culture II, voiced criticism of Vatican II, which, without exception, they credited as being the historical event that inaugurated the disappearance of the stories, devotions, and beliefs regarding purgatory. Also, members expressed frustration with their local parishes and parish authorities, as they felt they were not as supportive of devotions to purgatory as the apostolate leaders would have liked.

There are two types of purgatory apostolates. Publishing apostolates, initiated by authors who write books about purgatory and then tour churches and conferences to spread the message about purgatory, compose 30 percent of the apostolates. Web apostolates, which are more numerous, make up the remainder. Each type shares a similar pattern and strategy. The publications rely on old purgatory narratives, none of which is published later than 1930. The websites feature a "library" of what are deemed purgatory classics, like *Purgatory: Explained by the Lives and Legends of the Saints*, by Fr. F. X. Schouppe, S.J., which received in imprimatur in 1893; and the early modern-era treatises on purgatory by St. Catherine of Genoa and St. Alphonsus Liguori. Another common feature is an emphasis on educating Catholics about purgatory, and acknowledging that purgatory has been "forgotten," though Catholics are still obligated to believe in it. In the introduction to his book *Hungry Souls: Supernatural Visits, Messages and Warnings from Purgatory*, Gerard J. M. van den Aardweg notes that "in our culture today, of the three distinctions that traditional Christian doctrine teaches may follow death and judgment—Heaven, Hell, and Purgatory—only belief in Heaven or some such happy state has widely survived."[18] According to apostolate leaders, this is a mistake that must be corrected because a great many people will be going to purgatory. In one apostolate called "The Mission to Empty Purgatory," a mathematical calculation is used to determine how many souls are languishing in purgatory, and lists the number of prayers required for their release. The calculation also takes into consideration the number of future souls who will be in purgatory and publishes the number of prayers needed to account for the current birth rate.[19]

In addition to the emphasis on education, the apostolates tackle head-on the problem of purgatory, which is its materiality. For these authors, web editors, and apostolate leaders, the physicality of purgatory is not a problem but a mystery that has not yet been solved by science. In the Helpers of the Holy Souls apostolate, the editors speak directly about the physical suffering of the souls in purgatory. "In the discussion of this question, where so much is shrouded in impenetrable mystery, I shall present the reader with some points freely translated from the works of the learned Cardinal Bellarmine. It is certain that besides this pain of loss, there is another, which theologians call the pain of sense, which consists in something more than being deprived of the consoling presence of God." Later, the editor says that this sensible pain is fire, and in a "very high degree of probability, that it is a material fire, and not at all to be understood in a figurative sense." Within the same section the authors acknowledge that souls are immaterial, and that this presents an apparent conundrum, "if the fire be material, and such as we have here upon earth, how can it act upon disembodied souls? This we cannot tell; but, although it is beyond the reach of our comprehension, it may yet be true."[20]

A New Framing of Purgatory: Direct Insight into Spiritual Realms

The last chapter revealed how the late nineteenth witnessed a shift in the framing of purgatory from a punitive and often physical place of punishment to a more forgiving, abstract condition where souls suffered, not from material fire, but loss. Contemporary stories of purgatory in many ways appropriate old, punitive versions that focus on the material suffering of souls, but also are innovative in interesting ways. The recovery of purgatory as a real place of physical suffering reinforces the reality of a doctrine in decline but also provides information into hidden worlds. Through reading about souls who return from purgatory, Catholics report that they gain an understanding and "insight into spiritual realms."[21] Within a culture where ghosts and the supernatural pervade popular culture, texts that affirm the reality of the supernatural but also bear the stamp and legitimacy of the imprimatur help establish boundaries with respect to a spiritual realm and in many ways authorize practitioners to engage in practices that allow them to feel connected to the dead. In this way practitioners feel less anxiety about their connections with the deceased. This became evident to me during my interviews with author and apostolate minister Susan Tassone, whose writings about purgatory are bestsellers within the Catholic devotional literature market. Susan is a popular speaker within the Catholic conference circuit. On several occasions during her talks, she noted that when one was engaged in praying and working on behalf of the holy souls, one needed a strong prayer life.

I first became aware of Susan when I was conducting research at the archive of the Mundelein Seminary in Illinois. I had tracked down an eighteenth-century diary of a nun who reported her mystical contacts with the souls in purgatory. An online catalog indicated it was in the special collections at the archive, but when I attempted to retrieve it, it was checked out. This surprised me. The archivist indicated that a woman had checked it out as research for her own book about purgatory. About a year later, a similar incident occurred at the archive of the Archdiocese of Philadelphia. By this time I assumed it was Susan who was searching the archives and identifying the same books, periodicals, and pamphlets as me, but using them in a much different way. I had since read all of her books and publications. Her bibliographies indicated that we were traveling a similar research path. Several of the texts we each found, like *The Way of the Cross for the Holy Souls in Purgatory*, originally published in 1928, had expired copyrights. Susan had renewed the copyright and edited and republished it. Her own book, *Praying with the Saints for the Holy Souls in Purgatory*, was chock full of many of the sources I had also found— periodicals that were never cataloged, stories about everyday people and their interactions with their deceased relatives, and pamphlets detailing popular devotions and rituals for the holy souls. She brought them new life as contemporary publications and shared them with an eager audience. In my interviews with Catholics, Susan's name came up repeatedly. "I have revived my prayer life by following Susan's prayers and devotions" and "Susan's book about the thirty-day devotion of Gregorian chant has helped me pray for my father" are typical of the sentiments expressed by Catholics about Susan's work.

After one talk in a neighborhood church in a Chicago suburb in 2008, Susan, who is a "Vatican II Catholic," related the story of how she became a spokeswoman for the "holy souls." As she tells it, she was working in the corporate world and was not currently raising funds for the Church, yet her ability to amass millions of dollars in order to provide Masses for recently deceased friends brought her to the attention of the bishop, then the cardinal, and finally Pope John Paul II. She has had an audience with Pope John Paul II (and provided me with a picture of her presenting her book to him), and is a regular speaker on Catholic radio and television. Susan's apostolate began when she sought to console a colleague who had lost a loved one. She offered to have a Mass performed for her friend's soul. The man made a monetary contribution that she transferred to the Church. Several other colleagues requested Masses. Before she knew it, she had almost $100,000. She soon reached the $1 million dollar mark. Her discussion related a series of coincidences that transpired in her life, including a healing from an injury sustained in a car accident, after she began her work. In this way her talk resembled narratives of Providence in which the work of God is revealed through synchronicity and coincidences.

The issues of authority and the legitimacy of devotions to the holy souls were evident after Susan finished her talk. Several times she mentioned that her books have the imprimatur. The parish priest was sitting in the back of the church, listening to her presentation. After the talk, several parishioners explained to me that "the priest was not happy. The parishioners invited Susan to come, and he doesn't believe in purgatory, hell or in miracles." The cofounders of other purgatory apostolates report similar discomfort with their parish authorities. One apostolate minister noted that he was upset that his parish priest was not enthusiastic about starting a purgatory prayer group at his church. He said that he had the blessing of a cardinal, yet he lacked local support for his efforts. Despite the lack of support of many church authorities for contemporary purgatory apostolates, the leaders of these organizations continue in their efforts to promote devotions associated with purgatory and to republish old anecdotes and narratives about purgatory. They believe that they are providing guidelines for practitioners who, since Vatican II, lack a lexicon of the supernatural.

All of the online apostolates provide catechisms of purgatory. These take the form of either being republished, old catechisms of the Church, or websites that address questions about purgatory. They address what happens in purgatory, what it looks like, who suffers there, the nature of the punishments, and how it is that immaterial souls could suffer material punishments. They also provide guidelines for practitioners who wish to engage in devotions and prayers to relieve the suffering of the holy souls. They promise special rewards, and providential life events, revealing that the connections one makes with the souls in purgatory are real. In short, they provide an empirically based model of a world that nineteenth-century American bishop John England believed is hidden from us.

Gerard J. M. van den Aardweg's book *Hungry Souls: Supernatural Visits, Messages and Warnings from Purgatory* is important to the movement and is featured on many of the apostolate websites. Van den Aardweg, who has a PhD and is a practicing psychotherapist, frames old stories of purgatory within the context of modern parapsychology and his studies of near-death experiences. In reframing these, he provides readers with guidelines about how to interpret visitations of souls from purgatory and recommends that readers distance themselves from "spiritualists." He also gives readers a view into the otherworld. *Hungry Souls* is published by St. Benedict Press of Tan Books and is listed as one of the press's bestsellers. It is accompanied by a video that shares many of the features of a conventional ghost story. The video opens with the scene of a dreary, foggy night, and soon pans to a window that creaks open, to reveal something in the shadows that remains very ambiguous. Many of the pictures featured in van den Aardweg's book were taken at the purgatory museum in Rome and are utilized as empirical justification for the reality of purgatory. "The paranormal evidence displayed in the Little Museum of the church and some additional evidence, notably the burned hand in the corporale of Czestochowa in Poland, are instrumental in developing devotion to the suffering souls. These evidences also appeal to the modern mind, with its preference for concrete proof and witness testimony."[22]

Van den Aardweg's recasts old stories of purgatory and situates them within the contemporary context of the paranormal. In this way he updates the stories and makes them relevant to readers. Most of the purgatory narratives van den Aardweg recounts are very old, dating from the nineteenth century and earlier. One exception is the relatively recent story about the post-death experience of an Austrian named Hellmut Laun, who was pronounced dead after an automobile accident in 1929. He relates Laun's story as a near-death experience, which has become a convention familiar to contemporary readers:

> Time and space ceased to exist, the contract with the environment was broken off, every feeling extinguished. But now I experienced something extraordinary: at first faintly, yet increasingly more clearly it dawned upon me that I "was there" again. I woke up as it were in an immaterial space separated from the world and captured myself as "I." My self-awareness was absolutely identical with my being a person in the world and yet of a different nature. It is difficult to find the fitting words for that. I would rather say: I perceived again like previously in the world, but receptive, not of myself, by my own will, and yet actively, intensively, and with awe.[23]

The author's commentary focuses on the theme of the nature of the otherworld. One of the issues the anecdote illustrates is the apparent paradox that an immaterial body can experience material effects. His explanation reveals that there is a correspondence between this world and the otherworld: "Laun wrote this many years after the fact, from memory. The fascinating thing is that his memory, apparently an immaterial faculty, retains this experience, this perception of non-material realities, at all. He translates his retained perception of immaterial realities back into earthly words and material images: distance, space, Center, Sun. The words and images he uses do not transmit these realities directly; they can only approximate them. However, irrespective of these limitations, it is clear that the basic dimensions of the psyche turn out to be the same in the hereafter as in this life: the I, consciousness, thinking, feeling, longing for happiness and fulfillment, in other words, by death 'life is changed, not taken away.'"[24]

For van den Aardweg, the physicality of purgatory is a code that provides Catholics with important knowledge. "Tangible manifestations and communications from Purgatory are, so to speak, coded in the language of images and words we can understand, but that is only an approximation of the language of the hereafter." Offering another explanation about how apparently immaterial things, like thoughts and feelings, can produce material effects, he states, "On earth, immaterial motions of the soul may produce sensations similar to physical burning: desires can burn, love may set a heart aflame, and the like."[25] Other apostolate ministers, although not specifically using the language of "code" that van den Aardweg utilizes, nevertheless describe how the physical aspects of purgatory provide vital information for Catholics. First, physical evidence provides proof that it is real, and lack of attention to its physical reality is tantamount to denying it exists, according to apostolate leaders: "This would seem to represent a practical denial of Purgatory, because it weakens, in practice, one's understanding of just how much the souls in Purgatory suffer."[26] Second, the tradition previous to the Second Vatican Council affirms the physical nature of purgatory. Commenting on the language of "condition" that popes John Paul II and Benedict XVI used to characterize purgatory, one apostolate minister stated they were ignoring years of tradition that painted a much different picture. "Both John Paul II and Benedict XVI made such statements as individual theologians, not as popes. They have gone against the traditional teaching of the Church in this matter without sufficient proof, evidence etc. That being said, such statements only add fuel to the already dying fire of belief."[27] According to Mike Humphrey and Brian Bagley of the Helpers apostolate, the weight of tradition points to purgatory as a physical place: "there is a real fire in purgatory. All the saints talked about it."

Attention to the physicality of purgatory and the reality of visitations from souls, even as it provides practitioners with important information about the otherworld, is also fraught with spiritual danger. Apostolate

ministers warn of the dangers of invoking the dead and also establish
guidelines for prayers for the dead, which include attendance at recommended sacraments such as the Mass. Van Den Aardweg cautions readers
about dabbling in non-Church sanctioned devotional practices associated
with the dead. "Regarding reports (parapsychological and other) about manifestations of the dead, we must critically distinguish between real and
pseudo-communications, real and pseudo-apparitions." The author distinguishes the difference between these as being one of context. The context of spiritualism is dangerous and should be avoided, the author warns,
as Catholic devotion and spiritualism are confused within secular literature about parapsychology: "These two fundamentally different categories
are often confused in the 'scientific' parapsychological literature." In a chapter titled "Holy Soul, or Demonic Imposter?" van den Aardweg admon-
ished readers to stay away from practices like "channeling," séances, and
spiritualism. "Since many people, including many Catholics, are not free
from superstition and sometimes do not resist the wishful expectation
that some or other spiritualist medium will bring them in contact with
the dead, it is not superfluous to repeat that all ghosts of spiritualism are
always demonic frauds."[28] Anthony S. Pasquale, or Brother Anthony
Josemaria, FTI, also cautions the Catholic reader against "evoking" [*sic*]
the dead. "Evoking souls of the dead is expressly forbidden by God, there
can be no doubt that whatever spirits are sent are not from God. If they
are not from God, they are not from Purgatory." However, Josemaria
states that souls from purgatory, *sent* by God, but not *evoked* by prayers, do
provide insights into the supernatural and this is acceptable. "Devotion to
the holy souls, perhaps more than any other devotion, cultivates a supernatural point of view."[29] Toward the end of her lectures on purgatory,
Susan Tassone indicated that she regularly attended Mass and other sacraments. All of the apostolate ministers recommend the Mass as the most
effective sacrament and means of securing relief for the souls in purgatory, as well as a form of protection from spiritual danger. "The Sacrifice
of the Mass is the most important thing we can offer for the release of
a soul in Purgatory."[30]

The connections that practitioners establish with the holy souls through
prayer and devotions produce real-world effects in their lives. Guillaume
Cuchet argued that the nineteenth-century revival of purgatory in France
produced a thaumauturgic innovation that involved the belief that the holy
souls could intercede on behalf of the living. Intercessory prayer figures
prominently in the apostolate communities. Several apostolate ministers

address the question of whether or not the souls in purgatory can actually help the living, much like the saints can intercede on behalf of the living if requested to do so. In a section of his book, titled "Can the Souls in Purgatory Help Us?" Josemaria relates that the private revelations of several saints offer confusing messages about whether or not the holy souls can benefit the living. However, he concludes that the holy souls, by the grace of God, do help the living when asked through prayer: "The Holy Souls can do nothing on their own, but are *very often* inspired and directed by God *to those devoted to them*, both to receive and provide aid."[31] Other apostolate leaders, in addressing the issue, cite nineteenth-century texts that contain imprimaturs, using these to authorize this somewhat controversial issue. The Internet apostolate *The Suffering Souls* relates the experiences of the author of *Purgatory Explained*, written in 1893. After distributing his "little" books about purgatory, his son was cured of an illness. Later, his wife fell seriously ill. Remembering the cure of his son, he again distributed the books on the street and within the parish, and his wife was soon healed.[32]

Other apostolates list readers' testimonies of intercession. Events attributed to the intervention of the holy souls range from broken appliances and computers that get fixed after a practitioner prays for the holy souls and asks for their interventions, to more serious problems like the healings of life-threatening illnesses or broken marriages. One woman wrote that her husband had filed for a divorce and had already "moved on" with another woman. She prayed a novena (a nine-day prayer) for the holy souls and her relationship with her husband was restored. The testimonies are posted by people who indicate that they are from the United States, and by references to illnesses and situations generally attributed to advanced age, the posters appear to be either from the Vatican II or pre-Vatican II cohorts. "Mary Ann's" testimony is typical of the posts listed on the site: "I have many stories to tell of my encounters with the holy souls. I went to Catholic Schools, where we were encouraged to pray *for* the Holy Souls, and also *to* them. I have become somewhat disabled and cannot get around by myself too easily. It was my joy to go to Mass each morning, and then back to church for a visit between 3 P.M. and 4 P.M. in front of the Blessed Sacrament, to say Divine Mercy prayers. I have also for over 20 years [led] the Holy Hour (Eucharistic Adoration). I try to use my iPad to spread the Faith. I am on Facebook, putting my faith right out there. I have had many healings, visions, and encounters." For housebound and elderly Catholics, the Internet is a useful tool for connecting to faith communities and for sharing their religious experiences with others.

The intercession of the holy souls in practitioners' lives provides them with concrete evidence of the reality of purgatory and continues the tradition of "Providence" revealed in purgatory narratives. As revealed in the last chapter, in the nineteenth century Providence became an important framework for interpreting the connections established by practitioners with the holy souls through prayer. It mostly replaced the punitive image of purgatory that had dominated purgatory narratives for hundreds of years, and provided an important image of purgatory as a place populated with deceased friends and family, ready to help in the daily affairs of the lives of practitioners. Coincidences and miraculous phenomena, manifesting as real events, assure practitioners of the efficacy of their prayers and in turn provide another form of evidence for purgatory. Internet pages listing the copious testimonies of these events are important means of legitimation. Susan Tassone begins her public lectures with an account of her own healing and the series of coincidences that have led up to it. In my interviews with apostolate leaders, without exception they detailed the series of what they termed "apparent coincidences" that led them to their work. This harkens back to the association of priests who formed the periodical *The Poor Soul's Advocate* in the late nineteenth century, who also credited a seemingly coincidental set of circumstances for the formation of their magazine. Although they term these events coincidences, they actually interpret them to be the intervention of God, initiated by the prayers of the holy souls, on their behalf.

Voltaire in Hell: The Criticism of Vatican II

To varying degrees all of the members of the purgatory apostolates credit the Second Vatican Council as being the definitive historical event that eliminated belief in and devotions to the holy souls in purgatory. According to them, Vatican II represents the triumph of the modernizing tendencies that had been pushing at the edges of the Church since the Enlightenment, and, through the efforts of progressive theologians, finally pushed through and dictated a new framework, the new "spirit" of the Catholic Church. Most of the apostolate ministers insist that their apostolates are in line with the spirit of Vatican II and they actively seek the authorization of their parish priests, bishops, and cardinals. However, their statements indicate that they believe that Vatican II and the ethos of the contemporary Church are apathetic to belief in purgatory. Other apostolate leaders are more vocal in their assessments of Vatican II and the contemporary

Church and its effect on belief in the doctrine of purgatory. They believe that the progressive theologians and leaders of the Second Vatican Council have fallen into the heresies of modernism. An examination of each of these positions, from the belief that the Church is in error with respect to modernism and perhaps even subject to diabolical forces, to the belief held by the majority of the apostolate members that the changes of Vatican II represent unintended consequences that had the unfortunate effect of eliminating belief in purgatory, reveals an underlying cohesive position: the Church has become a service organization focused on earthly affairs such as administering to the poor, which is laudatory; however, the connection to the supernatural has been severed, and the stories of purgatory are fading. For the apostolate ministers, there is a connection between the stories of purgatory and the reality of the supernatural. If the stories disappear, so does the link to the supernatural. The ministers are unified in their assessments: they trace the problems back to the effects of the European Enlightenment, if not specifically, than allegorically.

In his account of Hellmut Laun's travel to purgatory, van den Aardweg relates how a soul that appeared to be trapped in flames desired to come toward Laun, but was prevented from doing so. "On my way to the Center [heaven] I saw—as I clearly remember—a man; not in his body, and yet I saw him very real. This man, or rather this spiritual being, had its gaze fixed on that Center with an unquenchable craving, with a longing while at the same time caused deep pains. When I look back today, only his face, stiffened in pain, is clearly in my memory." Van den Aardweg comments, "He thinks the unhappy figure was Voltaire. The suggestion was that he was in Hell, as there was no hope for him to come nearer to the Center."[33] Van den Aardweg provides further commentary about Voltaire later in the text. He cites the works of nineteenth-century Catholic apologist, author, and prelate Louis Gaston de Ségur, whom van den Aardweg notes received papal recommendations, and who wrote, "Everyone knows that Voltaire expired in a fit of rage and despair. One can still see, in Paris, the room where this tragic scene took place." François-Marie Arouet, or Voltaire, was the French satirist, historian, and philosopher whose name is synonymous with the French Enlightenment: "Voltaire was the prototype and role model for the freethinkers of that time."[34]

The presence of Voltaire trapped in hell illustrates a common narrative that apostolate ministers related about Catholic history. Although they reflect varying degrees of historical knowledge about Church history, all identify Vatican II as the culmination of events that transpired during the

Enlightenment, as represented by the figure of Voltaire. Significantly, the apostolate ministers who were from the millennial cohort, born between 1979 and 1987, were the most articulate spokespersons of this narrative. One young Catholic monk and minister of a popular web apostolate stated that the Enlightenment gained traction after Vatican II: "Such teachings as Purgatory are regarded by post-Enlightenment secularists with complete scorn. We live in a post-Christian West, in the ruins, you might say, of Christendom. In this toxic milieu, pride often leads us to dim down the message of the Gospel, to accommodate the Catholic Faith to the spirit of the age, rather than fighting the good fight and militating against whatever detracts from the truths of our Faith. Alas, priests and bishops are not immune from pride and the desire for human respect."[35] Older members of the apostolates repeat the same narrative: "In the 19th century, under the influence of the Enlightenment, 'modern' minds were already doubting these truths of the Catholic Faith."[36]

The nineteenth and early twentieth centuries encompassed key historical moments in the Catholic Church's relationship to the values that emerged from the Enlightenment, such as the connection between reason and faith. In the United States, early-nineteenth-century Catholics like Bishop John England and other important American Catholics such as Charles Carroll, who signed the Declaration of Independence and whose Catholic family was the wealthiest family in the American colonies, were advocates of Enlightenment values. The presence of "modernist" or progressive Catholics within the Church did present a challenge to the hierarchy, and in 1848 Pope Pius IX wrote the *Syllabus or Errors* and an accompanying encyclical, *Quanta Curia*. These strongly worded documents, which identified as heresies the belief that reason informs revelation and that revelation changes with history, was an attempt to counteract the influence that the Enlightenment had on European society. Populist revolutions, erupting in 1848, spread throughout Europe and served as a further catalyst to Pius IX, as he viewed these developments as a challenge to Church authority. Fifty years later, Pope Pius X wrote another document that condemned values associated with the Enlightenment. In *Pascendi Dominici Gregis* (Feeding the Lord's Flock), he declared that "modernism" was the culmination of all heresies. These documents attest to the fact that progressive forces did present a significant challenge to the Church hierarchy, as it was interpreting its role during those years. Several apostolate ministers believe that the declarations of Vatican II reversed the efforts of popes Pius IX and Pius X to combat Enlightenment thought. What "began to germinate during the so-called 'Enlightenment' and are summed up by the word 'Modernism,' reached its culmination during Vatican II."[37]

The narrative told by the apostolate ministers is one of the decline of purgatory, inextricably linked to Enlightenment values that spread and culminated at the Second Vatican Council, and directly affected belief in purgatory as an otherworld destination. Apostolate ministers related that during Vatican II the interpretation of the Church changed. Its link to the supernatural was lost. The Church was interpreted as "pastoral" and focused on worldly affairs, instead of being, as one apostolate minister suggests, "the keepers of the keys of Peter." The keys of Peter, in popular iconography and in narratives, open the gate to the otherworld. Brother Maria reflects this view: "In the confusion that has entered the Church since Vatican II, certain dogmatic realities have become unpopular. Anything that speaks of the arduous or difficult, God's justice, the malice of sin and its punishment in the hereafter (whether in Purgatory or Hell), has been tossed out of the program of catechetics, preaching, and popular devotion."[38] Another Internet apostolate implicates Vatican II directly in this regard, stating that one of the errors of the Council was that it had "an overly strong focus on the dignity of man coupled with an *over-emphasis* on the natural virtues (as opposed to the supernatural virtues of Faith, Hope, and Charity which come from God alone rather than nature). This ignores original sin and the need for supernatural grace, leading to a sort of Utopianism that sees peace as possible without recognizing the Kingship of Christ, and seemingly gives the Church a new mission: peace on earth rather than the salvation of souls."[39] In less specific language, and being careful to not directly implicate the Church and Vatican II, other apostolate ministers reveal that the language of purgatory, and its stories, were lost after Vatican II. Answering a question posed by a reader about whether or not the Church was "rethinking" the doctrine of purgatory, an apostolate minister answered, "Over the past few decades members of the clergy or *teachers* have so de-emphasized Purgatory that folks have gotten the wrong idea."[40] One apostolate minister did not mention Vatican II but commented on the lost tradition of purgatory: "Today, there is little mention of Purgatory, even among Catholics."[41]

The Meaning of the Stories

Representations of purgatory were already on the decline before the Second Vatican Council, yet the purgatory apostolate ministers identify Vatican II as the historical moment when the belief in purgatory was eliminated from Church discourse. Today, apostolate ministers are recovering the latter version, often in full acknowledgment of the two traditions, stating that "there are two models of purgatory, the punishment model, and the healing model."[42] The punitive and material model of purgatory is important to some apostolate ministers as images and stories provide insight into the otherworld and help restore a connection to the supernatural that members of these communities feel has been lost. Brother Maria notes that the punitive version of purgatory provides incentive to moral action and reminds practitioners that there is justice. "That there is a Purgatory is a powerful witness to God's justice. In the days after Vatican II, it was common to throw out God's justice and speak only of his mercy. But if God is not just, He is not God."[43] According to Van den Aardweg, the images and physical manifestations of souls from purgatory act as a code or symbolic language that provides information about the otherworld, building a direct connection between the living and the dead.

Apostolate members are quite articulate about what the materiality of purgatory means to them—the stories of the physical visitations of souls offer a link to the supernatural, and their efforts to recover the lost stories of purgatory reveal an implicit criticism of the Church's acquiescence to secular culture. The membership of the apostolates reflects the diversity within American Catholicism itself—it spans age cohorts and reflects that most of the members belong to Culture II, not the more conservative Culture I. Therefore, the efforts of the apostolate ministers cannot only be framed as a conservative response to progressive movements within the Church. Significantly, the apostolate members are united in their criticisms of Vatican II and what they perceive to be the consequences of the Council for purgatory and the supernatural, which occur within a narrative that begins with the Enlightenment. While they applaud the contemporary Church's efforts to focus on issues like hunger and poverty, they believe that Church authorities have disregarded altogether its duty to "souls," and its emphasis on the supernatural. Their efforts to recover the stories of purgatory represent an attempt to restore this connection.

Historically, non-Catholics have criticized the Catholic Church for its emphasis on linking physical objects with sacred presence, so the apostolate minister's critique that the Church has eliminated references to the concrete aspects of purgatory is especially ironic. Purgatory as a material place has been linked to superstition, and this association is further engrained when Catholic popes describe purgatory in abstract terms. At least with respect to the doctrine of purgatory, modern Catholicism aligns with a

Protestant and modernist sensibility that privileges spirit over matter. Scholar Webb Keane notes that the underlying preference for spirit over matter is a basic assumption of European Protestant ontology, "where the value of the human is defined by its distinctiveness from, and superiority to the material world."[44] Dick Houtman and Birgit Meyer echo this in their assessment of the study of material culture: "This conceptualization entails the devaluation of religious material culture—and materiality at large—as lacking serious empirical, let alone theoretical, interest. This stance has long informed the study of religion."[45] Meyer also notes that although the "turn to materiality" in religious studies has ameliorated this situation somewhat, it still pervades popular discourse about religion. "It still lingers on in everyday parlance about religion in Western societies. The current fascination with current spirituality and New Age expresses a search for this kind of religiosity, while more outward-oriented, ritual-istic religions are branded as inferior, superficial, and even insincere."[46] Catholicism has long been viewed as the bastion of sacred materiality, yet the history of purgatory represents a case where the abstract has tri-umphed over the material. Additionally, within scholarship about religion, materiality and its link to the supernatural has only recently been identi-fied as a fruitful site of study, having long been ignored. Catholic historian Robert Orsi argues "While it is true that faith has not gone away, sacred presences have acquired an unsavory and disreputable aura, and this clings to practices and practitioners of presence alike."[47]

The purgatory stories that apostolate ministers are recovering focus almost exclusively on materiality and incorporate extra-textual evidence such as books scorched by fiery souls. Because these texts are imbued with the "unsavory" aura of materiality, Church authorities choose to distance themselves from them. However, it is clear that it is the materiality of the old purgatory stories that is vitally important to many apostolate ministers. At issue is the emphasis on the realism of the visits of the souls from purga-tory and the interpretation of purgatory as a place of physical suffering. The purgatory narratives offer an empirical model of the otherworld, and images and references to physicality are code and symbolic keys to a realm that is normally hidden. Within the language of metaphysical materialism, things that can be seen, felt, and touched are accorded the status of the real. These texts are not mere conveyors of information. They are under-stood by practitioners to be something much more.

Working within the *turn to materiality*, scholars of religion have addressed a variety of cultural forms and examined ways in which religion intersects with materiality to create meaning and support belief. These forms range from rituals, concrete structures and architecture, art and visual media, to apparitions and images. Although stories and texts have enjoyed relative prominence as subjects of study, an important sub-field within the study of religion is devoted to examining religious texts' performative and "iconic" aspects. Sacred texts and Scriptures are kissed, used in performance and ritual, sworn upon, displayed as objects, with practitioners encouraged to eat them. They have even been called "living." Other scholars have brought attention to how texts are employed in concrete ways through reading practices like "Lectio Divina" or sacred reading.[48] The purgatory narratives are unique from other sacred texts in several ways. At the heart of the narratives is an encounter between a living person and a deceased soul, which under any other context would be identified as a ghost. Yet these narratives are not interpreted as ghost stories. Additionally, these texts are old. With the exception of one or two contemporary encounters, the purgatory narratives date from before 1920, and most originate well before that, generally from 1600 through 1850.

In her nuanced analysis of the conversion narratives of St. Paul and Augustine, Paula Fredriksen elaborates about how traditional religions utilize the past to fashion the present. "Any traditional religion which sees its origins in a discrete historical revelation will hold consonance with the past to be the ultimate criterion of legitimacy. Put differently, the present is legitimate only to the degree that it rearticulates and reaffirms the past. But the past is not thus preserved so much as remade in the image of the present: The past is too important, in a sense, to be allowed to exist."[49] Fredriksen's analysis is helpful in considering the work of recovery in which ministers of the purgatory apostolates are engaged. Contrary to interpretations of Vatican II as being part of a continuous tradition, as advocated by Joseph Ratzinger and others, the work of the apostolate ministers to reframe the present with recourse to old purgatory books points to a perceived rupture in tradition that must be ameliorated. The statements of apostolate ministers indicate that they are hoping to fill in the gaps lost after Vatican II, that is, to re-establish the connection to the supernatural. The materiality or reality of purgatory conveyed in the old purgatory books is important to this project.

Generally, when scholars address the materiality of texts, they examine how texts function in rituals or as objects to be displayed. In other words, texts are examined in their capacities that exceed their semantic meanings. Unique to the old texts of purgatory is that their semantic meaning concerns the materiality of purgatory and often, extra-textual evidence helps corroborate the meanings of the texts. Additionally, the subject of the texts is an encounter between a deceased soul and a living person, which, if viewed from a dominant materialist paradigm, is an *impossible* encounter. It is also a paranormal and supernatural event. Scholar Jeffrey Kripal, writing about other impossible encounters in the works of authors of the supernatural, argues that "authors who write about seemingly impossible things...make these impossible things possible through their writing practices."[50] In some ways Kripal's work aligns with that of Paul Griffiths and Wesley Kort, who write about religious writing and reading practices. These scholars point to the real world effects that these narrative practices engender. Kripal, however, is writing about mostly contemporary authors. His analysis and theory of religion is helpful in understanding how the purgatory texts function within apostolate communities, and the authors he describes, such as Jacques Vallee and Bertrand Meheust, utilize similar language as several apostolate ministers, particularly van den Aardweg. For Kripal, supernatural phenomena "are, in the end, like the act of interpretive writing itself, primarily semiotic or textual processes."[51] By attending to the semiotic nature of the supernatural, Kripal articulates a theory that accounts for the perceived real-world effects these texts produce in the lives of practitioners.

Writing about Meheust, whose work details the early history of the paranormal, Kripal argues that "for Meheust, the symbolic function is about communication between different orders of reality, orders so different that they cannot communicate to one another in any straightforward or simple way. As an expression of the symbolic function, then, the religious image, the myth, or, in some cases, the dream does not work like a simple word or a precise number. Its meaning is not, and *cannot*, be a straightforward one."[52] In other words, the very nature of the supernatural encounter is symbolic and therefore must be interpreted. The act of interpretation, according to Kripal, opens a space that is charged with meaning for the practitioner. Paraphrasing Meheust, Kripal writes, "Such symbols are relays, as it were, from something invisible and structurally unknowable, something truly alien, to our own local forms of culture and consciousness." He follows this with his own assessment, *"to the extent that it permits at least some type of communication across radically different metaphysical orders, the symbolic function renders the impossible possible"*[53] (author's emphasis).

The apostolate ministers, while insisting on recovering the texts that focus on concrete versions of purgatory, do not insist that the narratives correspond in a direct way to reality. Instead, the narratives function as "code" and "symbol" of the other world. In a very real sense, they act as models in the way that models are employed by scientists as replicas of reality. Just as scientists utilize real models to engage with and understand concrete situations, so practitioners utilize purgatory narratives of the past. The narratives function as empirical models of the otherworld that provide vital information about the supernatural and provide a direct link to this world. Through reading and interpreting the texts, the impossible—interactions with deceased loved ones and a view of life after death—is revealed to be possible. Much of the purgatory literature details devotions and rituals and intercessory prayer that are intended to help practitioners establish connections to deceased loved ones. Providential events and apparent miracles reinforce these connections.

The narratives work to facilitate connections with the supernatural, confirming Kripal's analysis of the supernatural as semiotic. Kripal further argues that scholars of religion have tended to ignore the supernatural in religious discourse. He identifies a pervasive ethos of materialist thinking that functions as a framework that dictates the parameters of the discipline of religious studies. "The sacred as sacred—or what we have encountered here as the psychical and the paranormal as the experiential core of comparative folklore, mysticism, and mythology—is precisely what has been eclipsed in the contemporary study of religion."[54] He is a strong advocate for rethinking this misunderstood aspect of religion. "Whatever paranormal phenomena are, they clearly vibrate at the origin point of many popular religious beliefs, practices, and images—from beliefs in the existence, immortality, and transmigration of the soul; through the felt presence of deities, demons, spirits, and ghosts; to the fearful fascinations of mythology and the efficacy of magical thinking and practice. But if the paranormal lies at the origin point of so much religious experience and expression, is should also lie at the center of any adequate theory of religion."[55] Brother Maria noted the "scorn" with which progressive Catholics viewed old narratives of purgatory, revealing that an antimaterialist bias has not only infected scholars of religion but also religious practitioners.

Providence and Miracles at an All Souls' Day Mass

In November 2008, Susan Tassone invited me to hear her speak in Chicago. Her lecture corresponded with my attendance at the annual meeting of religious studies scholars, the conference of the American

Academy of Religion. At that point Susan had been dubbed by many Catholics as "the purgatory lady" due to her many appearances on Catholic television and radio. I had not met her yet, and she would be giving her lecture after a Mass for the Holy Souls which was being held at a Polish Catholic church. Speaking with her on the phone before I left, I commented, "Susan, we will meet on All Souls' Day. Isn't it a coincidence that I will be there on the day when the holy souls are most remembered?" "That is not a coincidence, Diana," she replied as a matter of fact. "I will see you then."

I brought my sister-in-law, Brigid. As we entered the church, we were struck by the gravity of the atmosphere. The seriousness of the occasion was made present by somber decor. From the large candles that dotted the periphery of Church, to the cavernous stone walls, to the frigid tempera-ture of the old church—all of the elements worked to convey a sense of solemnity. Incense conveyed a sense of decorum but also, in the darkness, hung low in the air like fog, giving the appearance of a very dreary night. Brigid and I had arrived late, and as we attempted to take our seats a man walked up and requested that we present the "gifts" at the altar. The gifts, or offerings, are comprised of the money that parishioners place in a bas-ket that gets passed from person to person. They are presented at the altar before the priest dispenses the Eucharist, which is the central sacrament of the Mass. We were surprised to be incorporated into the service but we happily obliged. As we returned to our seats I realized that we were attend-ing a Mass for the Holy Souls.

The service continued with the extinguishing, one by one, of candles that represented congregation members who passed away during the year. As each candle was put out, a bell tolled. The bell rang and echoed off the stones of the church walls, and congregants responded to a prayer for each soul, in an effort to help it on its way to heaven and to alleviate its possible sufferings in purgatory. Most of the congregants were praying inaudibly, although I could hear several praying in Polish. I looked around the con-gregation to see if I could recognize Susan, as I had seen her in photo-graphs. There were about 100 people in attendance, and Brigid had mentioned that she had been to the church a few times in the past. Brigid's grandparents were Polish American, and the church serviced a Polish American community and most likely other Catholic communities from Eastern Europe. I later found out that the church also operated a school for teaching the Polish language and it also supported a Polish dancing club. It was obviously a very vibrant Catholic community. I also noticed that it was a Saturday night Mass and I was impressed that there were so many parishioners in attendance. I was looking forward to hearing Susan's presentation and interviewing the parishioners about their beliefs about purgatory.

After the service, the priest walked to the back of the church and took a seat, and Susan walked to the front and began talking about purgatory and her apostolate. There were about seventy people in the audience, and when I later spoke with them, they revealed a familiarity with Susan's work and also with other purgatory apostolates. Jim, a former union organizer for thirty years, explained how he had stopped going to church due to the grief he suffered after two of his children died from Agent Orange poisoning. His belief was restored, however, after he began to read about purgatory, mostly because of Susan's books, and because of miracles he witnessed in his neighborhood church. His wife, Jane, nodded her head and told me about the statue of Jesus, in the same church, that moved, bled, and cried. "When we walk in, his eyes are open and by the time we leave his eyes are closed." Jim nodded in agreement and smiled. The couple told me that they follow Susan wherever she speaks in Illinois, like several other people with whom I spoke.

Jim and Jane indicated that they had to insist that Susan visit their church to speak. Issues of power were evident throughout the evening. Susan had introduced me as a "PhD who has come to hear me speak" and as a professor. She also mentioned that her books have the imprimatur of her bishop. Later, she explained to me that she mentioned my presence to show that purgatory was worthy of scholarly attention. On the one hand, the parishioners suggested that they had to gently insist that Susan be invited to speak at the church, and on the other hand Susan said that she was invited by the priest and her ideas of purgatory were in line with the catechism of the Church. The tensions with local parishes that apostolate ministers had mentioned in their interviews with me were palpable that night.

At the end of the evening, Susan asked Brigid and me for a ride back to her apartment. The night air was cold and frigid as Brigid and I hoisted Susan's suitcase full of books into the trunk of the car. Susan happily related the details of her ministry. She said that she never really set out to do purgatory apostolate work, and that when she begin she was shy and nervous in front of audiences. However, she found that her presentations were very effective. Her presentation that night and her success as a speaker defy her characterization of herself as nervous, and Brigid and I were amused by her humility. She was careful to state that her writings confirmed the view of purgatory as a process, not as a place or as a place of punishment. For the cover of one of her books, she requested that the holy souls not be engulfed in flames. In that sense, Susan was not like most of the apostolate ministers. Even as she revived the books of the past, she was careful to focus on the ones that confirmed the version of purgatory as a process, best articulated by Frederick Faber in the nineteenth century.

That meeting was many years ago. In the meantime, I've heard Susan several times speaking on Catholic radio, and just recently her publisher informed me that she was scheduled to appear on a special television show about purgatory on a cable network. My last actual conversation with her occurred after my family and I experienced a house fire. The fire burned down our residence and everything within it, except my research, which was in the only room untouched by the fire, above the garage. Thankfully, my family and I were fine, as we were away at the time. A kind colleague had reached out to us and allowed us to stay in his beach house, which went a long way in helping soothe the shock from the fire. I spent a lot of time on the beach with my children, playing in the surf and looking at the waves. The occupants in the neighboring beach house, dubbed "Terrapin Station," were having a wonderful time. Their music was loud, but thankfully tasteful. They apparently enjoyed one tune, because they played it over and over again. Coincidentally, it was a song that my deceased father had loved. I always associated the song with him, although I didn't know what it was about.

On one particular day, as I was picking through shells in the sand and the song was blaring—it was "Box of Rain" by the Grateful Dead—I found a shell that looked exactly like a skull. This experience was disconcerting, especially because the repeated sounds of the song had been bringing up memories of my father. I took the shell inside and searched for the song on the Internet. Apparently, band member Bob Weir had written the song about his own father who had died of cancer, and it was about his desire to ease his father's pain. My father had also died of cancer, and my experience had been similar, as, I am certain, it would be for anyone who has lost a loved one to cancer. I was struck by the synchronicity of the events, and the timing of finding out about the meaning of the song. A few hours later, out of the blue, Susan called me.

"Diana, are you OK? I've had some bad things happen in my life, and I thought that you might have also."

"I am OK," I replied, but I told her about the fire, and how it had been a shock, but most important I shared with her the strange song playing repeatedly and about picking up the skull-shell, and how it was all very strange and macabre. She was very consoling. "At times like these, the souls come around. They will let you know through these signs. Your father knows you have gone through a hard time. He is there with you."

Her words struck me. I didn't reply, as I couldn't, so we hung up the phone and I wondered at the strange coincidences of that day. That was the last time I spoke with Susan.

Conclusion

The purgatory apostolate movement is not large. However, its members have articulated a common goal, which is to address what they perceive to be a lack of knowledge about the doctrine of purgatory among Catholic practitioners. They are doing this, without exception, through reviving purgatory texts of the past, or, like Susan Tassone, writing contemporary books about the tradition of purgatory established by Catholic saints and theologians of the past. Although most of them align themselves completely with the magisterium of the Catholic Church, which is its official governing body, they also articulate an interpretation of Catholic history that suggests that the doctrine of purgatory has been forgotten, particularly after the reforms of the Second Vatican Council. In their efforts to revive knowledge of the doctrine, they pay particular attention to purgatory's material and spatial aspects, such as its fire. Along with scholastic William of Auvergne, who wrote that it appears illogical that an incorporeal soul can be burned by the fires of purgatory, yet it is so, contemporary apostolate leaders Brian Bagley and Michael Humphrey cite the work of Robert Bellarmine, a Catholic saint and Doctor of the Church, as a means to tackle this problem. On the fires of purgatory, they state: "it is a material fire, and not at all to be understood in a figurative sense."[56]

Conclusion

PURGATORY REDUX

RECENTLY, A COLLEAGUE stopped by my office. As we were chatting he told me that his father had passed away within the last year and then he asked me if purgatory was still a doctrine of the Church. When I affirmed that it was, he looked sad and explained that he wished that his father knew this just prior to his death, as his father had been confused by the Church's 2007 clarifications regarding limbo. His father thought that the Catholic Church no longer supported belief in purgatory, and was, according to my colleague, upset by the news. We continued our discussion, and I explained the problem of purgatory's materiality and how it has been variously described as a place with material fire, or as a condition of a soul experiencing the pain of loss. My colleague seemed perplexed.

"How does one represent a *condition of soul?*" he asked. He continued, looking confused, "What, even, does that mean?"

That is the question, of course. In the preceding pages I have shown that after the doctrine of purgatory was codified, issues of its materiality and its location became urgent as mariners began to map their journeys to distant lands and did not find purgatory, heaven, or hell. Coeval with this development were the efforts of the scholastic theologians who incorporated the logic and philosophy of Aristotle into their theological reflections, and found that the problem of purgatory was a logical conundrum within the burgeoning frameworks of metaphysical dualism. Upon examining instances where the problem of purgatory's materiality was most egregious, as in the case of St. Patrick's Purgatory in Ireland, it became apparent that earthly purgatories, and later spatial purgatories, caused logistical and political problems. Efforts to downplay these, or in some cases to completely erase them—as happened in the case of St. Patrick's Purgatory and its legendary as referenced by John England—became more frequent after the French Enlightenment. William Faber and other, more contemporary spokespersons for the Catholic Church have emphasized a "new version" of purgatory as a condition of soul experiencing the pain of loss, against an older, punitive version emphasizing real fire and sensible suffering.

Returning to my colleague's question, however, reveals that if one scratches the surface of this problem, the problem itself is revealed to be a phantom that fades away to expose issues of power and context. After all, how does one conceive of a post-death punishment or expiation that is a condition? A condition is the state of some *thing*. In the case of purgatory, that *thing* happens to be a soul. With respect to a soul's expiation, how does one think through the difference between an abstract pain and a material pain? There is no other recourse than to represent pain or expiation in some manner that utilizes materiality. Historically, with respect to those who have represented purgatory, some have insisted in representing it in abstract terms, while others insist on a completely different type of representation, where fire is thought to be real, not figurative.

Those who insist on robust, visceral representations of purgatory link these to its objective reality. Simply stated, material things convey realism. The effort to restore a spatial version of purgatory—along with its material supports such as privileged altars, paintings and iconography of suffering souls, and books and periodicals filled with anecdotes about souls in purgatory—is an attempt to restore a doctrine that has been forgotten by a majority of contemporary Catholics. These efforts belong to an impetus firmly established within the cultural tradition of Catholicism, where material objects like saints' statues and icons promote an engagement with sacred presence. Yet within a cultural ethos of modernism in which sacred presences are suspect, the objects associated with presence are regarded with skepticism, as Robert Orsi has argued:

> Of all aspects of religion, the one that has been clearly most out of place in the modernizing world—the one that has proven least tolerable to modern societies—has been the modern presence of the gods to practitioners. The modern world has assiduously and systematically disciplined the senses not to experience sacred presence; the imaginations of moderns are trained toward sacred absence.[1]

Interestingly, what initially led me to study the history of purgatory was its frequent appearance in popular culture where there is no question as to the status of its reality, as it is presented as *fiction*. I wondered what accounts for the frequent representation of purgatory within popular culture? What I found was that the most popular and lucrative films about the supernatural contain overtly Catholic themes, and specifically pre-Conciliar, medieval themes. In the introduction to this book I mentioned the movie *The Sixth Sense*, which currently occupies first place among these movies. Much of the important action in the movie occurs in a Gothic Cathedral, and Cole Sear, the child who sees dead people, utilizes a Latin prayer of the pre-Conciliar era. Leaving aside how an eleven-year-old would know this prayer, it is apparent that purgatorial themes and a medieval Catholic aesthetic are as attractive now as they were in the nineteenth century, when Protestant converts extoled the beauty of Catholicism's aesthetic charms and attempted to recreate the Gothic style made popular by architect Augustus Pugin.[2] Even as it is true that moderns do not expect or even desire to encounter the sacred within objects and things, they certainly enjoy being entertained by sacred presences in films and books. This was the case in the nineteenth century as well, when Catholic purgatory periodicals, which told ostensibly real stories about visits from souls in purgatory, were bought and sold in the marketplace alongside Gothic novels and serials that told the same stories, but were presented and received as fiction.

One of the most well-known examples of a fictional purgatory occurs in the book *A Christmas Carol* by Charles Dickens, written in 1843, yet still popular today. In the opening chapter of the book, Dickens's character Ebenezer Scrooge meets his deceased partner, Jacob Marley, as a ghost. Marley's ghost is destined to do penance where he had sinned and occupies a terrestrial form of penance much in line with the purgatory promoted by scholastic theologian William of Auvergne. (See fig. 6-1.) He even adheres to William's criteria of only being able to "appear" as a warning, as he indicates to Scrooge, "How it is that I appear before you in a shape that you can see, I may not tell."[3]

At the time that Dickens was writing in England, the doctrine of purgatory had long been eradicated in the Anglican Church. Yet the resonances with earlier forms of purgatory are unmistakable:

> "Man of the worldly mind!" replied the Ghost, "do you believe in me or not?"
>
> "I do," said Scrooge. "I must. But why do spirits walk the earth, and why do they come to me?"
>
> "It is required of every man," the Ghost returned, "that the spirit within him should walk abroad among his fellowmen, and travel

FIGURE 6-1 Detail of a soul roaming the earth in chains. Juda Tadeas Supper, Virgin with Infant Jesus and St. Laurence, around 1750. Chornice (Czech Republic, Moravia), St. Laurence Church. Reprinted with the permission of the Department of Art History, Faculty of Arts, Masaryk University Brno, photo Tomasz Zwyrtek.

far and wide; and if that spirit goes not forth in life, it is condemned to do so after death. It is doomed to wander through the world—oh, woe is me!—and witness what it cannot share, but might have shared on earth, and turned to happiness!"

Again the spectre raised a cry, and shook its chain and wrung its shadowy hands.

"You are fettered," said Scrooge, trembling. "Tell me why?"

"I wear the chain I forged in life," replied the Ghost. "I made it link by link, and yard by yard; I girded it of my own free will, and of my own free will I wore it."[4]

One does not have to go as far back as the nineteenth century, or even 1999, the year when *The Sixth Sense* was released, to view representations of purgatory in popular culture. As I write this, the television series "Sleepy Hollow" has just been renewed and is among the most highly rated programs of 2013. A major premise in the television series is that the characters are suffering in purgatory. I live in the town where the series is being filmed, and many of my students seek work as extras on the set. Their questions about purgatory reveal ignorance about the doctrine and also a genuine curiosity about possible afterlife states. Questions about the reality of an afterlife inevitably follow our discussions. Although the purgatory represented in "Sleepy Hollow" is clearly fictional, the questions that the series inspires concern its reality and point to the capacity of fictional representations of the sacred to inspire reflection on their possible reality.

Purgatory clearly has a place as a fictional reality within popular culture. What has become of the Catholic doctrine of purgatory, however, is a different story altogether, one I hoped to have shed a little light on in the preceding pages. I hope to have allowed the sources and the ministers of the purgatory apostolates to speak. They've told a story of mourning for a doctrine that was once a part of the lives of all Catholics, wherever they lived.

Notes

INTRODUCTION

1. Richard Owen, "The Fires of Hell Are Real and Eternal, Pope Warns," *The Times* (London), March 27, 2007.

2. Ibid.

3. The International Theological Commission, on April 22, 2007, published "The Hope of Salvation for Infants Who Die without Being Baptized," which presented the view that unbaptized infants were subject to God's mercy and therefore one could be hopeful that they would go to heaven. Limbo is not, nor ever was, an official doctrine of the Catholic Church, although influential Catholics like Augustine of Hippo did hold the belief that the afterlife destination of unbaptized infants was not heaven, but a form of hell where they were not tortured (the "lip of hell"). Because unbaptized infants are assumed to be innocent of sin, though according to Catholic theology they are still in a state of original sin, they present a test case for speculation regarding their afterlife destinations. For a discussion of these speculations within the era of early Christianity, see Jeffrey Trumbower, *Rescue for the Dead: The Posthumous Salvation of Non-Christians in Early Christianity* (New York: Oxford University Press, 2001). I am grateful to Isabel Moreira for referring me to this source.

4. Nick Pisa in Rome, "Pope Ends State of Limbo after 800 Years," *The Telegraph* (London), April 23, 2007; Edmund MacCaraeg, "The Pope Abandons Limbo! Will Purgatory Follow?" April 26, 2007, accessed April 29, 2013, http://www.ucg .org/commentary/pope-abandons-limbo-will-purgatory-follow/.

5. Sister Mary and I have laughed about this incident several times since it occurred. She encouraged me to include it in this introduction.

6. *Council of Trent, The Canons and Decrees of the Sacred and Ecumenical Council of Trent: Celebrated under the Sovereign Pontiffs, Paul III, Julius III and Pius IV* (1848) (Ithaca: Cornell University Library Press, 2009), 233.

7. "Purgatory Inflames Hearts with God's Love, Pope Says," *Catholic News Agency*, Vatican City, January 12, 2011.

8. Cindy Wotten, "Purgatory Is a Process, Not a Place, Pope Says at General Audiences," *Catholic News Service*, January 12, 2011.

9. In an excellent analysis of Catholic concepts of hell, purgatory, and limbo, Henry Ansgar Kelly notes that "in recent times the idea of situating hell, purgatory, and the two limbos seems to have faded, along with all ideas of spatial location, in favor of purely spiritual states, there seems to have developed the idea of purgatory and the limbo of infants being more marginal to heaven than to hell" (132). "Hell with Purgatory and Two Limbos: The Geography and Theology of the Underworld" in Isabel Moreira and Margaret Toscana, eds., *Hell and Its Afterlife* (Farnham, Surrey, UK: Ashgate, 2010), 121–136. Thanks to Isabel Moreira for directing me to this article and anthology.

10. Historical overviews of Western beliefs about death include Philippe Ariès, *The Hour of Our Death: The Classic History of Western Attitudes towards Death over the Last One Thousand Years*, trans. Helen Weaver (New York: Vintage, 1982); Michel Vovelle, *La Mort et L'Occident de 1300 a nos jours* (Paris: Gallimard, 2000); Colleen McDannell and Bernhard Lang, *Heaven: A History*, 2nd ed. (New Haven: Yale University Press, 2001); Guillaume Cuchet, *Le Crépuscule du Purgatoire* (Paris: Armand Colin, 2005).

11. "A True Story about Purgatory Involving One of Our Priests," Shrine of St. Jude, http://www.shrineofsaintjude.net/home1601.html, accessed March 29, 2013.

12. Fr. Paul Stretenovic, "The Physical Suffering of Purgatory," *Tradition in Action*, http://www.traditioninaction.org/religious/e047-Purgatory.htm, accessed March 29, 2013.

13. The "hermeneutic of discontinuity" is a term that suggests that a new church was instituted after Vatican II that is discontinuous with the past. As the newly elected Pope Benedict XVI, Cardinal Joseph Ratzinger, in his address of December 22, 2005, to the Roman Curia, advocated interpreting the vast changes consequent to the Second Vatican Council as positive transformation, rather than as rupture or discontinuity.

14. Almost all surveys of American Catholicism reference the Second Vatican Council as the most significant event for Catholicism in the twentieth century. See Patrick Carey, *Catholics in America: A History* (Lanham, Md.: Rowman & Littlefield, 2008); James O'Toole, *The Faithful: A History of Catholics in America* (Cambridge, Mass.: Harvard University Press, 2010); James O'Toole, ed., *Habits of Devotion: Catholic Religious Practice in Twentieth-Century America* (Ithaca: Cornell University Press, 2005).

15. For the variety of ways the Council has been interpreted, see in particular chapter 9 of Carey's *Catholics in America* and chapter 5 of O'Toole's *The Faithful*; for an examination of how the changes were experienced by Catholic women, see Colleen MacDannell, *The Spirit of Vatican II: A History of Catholic Reform in America* (New York: Basic, 2011); for a compelling examination of how these changes intersected with issues of class and race, see John T. McGreevy, *Parish Boundaries: The Catholic Encounter with Race in the Twentieth-Century Urban North* (Chicago: University of Chicago Press, 1998); for an overview see also

Ralph Wiltgen, *The Rhine Flows into the Tiber: A History of Vatican II* (Charlotte: Tan, 1991).

16. Robert Orsi, *Between Heaven and Earth: The Religious Worlds People Make and the Scholars Who Study Them* (Princeton: Princeton University Press, 2005). Orsi provides a compelling description of the connection between the material culture of Catholicism and sacred presence in the Catholic worlds he describes.

17. Within Catholic culture, the souls in purgatory are referred to as "holy" because practitioners believe they are saved and will eventually go to heaven.

18. "About Us," *Spirit and Life*, http://www.benedictinesisters.org/spirit-and-life-magazine-aboutus.php, accessed March 26, 2010.

19. Dick Houtman and Brigit Meyer, eds., *Things: Religion and the Question of Materiality (The Future of the Religious Past)* (New York: Fordham University Press, 2012), 393n2.

20. Carey, *Catholics in America*, 116.

21. The Mystical Body of Christ (*Mystici Corporus Christi*) is a Catholic doctrine that declares all baptized souls are part of the Church, including those in heaven (the Church Triumphant), those in purgatory (the Church Suffering), and those on earth (the Church Militant).

22. "New Rite for Funerals Slated in Archdiocese," *The Georgia Bulletin* (Sept. 22, 1966), http://www.georgiabulletin.org/local/1966/09/22/c/#.UcXghfZ36nY, accessed June 21, 2013.

23. Carey, *Catholics in America*, 18.

24. Interview with anonymous practitioner, University of North Carolina Library, May 10, 2010.

25. O'Toole, *The Faithful*, 209.

26. Ibid.

27. Carey, *Catholics in America*, 116.

28. The following are studies of the changes of Catholic devotional practices in the twentieth century, noting the decline in many before the Second Vatican Council: Joseph P. Chinnichi, "The Catholic Community at Prayer, 1926–1976," in *Habits of Devotion: Catholic Religious Practice in Twentieth-Century America*, ed. James O'Toole (Ithaca: Cornell University Press, 2004); James P. McMartin, *Prayers of the Faithful: The Shifting Spiritual Life of American Catholics* (Cambridge, Mass.: Harvard University Press, 2010).

29. Pius XII, *Mystici Corporis Christi (On the Mystical Body of Christ)*, Encyclical letter, Vatican City, June 29, 1943.

30. Annibale Bugnini, *The Reform of the Liturgy, 1948–1975* (Collegeville, Minn.: Liturgical Press, 1990), 773. For an overview of the issues, criticisms and otherwise, of the reforms, see John F. Baldovin, *Reforming the Liturgy: A Response to the Critics* (Collegeville, Minn.: Liturgical Press, 2009); also, Thomas M. Kocik, "The 'Reform of the Reform' in Broad Context: Re-Engaging the Living Tradition," *Usus Antiquior: A Journal Dedicated to the Sacred Liturgy* 3, no. 2 (July 2012): 102–114.

31. The parallel church consists of groups of Catholics who feel that Second Vatican Council was illicit and that the pope's chair is vacant. These groups are called *sedevancantists* (*sede vecante*, the seat is vacant). *Sedeprivationism* describes the thesis of Dominican theologian Michel Louis Guérard des Lauriers who argued that the popes from Angelo Giuseppe Roncalli (John XXIII) to the present are invalid popes because they have embraced principles of modernism, which had been declared heresies by several earlier popes.

32. Benedict XVI, Christmas Address of His Holiness Benedict XVI to the Roman Curia, December 22, 2005.

33. Brian W. Harrison, O.S., "The Postconciliary Eucharistic Liturgy: Planning the Reform of the Reform," appendix 3 of *The Reform of the Reform: A Liturgical Debate: Reform or Return?* by Thomas Kocik (San Francisco: Ignatius, 2003).

34. Benedict XVI, Letter to the Bishops to accompany apostolic letter *Summorum Pontificum* (On the Supreme Pontiffs), July 7, 2007.

35. James D. Davidson, *The Search for Common Ground: What Unites and Divides American Catholics* (Indiana: Our Sunday Visitor, 1997). Davidson, a sociologist at Purdue University, studies American Catholics.

36. Ibid., chapter 7.

37. Ibid.

38. "A Traditionalist Avant Garde: Its Trendy to Be Traditionalist," *The Economist*, December 15, 2012, http://www.economist.com/news/international/21568357-its-trendy-be-traditionalist-catholic-church-traditionalist-avant-garde, accessed December 30, 2012.

39. See the following for an examination of nineteenth-century Catholic converts: Patrick Allitt, *Catholic Converts: British and American Intellectuals Turn to Rome* (Ithaca: Cornell University Press, 1997).

40. M. Night Shyamalan, *The Sixth Sense*, http://www.awesomefilm.com/script/sixth-sense.html, accessed June 14, 2013.

41. Ibid.

42. An apostolate is a ministry in which laity perform services that help fulfill the goals of the Catholic Church. Apostolate leaders publish books, form websites, or feed the hungry, among other things.

43. Isabel Moreira, *Heavens Purge: Purgatory in Late Antiquity* (New York: Oxford University Press, 2010), 5.

44. Victor Turner, "Betwixt and Between: The Liminal Period in Rites of Passage," in Victor Turner, *The Forest of Symbols: Aspects of Ndembu Ritual* (Ithaca: Cornell University Press, 1967), 93–111.

45. Judith Butler, *Gender Trouble: Feminism and the Subversion of Identity* (New York: Routledge, 2006). Butler complicates notions of the stability of gender in her work by attending to so-called liminal identities.

46. Mary Douglas, *Purity and Danger: An Analysis of the Concepts of Pollution and Taboo* (New York: Routledge, 2002).

47. David Chidester, "Material Terms for the Study of Religion," *Journal of the American Academy of Religion* 68, no. 2 (June 2000): 374.

48. The list of scholars working in the field has grown considerably. Of note is a journal dedicated to the subject, edited by David Morgan, Brent Plate, Birgit Meyer, and Crispin Paine: *Material Religion: A Journal of Objects, Arts and Belief* (London: Berg). The field is diverse with scholars working on issues as varied as place, such as Thomas Tweed, *Crossing and Dwelling: A Theory of Religion* (Cambridge, Mass.: Harvard University Press, 2008) to neuroscience, Ann Taves, *Religious Experience Reconsidered: A Building Block Approach to the Study of Religion and Other Special Things* (Princeton: Princeton University Press, 2009); also see Manuel A. Vásquez, *More Than Belief: A Materialist Theory of Religion* (New York: Oxford University Press, 2011), 3–4.

49. Jeremy Biles, "Out of This World: The Materiality of the Beyond," in *Religion and Material Culture: The Matter of Belief*, ed. David Morgan (New York: Routledge, 2010), 135–152. There is also a society, SCRIPTS, devoted exclusively to materiality and texts, which publishes a journal called *Postscripts: The Journal of Sacred Texts and Contemporary Worlds*, edited by Elizabeth Castelli.

50. Biles, "Out of This World," 141.

51. Jacques Le Goff, *The Birth of Purgatory* (Chicago: University of Chicago Press, 1986), 240. First published in 1981 as *La Naissance du Purgatoire* by Gallimard, Paris.

52. Carol Zaleski, "St. Patrick's Purgatory: Pilgrimage Motifs in a Medieval Otherworld," *Journal of the History of Ideas* 46, no. 4 (Oct.–Dec. 1985): 484.

53. Isabel Moreira points out that the medieval term "visio" was usually qualified by terms such as "corporalis" or "spiritualis" to distinguish between types of sight. Also see Isabel Moreira, "Augustine's Three Visions and Three Heavens in Some Early Medieval Florilegia," *Vivarium* 34, no. 1 (1996): 1–14.

54. Courtnay Konshuh, "The Audiences of Three Medieval Visions," *Connotations* 20, no. 1 (2010/11): 23–33.

55. Le Goff, *Birth of Purgatory*, 206.

56. *The Birth of Purgatory* includes an appendix that surveys scholarship about purgatory from 1936 through the 1980s.

57. Peter Brown, "The End of the Ancient Other World: Death and Afterlife between Late Antiquity and the Early Middle Ages," *The Tanner Lectures on Human Values*, Yale University, October 23–24, 1996.

58. Le Goff, *Birth of Purgatory*, 109.

59. Moreira, *Heaven's Purge*, chapters 5 and 8.

60. Carl Watkins, "Sin, Penance and Purgatory in the Anglo-Norman Realm: The Evidence of Visions and Ghost Stories," *Past and Present* 175, issue 1 (2002): 3–33.

61. Carl Watkins, *History and the Supernatural in Medieval England* (Cambridge: Cambridge University Press, 2007), 9.

62. Ibid., 18.

63. Takami Matsuda, *Death and Purgatory in Middle English Didactic Poetry* (Suffolk: D.S. Brewer, 1997). Matsuda provides an overview of literature about purgatory that attends to the complexities of practices regarding purgatory.

64. Tomáš Malý and Pavel Suchánek have compiled a database of iconographic images and research from sixteenth-century Bohemia, Boravia, and Silesia. See http://www.phil.muni.cz/dejum/baroque/en/tomas-maly-pavel-suchanek.php.

65. Kristen Poole, *Supernatural Environments in Shakespeare's England: Spaces of Demonism, Divinity and Drama* (Cambridge: Cambridge University Press, 2011).

66. Guillaume Cuchet, "The Revival of the Cult of Purgatory in France (1850–1914)," *French History* 18, no. 1 (March 2004): 76–95. Cuchet, *The Twilight of Purgatory* (Paris: Armand Colin, 2005). Michel Vovelle argued that the seventeenth century was the great century of purgatory. See Vovelle, *Le Mort et L'Occident de* 1300 *a nos jours* (Paris: Gallimard, 1983), 308.

67. Carl, Watkins, *History and the Supernatural*, 19.

68. Ibid., 19.

69. Ibid., 228. The "long twelfth century" refers to historiographical discussions regarding social, political, and religious developments in the tenth and eleventh centuries contributing to "a new Europe" in the twelfth century. Periodization of these developments is difficult. See Thomas F. X. Noble and John Van Engen, *European Transformations: The Long Twelfth Century* (Notre Dame: University of Notre Dame Press, 2012).

CHAPTER I

1. Dante Alighieri, *Purgatorio: A New Verse Translation (English and Italian Edition)*, trans. W. S. Merwin (New York: Knopf, 2000).

2. Early sources link the name of the lake to various legends, the most famous of which is that St. Patrick killed a serpent whose blood colors the water of the lake. See Alice Curtayne, *Lough Derg: St. Patrick's Purgatory* (Dublin: Burns Oates, 1944), 3. Other legends state that the lake is colored with the blood of the serpent maimed by a Celtic warrior who lived prior to St. Patrick, named Fin Mac Coul. See Thomas Wright, *St. Patrick's Purgatory: An Essay on Legends of Purgatory, Hell, and Paradise, Current during the Middle Ages* (London: John Russel Smith, 1844).

3. For its medieval fame, see the works of Yolande de Pontfarcy, specifically *Saint Patrick's Purgatory: A Twelfth-Century Tale of a Journey to the Other World*, trans. J. M. Picard (Kill Lane, Blackrock, County Dublin, Ireland: Four Courts Press, 1985).

4. The current Catholic catechism identifies purgatory as the "final purification of the elect, which is entirely different from the punishment of the damned. The Church formulated her doctrine of faith on Purgatory especially at the Councils of Florence and Trent." *Catechism of the Catholic Church*, 2nd ed. Vatican: Libreria Editrice Vaticana, 2000, 1030–1032.

5. St. John Seymour, *St. Patrick's Purgatory* (Dundalk: Dundalgen, 1918) lists pilgrims' accounts. See also Michael Haren and Yolande de Pontfarcy, eds., *The*

Medieval Pilgrimage to St Patrick's Purgatory: Lough Derg and the European Tradition (Enniskillen: Clogher Historical Society, 1988), 12; see Jacques Le Goff's reference to Jacobus de Voragines's *Golden Legend*, edited by Theodore Graese (Dresden-Leipzig, 1846), 213–216; for medieval *exempla*, see Frederich Tubach, *Index Exemplorum: A Handbook of Medieval Tales* (Helsinki: Suomalainen Tiedeakatenia, 1969), 307.

6. *Caesarii Heisterbacensis monachi ordinis Cister-ciensis Dialogus miraculorum*, ed. Joseph Strange (Cologne, Bonn, and Brussels: Heberle, 1851), 2:347.

7. The cave has been shut down several times, but apparently this had only a little effect on the pilgrimage, which has been continual from at least the eighth century until today. In chapter 2 I will detail the first official papal suppression of the site, and the response to this by its Irish stewards.

8. Alessandro Scafi, *Mapping Paradise: A History of Heaven on Earth* (Chicago: University of Chicago Press, 2006), 125.

9. J. B. Harley and David Woodward, eds., "Chapter 18: Medieval Mappaemundi," in *Cartography in Prehistoric, Ancient, and Medieval Europe and the Mediterranean*, vol. 1 of *The History of Cartography* (Chicago: University Of Chicago Press, 1987), 307.

10. Evelyn Edson, *The World Map, 1300–1492: The Persistence of Tradition and Transformation* (Baltimore: Johns Hopkins University Press, 2007), 31.

11. Martin Luther, *Commentary on Genesis*, trans. John Nicholas Lenker (Minneapolis: The Luther Press, 1910), part 2 "of Paradise."

12. Edn, *The World Map*, 15.

13. As I finished my manuscript, I found that Sara V. Torres also considered the place of purgatory within the medieval imagination. See her "Journeying to the World's End? Imagining the Anglo-Irish frontier in Ramon de Perellós's Pilgrimage to St. Patrick's Purgatory," in *Mapping Medieval Geographies: Geographical Encounters in the Latin West and Beyond, 300–1600*, ed. Keith Lilley (Cambridge: Cambridge University Press, 2014), 300–324.

14. Michael P. Carroll, *Irish Pilgrimage: Holy Wells and Popular Catholic Devotion* (Baltimore: Johns Hopkins University Press, 1999), fig. 9: St. Patrick's Purgatory Map.

15. Glyn S. Burgess and Clara Strijbosch, eds., *The Brendan Legend: Texts and Versions* (Leiden and Boston: Brill, 2006).

16. The following anthology discusses the historical contexts of the *Navigatio* and the relations between belief and texts: Burgess and Strijbosch, *The Brendan Legend*, NR; J. S. Mackley, *The Legend of St. Brendan: A Comparative Study of the Latin and Anglo-Norman Versions* (Leiden and Boston: Brill, 2008); The Marquess of Bute (John P. C. Stuart), "Brendan's Fabulous Voyage," *The Scottish Review* 21 (Jan. and April 1893): 35–73; "St. Brendan," *County Louth Archeological Society Journal* 2 (1909): 109–123. Additionally, see Eileen Gardiner's comprehensive bibliography of visions and texts relating to medieval European afterlife beliefs: "Hell Online," http://www.hell-on-line.org/BibJC.html, accessed May 1, 2013.

17. Henry Jones, *St. Patrick's Purgatory: Containing the Description, Originall, Progresse, and Demolition of That Superstitious Place* (1647), 8.

18. Ibid., 8.

19. Margaret Burell, "Hell as a Geological Construct," *Florilegium* 24 (2007): 38.

20. Ibid., 41.

21. Burrell, "Hell as a Geological Construct"; Howard Rollin Patch, *The Other World according to Descriptions in Medieval Literature* (New York: Octagon, 1970), chapter 5; for early modern associations of hell with geographical locations, see also Kristen Poole, "When Hell Freezes Over: The Fabulous Mt. Hecla and Hamlet's Infernal Geography," in *Supernatural Environments in Shakespeare's England: Spaces of Demonism, Divinity, and Drama* (Cambridge: Cambridge University Press, 2011); Bruce Gordon and Peter Marshall, eds., "The Map of God's Word: Geographies of the Afterlife in Tudor and Early Stuart England," in *The Place of the Dead: Death and Remembrance in Late Medieval and Early Modern Europe* (Cambridge: Cambridge University Press, 2000).

22. Maire MacNeill, *Festival of Lughnasa* (Dublin: Folklore of Ireland Council, 2008), 21; Jacques Le Goff, *Birth of Purgatory* (Chicago: University of Chicago Press, 1986), 207.

23. "Catherine of Siena to Don Giovanni of the Cells of Vallombrosa," in Vida Dutton Scutter, *Catherine of Siena as Seen in Her Letters* (New York: E. P. Dutton, 1905), 264.

24. Niccolò Tommaseo and St. Catherine of Siena, *Le Lettere Di S. Caterina Da Siena: Ridotte a Miglior Lezione, E in Ordine Nuovo Disposte Con Proemio E Note* [Catherine of Siena to Don Giovanni, a monk in the Certosa at Rome, who was sorely tempted and in great trouble of mind, because he could not obtain permission to make a pilgrimage to St. Patrick's Purgatory in Ireland] (Charleston, S.C.: Nabu, 2010), 4:50.

25. Caesarius of Heisterbach, *Caesarius of Heisterbach, Dialogus Miraculorum, XII. 23, in Caesarii Heisterbacensis Monachi Ordinis Cisterciensis Dialogus Miraculorum*, ed. Joseph Strange, 2 vols. (Cologne: J. M. Heberle, 1851), chapter 32. For cases of revenants seeking absolution from sin by performing earthly penances, see Carl Watkins, "Sin, Penance and Purgatory in the Anglo-Norman Realm: The Evidence of Visions and Ghost Stories," in *Past and Present* (2002) 175, no. 1: 3–33, 23–24 and n64. Also, for revenants seeking penance, see Carl Watkins, *History and the Supernatural*, 182–193; see also Le Goff, *Birth of Purgatory*, 61–95. I have relied on Jacques Le Goff's translation of this story in *The Birth of Purgatory*, 301.

26. William of Newburgh, Historia rerum Anglicarum, vv. 22–24, in *Chronicles of the Reigns of Stephen, Henry II, and Richard I*, ed. Richard Howlett (Rolls Series, London, 1884–1889), 4: ii, 4:475. This story is described by Nancy Caciola in "Wraiths, Revenants and Ritual in Medieval Culture," *Past and Present* (1996): 152:3–45.

27. Isabel Moreira, *Heaven's Purge: Purgatory in Late Antiquity* (New York: Oxford University Press, 2010), introduction and chapter 1.

28. Medieval conceptions about salvation were not uniform and were diverse even among seemingly homogenous demographics, such as clerics. See Watkins, *History*

and the Supernatural, 21. Jean-Claude Schmitt addresses visionary literature of after-life places of expiation. His work also confirms the diversity of medieval conceptions of the afterlife and its connection with penance. See Schmitt, *Ghosts in the Middle Ages: The Living and the Dead in Medieval Society* (Chicago: The University of Chicago Press, 1998), chapter 8.

29. "Anglo-Saxon Penetentials: A Cultural Database," http://www.anglo-saxon.net/penance/LAUD482_14b.html#Y44.02.01, accessed June 16, 2012.

30. Moreira, *Heaven's Purge*, 123.

31. Cyrile Vogel, "Le Pelerinage Penitentiel," *Revue des Sciences Religieuses* 38, no. 2 (1964): 113–153.

32. Alan Ford and John McCafferty, eds., *The Origins of Sectarianism in Early Modern Ireland* (Cambridge: Cambridge University Press, 2012), 168.

33. The penitential climate of late antiquity and the early to late medieval eras is complex due to the variety of ideas of penance and its links to afterlife purgation occurring in diverse locations at diverse times. In this instance I have relied on the works of Isabel Moreira, *Heaven's Purge*, 154–155, and also Carl Watkins, "Sin, Penance and Purgatory in the Anglo-Norman Realm: The Evidence of Visions and Ghost Stories," in *Past and Present* 175, no. 1 (2002): 3–33.

34. Carl Watkins, "Doctrine, Politics and Purgation: The Vision of Tnúthgal and the Vision of Owen at St. Patrick's Purgatory," *Journal of Medieval History* 22, no. 3 (1996): 21. Watkins examines two visions in light of the shifting penitential theology.

35. Watkins, "Sin, Penance and Purgatory," 25; Megan McLaughlin, *Consorting with the Saints: Prayer for the Dead in Early Medieval France* (Ithaca and London: Cornell University Press, 1994), 153.

36. Watkins, "Doctrine, Politics and Purgation," 236.

37. The terms "schools of satisfaction" and "retreats of penance" are found in the writings of the seventeenth-century Irish poet Aodh Mac Aingil, who decried the suppression of locations of penance in Ireland. See Tadgh O Dushlaine, "Going for Baroque: The Irish Spiritual Reformation 1600–1800," *Religion and Literature* 28, nos. 2/3. For the Irish context of penance, see Fred Van Lieburg, ed., "From Late Medieval Piety to Tridentine Pietism? The Case of 17th Century Ireland," in *Confessionalism and Pietism: Religious Reform in the Early Modern Period* (Mainz: Veröffentlichungen des Instituts für Europäische Geschichte, 2006).

38. Within the historiography of Lough Derg, some scholars argue that the penitential elements of the location were a later development and that it was Continental influence that brought attention to, or perhaps even created, the pilgrimage. Michael Carroll writes, "St. Patrick's Purgatory was primarily a European pilgrimage site, which just happened to be in Ireland, and the popularity of this site was tied to issues and processes that had more to do with what was going on in Europe generally than to anything that was happening in Ireland in particular."

See Carroll, *Irish Pilgrimage*, 84. This conclusion is tempting as the two earliest accounts of the pilgrimage are in Latin and there is a dearth of indigenous sources about Lough Derg until the early modern era. However, it is not conclusive and other historians, such as Alice Curtayne, maintain that the location had been a pre-Christian Celtic site of penance. See Curtayne, *Lough Derg*.

39. A. G. Little, ed., *Liber exemplorum ad usum praedicantium saeculo xiii compositus a quondam fratre minore Anglica de provincial Herberniae* (Aberdeen, 1918), 57. This story is described by Colman O Clabaigh, OSB, in "Anchorites in Late Medieval Ireland," *Anchoritic Traditions of Medieval Europe*, ed. Liz Herbert McAvoy (Woodbridge: Boydell, 2010), 153–177.

40. Clabaigh, "Anchorites in Late Medieval Ireland," 173.

41. Gerald of Wales, *The History and Topography of Ireland*, trans. John O'Meara (London: Penguin Classics, 1983).

42. Ibid., 101.

43. Ibid., 61.

44. I use this translation: Pontfarcy, *Saint Patrick's Purgatory*.

45. Ibid., 54.

46. Haren and Pontfarcy, *The Medieval Pilgrimage to St Patrick's Purgatory*, 48–49.

47. Colmán Ó Clabaigh, OSB, "Anchorites in Late Medieval Ireland," in *Anchoritic Traditions of Medieval Europe*, ed. Liz Herbert McAvoy (Woodbridge: Boydell, 2010), 159; Tom Licence, *Hermits and Recluses in English Society, 950–1200* (Oxford: Oxford University Press, 2011).

48. Robert Easting, *St. Patrick's Purgatory: Two Versions of Owayne Miles and the Vision of William of Stranton Together with the Long Text of the Purgatorio Sancti Patricii*, edited by Robert Easting (Oxford: Published for The Early English Text Society by The Oxford University Press, 1991).

49. Chapter 2 will reveal how the cave became associated with each island. Today, the penance is done in a church on Station Island.

50. Haren and Pontfarcy, *The Medieval Pilgrimage to St Patrick's Purgatory*, 55.

51. Curtayne, *Lough Derg*, 12.

52. Jones, *St. Patrick's Purgatory*.

53. Haren and Pontfarcy, *The Medieval Pilgrimage to St Patrick's Purgatory*, 50.

54. Ibid., 50.

55. Gregory of Tours, *The History of the Franks*, trans. Lewis Thorpe (Harmondsworth: Penguin Classics, 1983); for a treatment of the Irish rites of enclosure and the Irish anchoritic tradition, see Colmán Ó Clabaigh, OSB, "Anchorites in Late Medieval Ireland."

56. Ludwig Bieler, *Irish Penitentials (Scriptores Latini Hiberniae) (English and Latin Edition)* (Dublin: Dublin Institute for Advanced Studies, 1963), 279.

57. R. B. Easting, "Peter of Cornwall's Account of St. Patrick's Purgatory," *Analecta Bollandiana* 97 (1979): 413; Haren and Pontfarcy, *Medieval Pilgrimage to St Patrick's Purgatory*, 13n18.

58. Terence Dewsnap, *Island of Daemons: The Lough Derg Pilgrimage and the Poets Patrick Kavanagh, Denis Devlin, and Seamus Heaney* (Cranbury, N.J.: Associated University Presses, 2008), 25.

59. William Camden, *Brittania*, trans. Philemon Holland (Bristol: Thoemmes, 2003), s.v. "The County of Donegal or Tir-Conell."

60. See Tadhg Ó Dúshláine, "Lough Derg in Native Irish Poetry," *Clogher Record* 13, no. 1 (1988): 76–84.

61. See Michelle O'Riordan, *Irish Bardic Poetry and Rhetorical Reality* (Cork: Cork University Press, 2007); and Salvador Ryan, "A Slighted Source: Rehabilitating Irish Bardic Religious Poetry in Historical Discourse," *Cambrian Medieval Celtic Studies* 48 (2004): 75–99. The bards, however, were not the first poets to keep the history of ancient traditions alive. Filid were a class of pre-Christian poets charged with similar duties as the bards, but either disappeared prior to the medieval era or were integrated into the bardic tradition.

62. Quoted from Próinseas Ní Chatháin, "The Later Pilgrimage—Irish Poetry on Loch Derg," in *The Medieval Pilgrimage to St. Patrick's Purgatory*, ed. Haren and Pontfarcy.

63. Using folklore as a historical method, in an Irish context, is most persuasively addressed in Guy Beiner, *Remembering the Year of the French: Irish Folk History and Social Memory* (Madison: University of Wisconsin Press, 2007); and in Michelle O'Riordan, *Irish Bardic Poetry and Rhetorical Reality* (Cork: Cork University Press, 2007).

64. Aodh Mac Aingil, *Scáthán Shacramuinte na Haithridhe*, ed. Cainneach O Maonaigh (Dublin: Dublin Institute for Advanced Studies, 1952), 127–128.

65. Quoted and translated by Tadhg Ó Dúshláine in "Going for Baroque," 37–55; also see Bernadette Cunningham and Raymond Gillespie, "The Lough Derg Pilgrimage in the Age of the Counter-Reformation," in *Éire-Ireland* 39, no. 3 (2004): 167–179.

66. Translations by Dúshláine, "Lough Derg in Native Irish Poetry."

67. Ibid., 81.

68. Ibid., 83.

69. Jones, *St. Patrick's Purgatory*, 9; mss. "Hilern Derm Macevan St. Patrick's Rhyme."

70. Pontfarcy, *St. Patrick's Purgatory*, 24–26; and Curtayne, *Lough Derg*.

71. Jones, *St. Patrick's Purgatory*, 9. The original cave was on Saint's Island, and in chapter 2 I will address the opening of a new cave on the neighboring Station Island.

72. Ibid.

73. Kristen Poole, "When Hell Freezes Over," 122.

74. Curtayne, *Lough Derg*, 29.

75. Pontfarcy, *Saint Patrick's Purgatory*, 44.

76. Pontfarcy, *Saint Patrick's Purgatory*, 44–45.

77. Ibid., 52.
78. In addition to the Picard translation, my discussion of the *Treatise* is also based on these translations: Cornelis M. Van der Zanden, ed., *Étude sur le purgatoire de Saint Patrice, accompagnée du texte latin d'Utrecht et du texte anglo—normand de Cambridge* (Amsterdam: H. J. Paris, 1927), which is based on the oldest extant version of the manuscript. See also R. B. Easting, ed., *St. Patrick's Purgatory: Early English Text Society* 298 (Oxford: Oxford University Press, 1991).
79. Victor Turner and Edith Turner, *Image and Pilgrimage in Christian Culture: Anthropological Perspectives*, repr. (New York: Columbia University Press, 2011), 126. It was Marie de France's popular French translation of H. Saltrey's account of the purgatory that contributed to its medieval reception as a knight's adventure. Marie De France and Thomas Atkinson Jenkins, *"L'Espurgatoire Seint Patriz," of Marie De France an Old-French Poem of the Twelfth Century, Published with an Introduction and a Study of the Language of the Author* (Philadelphia: A. J. Ferris, 1894).
80. Pontfarcy, *St. Patrick's Purgatory*, 54.
81. Ibid., 55.
82. Haren and Pontfarcy, *The Medieval Pilgrimage to St. Patrick's Purgatory*, 54–73.
83. Guillaume Cuchet, "The Revival of the Cult of Purgatory in France (1850–1914)," *French History* 18, no. 1 (March 2004); Isabel Moreira, *Heaven's Purge: Purgatory in Late Antiquity* (New York: Oxford University Press, 2010); Le Goff, *Birth of Purgatory*; and Stephen Greenblatt, *Hamlet in Purgatory* (Princeton: Princeton University Press, 2002). Carol Zaleski includes the *Treatise* in a genre of visionary literature she calls return-from-death narratives or the Drythelm line. See Carol Zaleski, *Otherworld Journeys: Accounts of Near-Death Experience in Medieval and Modern Times* (New York: Oxford University Press, 1988).
84. Le Goff, *Birth of Purgatory*, 200. See Isabel Moreira's section on the early use of the term "purgatory," *Heaven's Purge*, 262n44.
85. Watkins, "Doctrine, Politics and Purgation," 232.
86. Zaleski, *Otherworld Journeys*, 484.
87. Courtnay Konshuh, "The Audiences of Three Medieval Visions," *Connotations* 20, no. 1 (2010/11): 23–33.
88. Ludwig Bieler, "St. Patrick's Purgatory: Contributions towards an Historical Topography," *The Irish Ecclesiastical Record* 93 (1960): 137–144.
89. "While *Saint Patrick's Purgatory* is clearly related to Irish Christianity and the cult of Saint Patrick, it is doubtful whether in the twelfth century it had the same Catholic and Irish nationalist overtones that it acquired subsequently and still carries with it today" (LeGoff, *Birth of Purgatory*, 199); and Zaleski notes that there is "little that is characteristically Irish in either their otherworld topography or their way of characterizing pilgrimage" (Zaleski, "St. Patrick's Purgatory:

Pilgrimage Motifs in a Medieval Otherworld Vision," *Journal of the History of Ideas* 46, no. 4 [1985]: 469).

90. Victor Turner and Edith Turner, *Image and Pilgrimage in Christian Culture: Anthropological Perspectives* (New York: Columbia University Press, 1995), 108, 102.
91. Curtayne, *Lough Derg*, 42.
92. Ibid., 44.
93. Joseph McGuiness, *St. Patrick's Purgatory: Lough Derg* (Blackrock, County Dublin: Columba, 2000), 80.
94. Dewsnap, *Island of Daemons*, 74.
95. Dushlaine, "Going for Baroque," 39.

CHAPTER 2

1. Jacques Le Goff, *The Birth of Purgatory* (Chicago: University of Chicago Press, 1986), 242; originally William of Auvergne, *De Universo*, chapter 60. Also this English translation does cover William's philosophy that underpins his understanding of the soul, but it does not cover the chapters of the *De Universo* that deal specifically with purgatory. See also Roland J. Teske, *Universo* (1998); and William of Auvergne, *The Universe of Creatures*. Medieval Philosophical Texts in Translation 35 (Milwaukee: Marquette University Press, 1998). "Heretical around the edges" is a reference to Patrick Kavanagh's poem about Lough Derg. See Patrick Kavanagh, *The Complete Poems of Patrick Kavanagh*, edited by Peter Kavanagh (New York: Peter Hand, 1972).
2. James Bono, "Medical Spirits and the Medieval Language of Life," *Traditio* 40 (1984): 91–130.
3. Nancy Caciola, "Wraiths, Revenants and Ritual in Medieval Culture, Past and Present," no. 152 (August 1996): 9.
4. See Thomas F. X. Noble and John H. Van Engen, *European Transformations: The Long Twelfth Century* (Notre Dame: University of Notre Dame Press, 2012).
5. Le Goff, *The Birth of Purgatory*, 240.
6. *Annals of Ulster*, 1497.
7. Monsignor Richard Mohan, prior of Lough Derg, in a discussion with the author, May 2012.
8. Carl Watkins, *History and the Supernatural in Medieval England* (Cambridge: Cambridge University Press, 2007), 187.
9. Jean Claude Schmitt, *Ghosts in the Middle Ages* (Chicago: University of Chicago Press, 1998), 11.
10. Carol Zaleski, *Otherworld Journeys: Accounts of Near Death Experience in Medieval and Modern Times* (New York: Oxford University Press, 1988). In chapter 1 of this definitive study, Zaleski examines Gregory I's *Dialogues* as one of the models for future otherworld journeys.

11. The "Roman bathhouse ghost" story, originally related by Gregory I in his *Dialogues*, has been examined by Schmitt, *Ghosts in the Middle Ages*, 32; Le Goff, *The Birth of Purgatory*, 92; and Stephen Greenblatt, *Hamlet in Purgatory* (Princeton: Princeton University Press, 2002), 114.

12. Saint Gregory the Great, *Dialogues*, trans. Odo John Zimmerman, OSB (New York: The Catholic University of America Press, 1959), 4:57.

13. Schmitt, *Ghosts in the Middle Ages*, 8.

14. Yolande de Pontfarcy, *Saint Patrick's Purgatory: A Twelfth Century Tale of a Journey to the Other World*, trans. J. M. Picard (Kill Lane, Blackrock, County Dublin: Four Courts Press, 1985), 45.

15. Ibid.

16. For an overview of this activity, see Watkins, *History and the Supernatural in Medieval England*, 191.

17. Watkins, *History and the Supernatural in Medieval England*, 192.

18. Alan Bernstein writes about the influence of the Arabic philosopher Avicenna on William's work. See Alan Bernstein, "Esoteric Theology: William of Auvergne on the Fires of Hell and Purgatory," *Speculum* 57, no. 3 (1982). Le Goff, in *Birth of Purgatory*, comments on scholarly assessments of William's hostility to Aristotle, which he believes have been overdrawn (241).

19. William of Auvergne, 2.3.24, 1:1067aD-bA. I am using de Mayo's translation here: Thomas Benjamin de Mayo, "The Demonology of William of Auvergne" (PhD diss., University of Arizona, 2006), 266. I am also using translations by Le Goff, Bernstein, and de Mayo, as well as commentary and the English translation (for philosophical context) by Roland J. Teske, *The Universe of Creatures* (Milwaukee: Marquette University Press, 1998). Also see Le Goff's treatment of William's philosophy in *The Birth of Purgatory*, 241–245; and William of Auvergne, *De Universo*, 2.3.24, 1:1067bH-1068aE.

20. De Mayo, "The Demonology of William of Auvergne" (PhD diss., University of Arizona, 2006), 267.

21. My discussion is informed by Alan E. Bernstein, "The Ghostly Troop and the Battle over Death: William of Auvergne, Christian, Old Norse, and *Irish Views*," in *Rethinking Ghosts in World Religions: Behind the Ghastly Smoke*, ed. Mu-chou Poo (Leiden: Brill, 2009).

22. I have relied on Bernstein's translations of William, in *Esoteric Theology*, 514–515; and the relevant passages in *De Universo* 2.1.60–65, 1:676–682.

23. William of Auvergne, *De Universo*, 682.

24. Bernstein, *Esoteric Theology*, 509.

25. Le Goff, *Birth of Purgatory*, 245. The disagreement on this issue between Le Goff and Bernstein is referenced in each of their texts: Le Goff, 245; Bernstein, *Esoteric Theology*, 515n29a. It is also mentioned in de Mayo's "Demonology," 195n74.

26. St. Thomas Aquinas, *Summa Theologica*, Supplement 69, 3.

27. Ibid.

28. Pope Innocent IV, "Letter to the Bishop of Tusculum" (March 6, 1254).

29. Ibid.

30. Alan E. Bernstein, "The Ghostly Troop and the Battle over Death," 145.

31. Watkins, *History and the Supernatural in Medieval England*, 192n87.

32. Schmitt, *Ghosts in the Middle Ages*, 10, 8.

33. Watkins, *History and the Supernatural in Medieval England*, 18.

34. Ibid., introduction.

35. John O'Donovan, *Annals of the Kingdom of Ireland by the Four Masters, from the Earliest Period to the Year 1616: Ed. from the Autograph. Manuscript with a Transl. and Copious Notes by John O'Donovan* (Dublin: Hodges, Smith and Co., 1848); see also Alice Curtayne, *Lough Derg: St. Patrick's Purgatory* (Dublin: Burns Oates, 1944), 21.

36. Curtayne, *Lough Derg*, 22.

37. Colmán Ó Clabaigh, OSB, "Anchorites in Late Medieval Ireland," in *Anchoritic Traditions of Medieval Europe*, ed. Liz Herbert McAvoy (Woodbridge: Boydell, 2010), 156.

38. Curtayne, *Lough Derg*, 28.

39. See Pontfarcy's discussion of the territorial fights between kings and bishops during this time, and the interesting place of knight John D'Courci, in Pontfarcy, *St. Patrick's Purgatory*, 24–26.

40. Victor Turner and Edith Turner, *Image and Pilgrimage in Christian Culture: Anthropological Perspectives* (Oxford: Blackwell, 1978), 132.

41. Daniel O'Connor, *Lough Derg and Its Pilgrimages: With Map and Illustrations* (Dublin: J. Dollard, 1979), 99.

42. Mircea Eliade, "Folklore as an Instrument of Knowledge," trans. Mac Linscott Ricketts, in *Mircea Eliade: A Critical Reader*, ed. Bryan Rennie (London: Equinox, 2006).

43. The serpent and its bones are mentioned in almost all histories of Lough Derg. Bishop Henry Jones, *St. Patrick's Purgatory* (1647) mentions the myth and the serpent several times. The legend of the Hag was related to Rev. Cesar Otway in *Sketches in Ireland: Descriptive of Interesting and Hitherto Unnoticed Districts in the North and South* (Dublin: William Curry, 1827), 102, 180–185; Thomas Wright, *St. Patrick's Purgatory: An Essay on the Legends of Purgatory, Hell, and Paradise, Current during the Middle Ages* (London: John Russell Smith, 1844). Wright offers in his work a compilation of the myths and their sources and he states that the tailbone is mentioned by Thomas Messingham in his *Florilegfium Insulae Sanctorum* (1624, 96).

44. Wright, *St. Patrick's Purgatory*, 4.

45. David N. Dumville, "'Beowulf' and the Celtic World: The Uses of Evidence," *Traditio* 37 (1981): 109–160.

46. Mircea Eliade, *The Myth of the Eternal Return or, Cosmos and History*, trans. Willard R. Trask (Princeton: Princeton University Press, 1965), 18.

47. Pontfarcy, *Saint Patrick's Purgatory*, 47–48.

48. The belief that demons haunted the island was recorded by Gerald of Wales as early as 118. See Gerald's *Topographia Hibernica* (1188),61.

49. Curtayne, *Lough Derg*, 28.

50. Turner and Turner, *Image and Pilgrimage in Christian Culture*, 123; and Carol Zaleski, "St. Patrick's Purgatory: Pilgrimage Motifs in a Medieval Otherworld," *Journal of the History of Ideas* 46, no. 4 (Oct.–Dec. 1985): 468.

51. Jones, *St. Patrick's Purgatory*, 7.

52. Ibid.

53. Turner and Turner, *Image and Pilgrimage in Christian Culture*, 106.

54. Jones, *St. Patrick's Purgatory*, 12.

55. Aubrey Gwynn and Richard Neville Hadcock, *Medieval Religious Houses: Ireland* (London: Longmans, 1970), 193; also see D. Canon O'Connor, *Saint Patrick's Purgatory, Lough Derg. Its History, Traditions, Legends, Antiquities, Topography and Scenic Surroundings, with Some Account of Its More Notable Pilgrims, and a Detailed Description of the Authorized Devotions Performed at Its Venerable Shrine* (Dublin: James Duffy, ca. 1879, revised ca. 1895, 1903), 34–37.

56. "St. Patrick's Purgatory, Lough Derg, Home Page, Welcome, Pilgrimages and Retreats," *Lough Derg*, http://www.loughderg.org/, accessed April 13, 2011.

57. Seamus Heaney, *Station Island* (New York: Farrar, Straus and Giroux, 1986).

58. "Pilgrim Reflections," *Lough Derg*, http://www.loughderg.org/about-us/pilgrim-reflections, accessed June 15, 2012.

59. William Butler Yeats, "The Pilgrim," in *The Collected Poems of W. B. Yeats* (Hertfordshire: Wordsworth Editions, 1994), 268.

60. Joseph McGuinness, *St. Patrick's Purgatory* (Dublin: The Columba Press, 2000), 68.

61. Canon O'Connor, *Saint Patrick's Purgatory*, chapter 3.

62. St. John D. Seymour, *Saint Patrick's Purgatory: A Mediaeval Pilgrimage in Ireland* (Dundalk: Dundalgan, 1918), lists six documents of his completion and later lists the manuscripts in various European libraries.

63. O'Connor, *Saint Patrick's Purgatory*, 27–32.

64. Ibid.

65. John D. Seymour Laurence, *Saint Patrick's Purgatory*, 67.

66. John D. Seymour, *Saint Patrick's Purgatory*, 67.

67. Ibid., 70.

68. Canon O'Connor, *Saint Patrick's Purgatory*, 109.

69. Ibid., 109–110. O'Connor mentions it in the text also in a footnote: "This Sermon is classed 'No. 30' and is preserved in the Library of San Clemente, Rome."

70. Ibid.

71. Council of Trent, Pope Pius IV, 25th Session (Dec. 4, 1563), Decree on Purgatory.

72. Curtayne, *Lough Derg*, 53.

73. Ibid., 54.

74. The original cave was on Saints Island. Ludwig Biele believed that it was at the end of the thirteenth century that the cave was moved to Station Island. Curtayne's theory confirms that the Irish caretakers were aware and stewarding two caves at the time of the closure in 1497.

75. Seymour, *St. Patrick's Purgatory*, 76.

76. Curtayne, *Lough Derg*, 55.

77. Ibid., 46.

CHAPTER 3

1. Caesar Otway, *Sketches in Ireland, Descriptive of Interesting and Hitherto Unnoticed Districts in the North and South* (Dublin: William Curry, jun. and Company, 1827), preface.

2. Patrick Carey, *An Immigrant Bishop: John England's Adaptation of Irish Catholicism to American Republicanism* (New York: United States Catholic Historical Society, 1979), v.

3. For an analysis of sources from this time period, see Bernadette Cunningham and Raymond Gillespie, "The Lough Derg Pilgrimage in the Age of Counter-Reformation," in *Aire-Ireland* 39, nos. 3 and 4 (Fall 2004): 167–179.

4. As recounted by Guy Beiner in *Remembering the Year of the French: Irish Folk History and Social Memory* (Madison: University of Wisconsin Press, 2007), 218.

5. R. D. Edwards, *Atlas of Irish History* (London: Methuen, 1973); and Marianne Elliot, *Partners in Revolution: The United Irishmen and France* (New Haven: Yale University Press, 1990), 8.

6. S. J. Connolly, ed., *Oxford Companion to Irish History* (Oxford: Oxford University Press, 1998), 438.

7. The "Oath of Abjuration" had been passed in England in 1657. In 1703 it was imposed on teachers, lawyers, politicians, and clergy. The oath demanded a renunciation of allegiance to the pope and certain Catholic beliefs. Most priests did not take the oath. See Connolly, *Oxford Companion to Irish History*, 2.

8. Rev. William P. Burke, *The Irish Priests in Penal Times: From the State Papers in H.M. Record Offices, Dublin and London, the Bodleian Library, and the British Museum* (Waterford: Harvey and Company, 1914), 464.

9. Ibid., 204. Lord Chesterfield writing to Bishop Chenevix at Wexford, January 29, 1755.

10. Burke, *The Irish Priests in Penal Times*, 198.

11. Carey, *An Immigrant Bishop*, 6.

12. Burke, *The Irish Priests in Penal Times*, 219.

13. Registration Act, 1704, ca. 7: An Act to Register Popish Clergy.

14. Burke, *The Irish Priests in Penal Times*, 210.

15. Ibid., 212.

16. Ibid., 208.

17. Charles Morris, *American Catholic: The Saints and Sinners Who Built America's Most Powerful Church* (London: Vintage, 1998), 31.
18. See W. H. A. Williams, *Tourism, Landscape, and the Irish Character: British Travel Writers in Pre-Famine Ireland* (Madison: University of Wisconsin Press, 2008), in which Williams describes that the common perception of the English about the Irish was formed by travelogues.
19. Elliot, *Partners in Revolution*, 15–16.
20. Ibid., 16.
21. James Morgan Read, "Atrocity Propaganda and the Irish Rebellion," *Public Opinion Quarterly* 2, no. 2 (1938): 229–244; see also Elliot, *Partners in Revolution*, 17.
22. Elliot, *Partners in Revolution*, 203.
23. *The Poor Man's Catechism* (1815) 1798.
24. Patrick Griffin, "Hidden Irish American History Uncovered at Notre Dame," in *Irish Central* (May 26, 2009), http://www.irishcentral.com/roots/hidden-irish-american-history-uncovered-at-notre-dame-237644001.html, accessed November 13, 2012.
25. This is how England is represented in the historical documents of the Diocese of Cork and Ross, Redemption Road, Cork Ireland. See "Notes on the Most Reverend John England," http://www.corkandross.org/priests.jsp?priestID=397, accessed May 11, 2011.
26. "The shipboard death rate for immigrants from other countries was typically about.5 percent" (Morris, *American Catholic*, 37).
27. It was, more accurately, a one-man and one-woman publishing house, as England worked with his sister, who accompanied him from Ireland. Additionally, there is little doubt there were also others who helped England with his press.
28. *The Catholic Miscellany* (1822).
29. *The Miscellany* continued to be published after John England's death, but ceased publication in 1861 due to fire in Charleston that damaged the press. It was revived in 1951 as *The Catholic Banner*. In 1990, Bishop David B. Thompson changed the name to *The New Catholic Miscellany*, and today it is known as *The Catholic Miscellany*, the official newspaper of the Diocese of Charleston, South Carolina.
30. Ibid.
31. *United States Catholic Miscellany* 20, no. 10 (1840).
32. John Gilmary Shea, *A History of the Catholic Church within the Limits of the United States: From the First Attempted Colonization to the Present Time* (Baltimore: J. G. Shea, 1886), 197; John England and Sebastian Gebhard Messmer, *The Works of the Right Reverend John England: First Bishop of Charleston* (Cleveland: Arthur H. Clarke), 4:212.
33. *Catholic Miscellany* 20, no. 10 (1840): 162.
34. Ibid.
35. Morris, *American Catholic: The Saints and Sinners Who Built America's Most Powerful Church* (New York: Vintage, 1998), 33; *The Times* (London), April 2, 1849; Graham

1999, 609; or Eileen Moore Quinn, "Entextualizing Famine, Reconstituting Self: Testimonial Narratives from Ireland," *Anthropological Quarterly* 74, issue 2 (2001): 72–88.

36. Suzanne J. Crawford O'Brien, "Well, Water, Rock: Holy Wells, Mass Rocks and Reconciling Identity in the Republic of Ireland," *Material Religion: The Journal of Objects, Art and Belief* 4, no. 3 (2008): 339.

37. John England, *The Works of the Right Reverend John England, First Bishop of Charleston*, collected and arranged by Ignatius Aloysius Reynolds (Baltimore: John Murphy & Company, 1849), 3:200.

38. Ibid.

39. *The Catholic Miscellany* (1822).

40. *The Catholic Miscellany* (1826), 311.

41. *The Catholic Miscellany* (1829).

42. *The Catholic Miscellany* 9.

43. *The Catholic Miscellany* 8, no. 3.

44. *The Catholic Miscellany* 9, no. 37 (March 7, 1827), 292.

45. *The Catholic Miscellany* 8, no. 3.

46. Ibid.

47. Luis Lopez Mendez, "South America: Observaciones sobre las leyes de Indias, i sobre de indepenci de Americas," *North American Review* 19, issue 44 (July 1824), 158–208: 159.

48. Ibid., 158.

49. Ibid., 174.

50. Ibid., 192.

51. Ibid., 187.

52. Henry Charles Lea, *A History of Auricular Confession and Indulgences in the Latin Church* (Philadelphia: Lea Bros., 1896), 65.

53. Mendez, "South America," 187.

54. Ibid., 192; Mendez cites Vicente Pazos Kanki, *Letters on the United Provinces of South America* (New York: Seymour, 1819), 88–99.

55. Ibid. But note that Mendez is quoting Pazos Kanki, *Letters on the United Provinces*, 91–92.

56. Jenny Franchot, *Roads to Rome: The Antebellum Protestant Encounter with Catholicism* (Berkeley: University of California Press, 1994), introduction. Franchot provides a detailed analysis of how American Protestants utilized an anti-Catholic historiography to portray Catholics as the antithesis of American progression.

57. Mendez, "South America," 158.

58. Franchot, *Roads to Rome*, 4.

59. The following works discuss Enlightenment and Catholicism: Kant, *Religion within the Limits of Reason Alone* (1793); D. A. Brading, *The First America: The Spanish Monarchy, Creole Patriots, and the Liberal State, 1492–1867* (Cambridge: Cambridge University Press, 1993); Franchot, *Roads to Rome*; Oded Heilbronner,

"Age of Catholic Revival," in *A Companion to Nineteenth-Century Europe: 1789–1914*, ed. Stefan Berger (Chichester: Wiley-Blackwell, 2009). For an overview of the "discourses" of disenchantment and contemporary treatments of the Enlightenment and the religions of "enchantment," see Michael Saler, "Modernity and Enchantment: A Historiographic Review," in *The American Historical Review* III, no. 3 (2006).

60. Mendez, "South America," 163.

61. Ibid., 186.

62. Ibid., 302.

63. Ibid.

64. John England, "On Certain Superstitions Imputed to Catholics," *United States Catholic Miscellany* 20, no. 10 (1840).

65. "The Purgatory of Saint Patrick in Lough Derg," in *The Irish Ecclesiastical Record* (Dublin: John Fowler, 1865), 1:494.

CHAPTER 4

1. Lynn Sharp, *Secular Spirituality: Reincarnation and Spiritism in Nineteenth-Century France* (Lanham, Md.: Lexington, 2006), 3.

2. Julie Byrne, "Roman Catholics and Immigration in Nineteenth-Century America" (Research Triangle Park, N.C.: National Humanities Center, 2012).

3. For Irish Catholicism and Irish diasporic religious practices, see the following: Emmet Larkin, "The Devotional Revolution in Ireland, *1850–75*," *The American Historical Review* 77, no. 3 (June 1972): 625–652; Emmet Larkin, *The Consolidation of the Roman Catholic Church in Ireland, 1860–1870* (Chapel Hill: University of North Carolina Press, 1987); Emmet Larkin, *The Historical Dimensions of Irish Catholicism* (Washington, D.C.: Catholic University of America, 1984); Ann Taves, *The Household of Faith: Roman Catholic Devotions in Mid-Nineteenth-Century America* (Notre Dame, Ind.: University of Notre Dame Press, 1990). Additionally, Cara Delay's article complicates Larkin's picture of a homogenous devotional revolution. See "The Devotional Revolution on the Local Level: Parish Life in Post-Famine Ireland," in *U.S. Catholic Historian* 22, no. 3, *Ireland and America: Religion, Politics, and Social Movements* (Summer 2004): 41–60.

4. Taves, *The Household of Faith*, 120.

5. Ibid., 25. Taves's table indicates this shift. Recorded devotions to souls in purgatory within prayer books increased from .07 percent to 63 percent.

6. Frederick William Faber, "Purgatory: The Two Catholic Views of Purgatory Based on Catholic Teaching and Revelations of Saintly Souls," in *All for Jesus* (Baltimore: John Murphy Company, 1853). Faber calls the material version of purgatory "that sensible neighborhood to hell"; sections on purgatory were also published by Paulist Press as a pamphlet called *Purgatory* in 1928, and received an imprimatur.

7. See John Henry Newman, "The Intermediate State," in *The Works of Cardinal Newman: Parochial and Plain Sermons* (1835) (Westminster, Md.: Christian Classics, 1966), 3:367–387.

8. John Henry Newman, "79: On Purgatory: Against Romanism" in *Tracts for the Times, Volume IV* (London: J.H. Parker, Oxford, 1840), 5. Although most of the tracts were officially credited to the members of the University of Oxford, Newman wrote many of the tracts. See Vincent Ferrer Blehl, S.J., *John Henry Newman: A Bibliographical Catalogue of His Writings* (Charlottesville: University of Virginia Press, 1978).

9. Newman, *On Purgatory*, 5.

10. Ibid. 14.

11. Ibid. 48. Newman refers to Jeremy Taylor's work *Dissuasive from Popery*, part 1, chapter 1, paragraph 4.

12. John Henry Newman, *An Essay on the Development of Christian Doctrine* (London: Longman's, Green, and Company, 1890), chapter 2, section 16.

13. See John Henry Newman, "Remarks on Certain Passages in The Thirty-Nine Articles," in *The Works of Cardinal Newman, Via Media* (1841) (Westminster, Md.: Christian Classics, 1978), 2:294; also Geoffrey Rowell writes about Newman and the Oxford Movement and purgatory in *Hell and the Victorians* (London: Oxford University Press, 2000), section 7.

14. Faber's works and pamphlets are still popular and being published by religious presses like Tan Books. Additionally, they are being published by lay ministers through their apostolate work, on websites, in countries including Ireland, Australia, and the United States. See chapter 5.

15. John Quinn, "The Zeal of a Convert: Father Frederick Faber," *Crisis Magazine: A Voice for the Faithful Catholic Laity* (Sept. 17, 2012), http://www.crisismagazine.com/2012/the-zeal-of-a-convert-father-frederick-faber, accessed December 12, 2013.

16. These statistics are taken from Melissa J. Wilkinson, *Frederick William Faber: A Great Servant of God* (Leominster: Gracewing, 2007), 185.

17. Ibid.

18. Faber, *All for Jesus*, 378.

19. Ibid., 380.

20. See the works of Rowell, *Hell and the Victorians*; Wheeler, *Heaven, Hell and the Victorians* (Cambridge: Cambridge University Press, 1994); Philippe Ariès, *The Hour of Our Death: The Classic History of Western Attitudes toward Death over the Last One Thousand Years* (New York: Vintage, 1982); Pat Jalland, *Death in the Victorian Family* (New York: Oxford University Press, 2000). Ann Douglas reveals that the softening of representations of hell could be attributed to the market whereby ministers had to compete for members. See Ann Douglas, "Heaven Our Home: Consolation Literature in the North United States: 1830–1880," in "Death in America," *American Quarterly* 26, no. 5 (Dec. 1974): 496–515. A good overview of American images of the afterlife is Gary Scott Smith's *Heaven in the American*

Imagination (New York: Oxford University Press, 2011) in which he notes that some theologians feared losing converts if they emphasized punitive images of hell (132).

21. Henry Ward Beecher, "The Heavenly State and Future Punishment: Two Sermons" (New York: J.B. Ford, 1871), 83.

22. Guillaume Cuchet, "The Revival of the Cult of Purgatory in France (1850–1914)," *French History* 18, no. 1 (March 2004): 80.

23. Samuel Edgar, *The Variations of Popery* (New York: R. Craighead, 1849), 490.

24. Ibid., chapter 17.

25. Ibid.

26. Ibid., 496.

27. William John Hall, *The Doctrine of Purgatory and the Practice of Praying for the Dead as Maintained by the Romish Church* (London: Henry Wix, 1843), v.

28. Ibid.

29. Lynn Sharp, "Echoes from the Beyond: Purgatory and Catholic Communication with the Dead" (paper presented at the Western Society for French History Conference, Irvine, Calif., Oct. 2003).

30. Ibid., 6.

31. *Liberateur de ames* (Dec.–Jan. 1882/83).

32. George Salmon, "Purgatory and Modern Revelations," in *The Eclectic Magazine of Foreign Literature, Science, and Art* (Dec. 1883): 792, 801.

33. Ibid., 789.

34. Ibid., 790.

35. George Salmon, "Lecture 13. Modern Revelations," Lectures Delivered in the Divinity School, University of Dublin, by George Salmon, D.D., 1888.

36. Ibid.

37. Pope Urban VIII, *Sanctissimus Dominus Noster* (March 13, 1625), Papal Archive.

38. Ibid.

39. Father H. Faure, S.M., *Consolations of Purgatory*, translated from the French by W. Humphrey Page, K.S.G., Privy Chamberlain to H.H. Pius X (New York: Benziger Brothers, 1912), vii.

40. Pope Pius IX, *Syllabus Errorum* (Dec. 8, 1864), Papal Archive.

41. *The Catholic Layman* 5, no. 50 (Feb. 16, 1856): 15–16.

42. Francesca Romana Koch, *I contabili dell'aldilà: La devozione alle anime del purgatorio nella Roma postunitaria* (Turin: Rosenberg & Sellier, 1992). I am indebted to William Christian for recommending this book.

43. The curator of the museum reports that they get four thousand visitors annually (2013).

44. All quotations taken from W. B. Seabrook, "Letter from Abroad: Fr. Jouet's Strange Museum, There Are More Things in Heaven and Earth Than Are Dreamed of in Our Philosophy," *The Star and Sentinel* (Gettysburg, Pa.) (June 30, 1909).

45. Ibid.

46. Ibid.

47. *L'Echo du purgatoire: Souvenez-vous et priez pour vos morts* (Ottawa: J.P. Laurin, 1918), 9.

48. Faure, *Consolations of Purgatory*, 56.

49. *L'Echo du Purgatoire*, 13.

50. Ibid.

51. Faure, Consolations of Purgatory, 55.

52. Ibid.

53. Charles Cashdollar, "The Social Implications of the Doctrine of Divine Providence: A Nineteenth-Century Debate in American Theology," *Harvard Theological Review* 71, issue 3–4 (Oct. 1978): 265–284; also see Newman's lectures on Divine Providence, "Particular Providence as Revealed in the Gospel," from his lecture in *Parochial and Plain Sermons.*

54. Nineteenth-century biographies of Montfort include Pere Dalin, *Life and Select Writings of Blessed Louise-Marie Montfort* (London: 1860); and Par M. L'Abbe Pauvert, *Vie du vénérable Louis Marie Grignion de Montfort* (H. Oudin Freres: Paris, 1875).

55. For Montfort's hymns, especially "Abandonment to Providence," see Alphonse Bossard and Stefano de Fiores, *Jesus Living in Mary: Handbook of the Spirituality of St. Louis de Montfort* (Litchfield, Conn.: Montfort, 1994).

56. Editions of the *Poor Souls Advocate* are kept by the Philadelphia Archdiocesan Historical Research Center and Archive; additionally, information about this periodical is also found in John C. Leffel, *History of Posey County, Indiana* (Chicago: Standard, 1913). I am thankful to Michael Widner of the Indiana Historical Society.

57. Father Francis B. Luebbermann, *The Poor Souls Advocate* (Sept. 30, 1888): 1.

58. Ibid., 5, 4.

59. Ibid., no 1, under "Prospectus."

60. Ibid., 19–20.

61. Ibid., 90.

62. Anselm Hohenegger, OSB, *Tabernakel und Fegefeuer: Handbuch der Erzbruderschaft der ewigen Anbetung des aller heiligsten Sakramentes unter dem Schutze des hl. B. Benedikt zur Rettung der armen Seelen im Fegefeuer, des 3. Ordens des hl. Benedikt und des St. Benedikts-Vereins für Priester* (Lambach: Perpetual Adoration, 1880).

63. The Knights of Columbus and Catholic Truth Society, *Catholic Encyclopedia: An International Work of Reference* (New York: Robert Appleton, 1912), 122.

64. Benedictine Sisters of Perpetual Adoration, *Tabernacle and Purgatory* 1, no. 3 (1905): 88.

65. Benedictine Sisters of Perpetual Adoration, *Tabernacle and Purgatory* 1, no. 2 (1905): 62.

66. Ibid., 28.

67. Benedictine Sisters of Perpetual Adoration, *Tabernacle and Purgatory* 1, no. 1 (1905): 30.

68. Benedictine Sisters of Perpetual Adoration, *Tabernacle and Purgatory* 3, 89.
69. Sharp, "Echoes from the Beyond," 5. In this chapter I discuss two publications called "L'Echo du Purgatoire." They are distinct as one is a pamphlet and the other is a periodical.
70. Francois Gay, ed., *L'Echo du Purgatoire*. This statement appears on the first page of the first issue.
71. Sharp, "Echoes from the Beyond," 7.
72. Benedictine Sisters of Perpetual Adoration, "Spirit and Life," http://www .benedictinesisters.org/spirit-and-life-magazine-home.php, May 6, 2013.
73. The Congregation of Helpers, "Bearers of Hope: The Helpers of the Holy Souls Celebrate 150 Years of of Worldwide Service," http://www.congregationofhelp-ers.org/page10.asp, accessed March 20, 2013. The original website is gone, but this cached version is available: http://web.archive.org/web/20081120052447/ http://web.archive.org/web/20081120052447/http://www.congregationofhelpers .org/page10.asp, accessed May 24, 2014.

CHAPTER 5

1. Mike Humphrey and Brian Bagley, eds., Helpers of the Holy Souls, http://www .helpersoftheholysouls.com/, accessed January 2, 2013.
2. These statistics provided by apostolate minister Mike Humphrey and Brian Bagley, in a phone interview with the author, Wilmington, N.C., April 13, 2013.
3. Interview with anonymous interviewee, Chicago, Ill., November 2, 2008.
4. Scott Richert, "Whatever Happened to Purgatory," About.com *Catholicism*, http://catholicism.about.com/b/2008/11/07/reader-question-what-happened-to-purgatory.htm, accessed November 7, 2008.
5. Charles Morris, *American Catholic: The Saints and Sinners Who Build America's Most Powerful Church* (New York: Vintage, 1998), 356.
6. Interview with anonymous practitioner, December 10, 2012.
7. Interview with Mike Humphrey, April 13, 2013.
8. Fr. Paul Sretenovic, "The Physical Suffering of Purgatory," http://www.traditio-ninaction.org/religious/e047-Purgatory.htm, accessed January 2, 2013.
9. Anthony Pogorelc and James Davidson, "One Church, Two Cultures?" review of *Religious Research* 42, no. 2 (Dec. 2000): 146–158; Eugene Kennedy, *Tomorrow's Catholics, Yesterday's Church: The Two Cultures of American Catholicism* (Liguori, Mo.: Liguori, 1995); William V. D'Antonio, James D. Davidson, Dean R. Hoge, and Mary L. Gautier, *American Catholics Today: New Realities of Their Faith and Their Church* (Lanham, Md.: Rowman & Littlefield, 2007).
10. This is based on my own study and Joseph McShane's study, "Mirrors and Teachers: A Study of Catholic Periodical Fiction between 1930 and 1950," in McShane, *U.S. Catholic Historian* 6, nos. 2/3, (Spring–Summer 1987): 181–198. Further research is required to trace the reasons for the decline in devotions to purgatory.

11. D'Antonio et al., *American Catholics Today*.

12. Kennedy, *Tomorrow's Catholics*.

13. Pogorelc and Davidson, "One Church, Two Cultures?"

14. James D. Davidson, "How American Catholics Think about the Church" (the 2009 Philip J. Murnion Lecture delivered at the Catholic University of America, June 26, 2009).

15. D'Antonio et al., *American Catholics Today*, 54.

16. Ibid.

17. Ibid., 56.

18. Gerard J. M. van den Aardweg, *Hungry Souls: Supernatural Visits, Messages and Warnings from Purgatory* (Charlotte, N.C.: Tan, 2009), x.

19. "The Mission to Empty Purgatory," http://www.mtep.com/status.htm, accessed April 13, 2012.

20. Helpers of the Holy Souls, "The Pains of Purgatory," http://www.helpersoftheholysouls.com/why_we_shouldhelp/1stmotivethepainsofpurgatory.htm, accessed February 10, 2013.

21. Interview with anonymous interviewee, Chicago, Ill., November 2, 2008.

22. Van den Aardweg, *Hungry Souls*, xix.

23. Ibid., 2.

24. Ibid., 3.

25. Ibid., 15.

26. Sretenovic, "The Physical Suffering of Purgatory."

27. Anonymous, email message to the author, April 17, 2013.

28. Van den Aardweg, *Hungry Souls*, 19.

29. Brother Anthony JoseMaria, FTI, *The Blessed Virgin Mary in England*, vol. 1, *A Mary-Catechism with Pilgrimage to Her Holy Shrines* (Bloomington, Ind.: IUniverse, 2008), 178, 176.

30. JoseMaria, *Mary-Catechism*, 178.

31. Ibid.

32. Suffering Souls, "The Holy Souls Will Repay Us a Thousand Times Over," http://www.sufferingsouls.com/part2.htm, accessed February 4, 2012.

33. Van den Aardweg, *Hungry Souls*, x.

34. Ibid., 140n4.

35. Email interview with Brother Maria, April 30, 2013.

36. Margaret C. Galitzin, "The Museum of the Poor Souls in Purgatory," in *Tradition in Action* (Nov. 12, 2011), http://www.traditioninaction.org/religious/e048-Museum_1.htm, accessed May 6, 2013.

37. Fish Eaters, "Traditional Catholicism 101: A Primer," http://www.fisheaters.com/traditionalcatholicism.html, accessed May 6, 2013.

38. Email interview with Brother Maria, April 30, 2013.

39. Fish Eaters, "Traditional Catholicism 101."

40. Mike Humphrey and Brian Bagley, phone interview.

41. Thomas W. Petrisko, *Inside Purgatory: What History, Theology and the Mystics Tell Us about Purgatory* (Pittsburgh: St. Andrew's Productions, 2000), introduction.

42. Helpers of the Holy Souls, "Are We Re-Thinking Purgatory?" http://www .askacatholic.com/_WebPostings/Answers/2006_09SEPT-APR2007/2007Apr AreWeReThinkingPurgatory.cfm, accessed May 6, 2013.

43. Email interview with Brother Maria, April 30, 2013.

44. Webb Keane, *Christian Moderns: Freedom and Fetish in the Mission Encounter* (Oakland: University of California Press, 2007), 204.

45. Dick Houtman and Birgit Meyer, eds., *Things: Religion and the Question of Materiality* (New York: Fordham University Press, 2012), 1.

46. Ibid.

47. Robert Orsi, *Between Heaven and Earth: The Religious Worlds People Make and the Scholars Who Study Them* (Princeton: Princeton University Press, 2006), 12.

48. Wesley Kort, *"Take, Read": Scripture, Textuality and Cultural Practice* (University Park: Pennsylvania State University Press, 1996); Paul Griffiths, *Religious Reading: The Place of Reading in Religious Practice* (New York: Oxford University Press, 1999).

49. Paula Fredriksen, "Paul and Augustine: Conversion Narratives, Orthodox Traditions, and the Retrospective Self," *Journal of Theological Studies*, n.s. 37 (1986): 34.

50. Jeffrey Kripal, *Authors of the Impossible: The Paranormal and the Sacred* (Chicago: The University of Chicago Press, 2010), 25.

51. Ibid.

52. Ibid., 213.

53. Ibid.

54. Kripal, *Authors of the Impossible*, 254.

55. Ibid., 253.

56. Brian Bagley and Michael Humphrey's citation of Robert Bellarmine, http:// www.helpersoftheholysouls.com/why_we_shouldhelp/1stmotivethepainsofpur gatory.htm, accessed January 25, 2014.

CONCLUSION

1. Robert Orsi, *Between Heaven and Earth: The Religious Worlds People Make and the Scholars Who Study Them* (Princeton: Princeton University Press, 2005), 12.

2. See Richard Louis Cleary, *Gothic Arches, Latin Crosses: Anti-Catholicism and American Church Designs in the Nineteenth Century* (Chapel Hill: University of North Carolina Press, 2006).

3. Charles Dickens, *A Christmas Carol*, ed. Max Bollinger (London: Sovereign, 2012), 23.

4. Dickens, *A Christmas Carol*, 23.

Index